Shared Space:
The Communities Agenda

About the Cover

The tree on the cover of this book can be found on the main path of the central park in Christchurch, New Zealand. I took this picture when I was there in July 2007 (their winter) to present a keynote address at the national conference of Local Government New Zealand. The organization was interested in our ideas on resilience, innovation and social clusters, and the application of these ideas to the work in which they are involved on the social, cultural, economic and environmental aspects of well-being.

I was both intrigued and inspired by this tree. From far, it looked like it had virtually no chance of survival and actually had died. But as I came closer, I began to see its incredible new growth. I remember thinking that this single tree embodied 'on the ground' the concept of resilience. Despite some clear threat, it not only was surviving but also was thriving. It was brimming with life – all it took was a set of open eyes to see it.

I realized at that moment that this was a crucial life lesson – about the many individuals, groups and communities we often pass by without valuing, let alone recognizing, their astonishing strengths and capacity to rebuild in the face of significant challenge.

Sherri Torjman

ISBN#: 1-55382-257-9

Published by:
The Caledon Institute of Social Policy
1390 Prince of Wales Drive, Suite 401
Ottawa, ON   K2C 3N6
CANADA

Phone: (613) 729-3340
Fax: (613) 729-3896
E-mail: caledon@caledoninst.org
Website: www.caledoninst.org

Acknowledgements

The author gratefully acknowledges the following individuals for their invaluable assistance:

Paul Born of the Tamarack Institute for coining the phrase "communities agenda," for his infectious enthusiasm and relentless optimism, and for pushing us all to dream big in the quest to reclaim our humanity.

Alan Broadbent of the Maytree Foundation for enabling this work through his support of the Caledon Institute of Social Policy, his stalwart commitment to social well-being and his strategic guidance.

Ken Battle of the Caledon Institute for his outstanding social policy leadership in Canada and for being a wonderfully supportive colleague over the past 22 years of our working relationship.

Sandy Houston and Colette Murphy from the George Cedric Metcalf Charitable Foundation for their significant contribution of financial and intellectual capital to the research that served as the foundation for this book.

Tim Brodhead, Katharine Pearson and Stephen Huddart from the J.W. McConnell Family Foundation for all the learning and inspiration from our long and valued partnership.

Anne Makhoul of the Caledon Institute for her passion about community initiatives and her unique ability to tell their stories.

Melanie Burston of the Caledon Institute for her good humour and incredibly hard work on the production of this book.

Mark Cabaj and Eric Leviten-Reid from the Tamarack Institute for their warm collegiality and brilliant contribution to strategic community practice.

Susan Scotti, Liz Huff, Donna Troop, Patrick Gibson and Jean Viel of Human Resources and Social Development Canada for their staunch commitment to place-based community solutions and for graciously providing many learning opportunities to share this work.

Alex Loshak from ALDI Corporate Publishers for his expertise and professionalism throughout the production process and to Robert Tippins from Carleton University for his efficient handling of the publication of this book.

Jack, Dan and Lisa Torjman for their love and unwavering support.

Thanks as well to all the gracious partners in Vibrant Communities and to the hundreds of community practitioners I have met over the years who continue to amaze and inspire.

Finally, a special note of appreciation to Karasima. I see you.

Sherri Torjman

Odida mlatigoo @uwo.ca

Table of Contents

Chapter 1

Reaching for Resilience

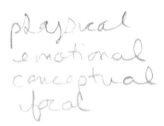

Shared space

Small words – big ideas.

Shared space is the physical place we live. It is our home, our block, our neighbourhood. It is the land we walk and the air we breathe. It is the schools, parks, streets, woods and rivers that make up our world.

Shared space is also an emotional place. It is a sense of belonging. It is the place that families and neighbours call home. It is the place we plant our hearts.

Shared space is a conceptual arena. It is a common vision and set of goals. It is a shared understanding of how communities can contribute to well-being and how they can carry out this work. It includes both what they do and how they organize in the face of complex challenges.

Shared space is the focal point for the communities agenda – whose goal is to promote resilience in order to build strong and vibrant communities. The term 'communities agenda' refers both to *what* communities can do to foster resilience and *how* best to undertake this work.

Resilience is the result of strategic actions undertaken in four independent, but associated, clusters related to sustenance, adaptation, engagement and opportunity. These resilience clusters comprise the substantive focus of the communities agenda. Its process focuses upon work in the shared space within and between resilience clusters and around policy.

The unique role of the communities agenda

This framework refers to the communities agenda as though there is a common understanding of the term. There is none, at least not formally. Perhaps informally and implicitly because there are so many exciting efforts being undertaken in communities throughout the country and, indeed, the world. There is a palpable energy and vibrancy that have never before been seen. The communities agenda is alive and well in practice, though not yet articulated in theory.

So why the need for an agenda and, more specifically, a communities agenda? With growing appreciation of the importance of place and the wide scope of innovative activity, it is time to acknowledge the profound transformation under way. The framework presented here seeks to capture the essence of these local efforts in order to help them advance strategically together. Its purpose is to provide a common conceptual starting gate.

The intent of a communities agenda is not to set out a single approach for how to embark upon work in the shared space. A uniform methodology is not only undesirable. It is also impossible. There is no best approach to making communities great places. Nor should there be. The precise focus will vary by community and rightfully will be different in every case.

The communities agenda is all about local expression within a shared understanding. The agenda is intended to impart conceptual rigour that is guided by – and that guides – effective practice in both substance and process.

The term 'agenda' usually implies a structured conversation with a clear purpose. But structured does not mean inflexible. In fact, flexibility is an essential element of the communities agenda. Structured means that the major signposts which guide community efforts – overall goals, methods and milestones – are consistent in their intent and approach. The distinctive expression of that intent is their unique poetry.

As noted, the goal of the communities agenda is to promote resilience in order to build strong and vibrant communities. But let there be no doubt. *The communities agenda in no way minimizes the need for a solid core of public goods and services. Community-based actions both supplement and complement – but do not replace – public policies focused upon economic and social well-being.*

While the communities agenda is a complement to government intervention, both community work and public policy are linked by shared purpose. They represent investment in the common good – the well-being of society and the individuals who comprise it. The difference is the primary target of intervention. The unique and crucial role of government is discussed in the later chapter on *Creating an Enabling Environment*.

The growing interest in 'place'

Recent years have seen growing interest in cities and communities as a focus of policy and investment. Recognizing the potential of place as a strategic focal point is not new. Voluntary action existed long before government programs were introduced to tackle major economic and social challenges. What *is* new is the sophistication of emerging community approaches, the scope of the work and the range of actors involved in these local efforts.

Before exploring these promising approaches, it is essential to address the age-old question: What is 'community'? Is it a neighbourhood, geographic region, group with similar history or even a loose network of individuals linked by common interest? All of the above. For the purposes of this framework, community is understood first and foremost as a geographic place. It is a region, city, neighbourhood or town.

While the primary defining feature of community is geography, its geometry is equally important. People come in all sizes, shapes and shades – and it is this fascinating diversity that comprises its social assets. No matter how the physical boundaries are drawn, community begins with people.

As the traditional anchors of life become more tenuous, many search for a sense of belonging. Neighbourhoods and communities – the physical and social space where people live – help fill that need.

The interest in communities derives from the recognition that quality of place directly affects the well-being and success of individuals and families. The healthy development of children, for example, depends in large part upon their social context. Dense networks and multiple relationships of trust, which can be built locally only in neighbourhoods and communities, have a strong positive impact upon health, social cohesion and financial well-being.[1]

On the economic front, communities and the regions they comprise are being recognized increasingly as the engines of nations. A national economy effectively is the sum of its regional economic activity.

Economic health and competitiveness, in turn, have a direct impact upon the availability and quality of employment. Both are prime determinants of prosperity – or poverty, as the case may be. Communities also foster learning and networking, which are core ingredients of innovation.

The key to competitiveness lies in the ability of local regions to attract highly skilled workers. In the current economy, knowledge and skills have become critical factors of production. In order to draw the talent they need to compete successfully, large urban centres in particular must pay more attention to quality-of-life factors than they did in the past.[2]

These centres are viable as strong economies only to the extent that they have a clean environment and social amenities, such as decent affordable housing, parks, trails, and recreational and cultural programs. Cities, communities and regions are becoming more aware of the need to establish and maintain their competitive advantage. The Prime Minister's External Advisory Committee on Cities and Communities, which issued its final report in 2006, concluded that sustainability actually is enhanced when decisions are made through a place-based lens.

But there are also reasons on the negative side of the equation to pay attention to communities. Most struggle with a range of stresses related to complex social and economic problems – racial tensions, persistent poverty, unemployment and underemployment, social exclusion, unstable housing tenure, homelessness, drug abuse and domestic violence – though these problems are not unique to large urban centres.

The communities agenda is rooted in resilience

The communities agenda sets out a framework for promoting strong and vibrant communities. The framework is shaped in large part by the concept of *resilience* – deemed crucial because it deals fundamentally with the ability not only to cope but also to thrive in the face of tough problems and continual change.

Equally important, the concept of resilience embeds a feeling of optimism about the future and the conviction that there is a better way to tackle complex challenges. The communities agenda carries with it an excitement about opportunity and a sense of passion about what is possible. It is an inherently forward-looking and positive agenda. It is this feeling of hope that underpins the communities agenda because it speaks fundamentally to the capacity and potential of local action – if it is sufficiently broad-ranging and strategic.

The notion of resilience is rooted in the thinking on sustainable development whose purpose is to improve the quality of life for all humanity. The term was defined in 1987 by the World Commission on Environment and Development as development that meets the needs of the present without compromising the ability of future generations to meet their own needs.[3]

The unique contribution of sustainable development is that it moves beyond conventional economic indicators as the sole barometer of a nation's well-being. It considers environmental, social and cultural domains as equally important factors in the societal equation. The communities agenda focuses primarily upon the social, cultural and economic dimensions of sustainable development.

Sustainable development basically says that wellness involves far more than wealth. A society is more than its economy.[4] Within the context of sustainable development, the focus upon economic growth and prosperity takes its place beside equally essential environmental, social and cultural objectives. It is concerned with clean air and water, nutritious food and decent shelter, good health and safe neighbourhoods, stable roots, and strong sense of self and belonging.

A central goal of communities – and indeed of nations – has been to create a well-functioning economy in order to reap the associated social benefits. Conventional wisdom dictated that a focus on prosperity and wealth creation would cause all boats to rise. The problem is that many paddlers have no boats. It has become increasingly apparent that social health is not merely the product of a strong economy. It is actually a *determinant* of a healthy economy. A productive economy requires a strong social infrastructure.[5]

Sustainable development has clear links to resilience, which is essentially about sustainability and the ability to survive in the face of shock, pressure, challenge and change. But while there is a general thrust, there is no single definition of resilience. It is a concept employed in fields as diverse as ecology science, organizational management, community development, mental health and child development.

The concept of resilience informs areas that vary widely (and wildly) from national fire and flood emergency preparedness to the cultivation of problem-solving skills in preschoolers. Its practical applications range from high-level activities to be carried out by national governments to personal steps that can be taken by individuals – though there appears to be a common thread of coping with, adapting to and thriving in the face of some pressure or threat.

The communities agenda sees resilience as its desired goal. The interactions that help achieve resilience derive from patterns in the fields of ecology and mental health.

Ecological interpretation

The ecological literature on resilience is probably the most widely known application of the concept.[6] In this stream of work, resilience is often paired with vulnerability – a state marked by a clutch of negative factors. The United Nations Environmental Programme focuses upon vulnerability and resilience as major anchor concepts in the climate change picture in particular.

In theory, these two dimensions can be understood as polar opposites on the spectrum of well-being. In practice, they are anything but equal opposites. They are points along a conceptual continuum. While the immediate priority is the vulnerability end of the continuum, the broader goal is to pay attention to the full range of actions that contribute to resilience. The concept of resilience has two meanings in the ecological literature, each of which reflects a distinct, but related, dimension of stability.[7]

The first component is more traditional and focuses upon stability near a desired steady state. This conceptualization is considered to be the engineering component of resilience in which ecological systems are seen to exist close to a stable equilibrium. Resilience is the rate at which a system returns to a steady state following a disturbance, such as an earthquake, tsunami, hurricane or oil spill.

The ecological dimension of resilience, by contrast, emphasizes the ability of an ecosystem to adapt to change. This dimension is concerned more with the process of change – with adaptability, variability and unpredictability.

From this perspective, resilience is understood as the magnitude of disturbance that can be absorbed before the system redefines its structure and processes – effectively how far it moves from its original steady state. A resilient ecosystem can withstand shocks and rebuild itself when necessary. These two interpretations highlight the tensions embodied in the concept with its opposing dualities of constancy and change, predictability and unpredictability.[8]

Resilience is the capacity to experience massive change and yet still maintain the integrity of the original. It is not about balancing change and stability. Neither is its purpose to reach an equilibrium state. Rather, resilience is about how big change and stability paradoxically work together.[9]

Some governments have tried to apply the notion of resilience to developing emergency preparedness or disaster plans. Resilience from this perspective is understood as the ability to withstand external pressures through effective preparation, coping and adaptation. UK Resilience, for example, is responsible for emergency preparedness, response and recovery. Emergencies may arise from natural disasters like floods or drought, diseases such as bird flu or terrorist attacks. Several critical resilience projects are under way to counteract the potential effects of chemical, biological, radiological or nuclear incidents.

The ecological stream of literature embodies a double notion of resilience as a capacity both to withstand outside pressures and to adapt to them. Resilience is the ability of a system to maintain its structure and function when subject to disruptive force. Its equally important adaptive capacity is the ability to accommodate successfully the impacts of change. *Survival* and *adaptation* are two distinct but intrinsically related components of this concept.

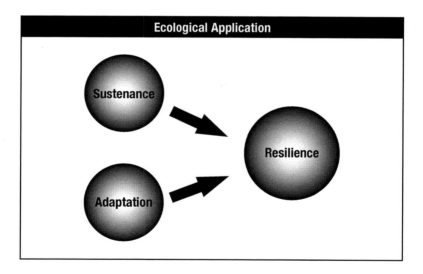

Mental health application

It is clear that the understanding of resilience has been inspired deeply by the study of ecology. But there is another major body of literature that builds on the concept of resilience. The mental health field is concerned with identifying the personal characteristics, behaviours, skills and competencies of individuals considered to be resilient.[10] These are people who have faced great personal challenge and have emerged relatively healthy and strong.

While the ecological interpretation of resilience focuses upon disruption or disturbance such as floods, fires, earthquakes or tsunamis, the mental health literature has its own representation of disruptive force – be it the death of a family member, domestic violence, disability or illness, alcohol and drug abuse, or other serious threat to emotional stability. Resilience is the ability to cope with stressful change, and perceived or actual threat.

> Do you know people who are survivors? Bad things happen: They lose their job, they get passed over for promotion or work with a micromanaging boss. Yet, through it all, they seem to bounce back, even thrive. Under the greatest adversity and change, they can stay focused and take action without becoming hopeless or helpless. In short, these people demonstrate resilience.[11]

As in the ecological interpretation of resilience, there is a vast and growing literature on its mental health application. The US-based Project Resilience initiative employs the term "resiliencies" to describe the categories of strengths mobilized in the struggle with hardship. It identifies seven resiliencies that guide the identification of internal strengths: morality, insight, independence, relationships, initiative, humour and creativity.[12]

Internal strengths, behaviours and competencies are only one side of the story from the mental health perspective. External factors such as caring adults, high expectations and possible opportunities make equally important contributions to resilience.

The mental health application of resilience focuses upon the interventions required to cultivate desirable personal qualities as well as the outside supports that promote this capacity. Caring relationships, for example, are considered as one way to help young people gain a sense of connection and confidence – both of which are essential internal qualities.

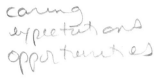

A resilience lens also sees professionals as partners rather than authorities, initiators and directors of the change process. It argues that professionals must understand that the impact of damage may not be as significant as the strengths and resources that previously have been ignored. The damage model of mental health paints individuals as lacking an ability to help themselves.

The challenge model, by contrast, acknowledges the negative effects of hardship but also recognizes the opportunity to respond constructively and creatively. It is more consistent with the resilience approach. It breaks with a long tradition of theory and practice, which emphasizes problems and vulnerabilities in children, families, communities and organizations burdened by adversity. The challenge approach acknowledges, and indeed celebrates, their power for self-help and healing.[13]

But the mental health literature goes beyond survival and coping. It implies that any person or group of individuals able to withstand difficult circumstances and handle them well is often emotionally stronger as a result. Resilience can be understood as a capacity not only to bounce back from adversity but also to be strengthened and improved by it.

The resilience approach is essentially a strength-based philosophy. There are echoes of this focus on capacity in the increasingly popular asset-based approach to community development.[14] This approach focuses upon the multiple and inherent strengths of communities. No matter how difficult or vulnerable their circumstances, there are always positive features upon which to build.

A related application of the concept of resilience can be found in the child development literature, which explores the factors that contribute to healthy outcomes.[15] Child development links to the mental health field through its identification of the qualities of resilient children – generally seen as optimistic, with a sense of meaning and purpose, confidence and self-esteem. They are able to get the social support they need to overcome challenges.

An extensive literature on nurturing resilience in children discusses how they can learn to cope in the world and make better decisions. While it is not feasible to teach children what to do in every conceivable situation, it *is* possible to prepare them to manage challenging circumstances when these invariably arise.

As in mental health, the work on child development moves beyond factors intrinsic to the individual. Research into resilience in families is investigating the role of non-income resources and behaviours that help low-income households cope with poverty and insulate their children from its risks and negative effects.[16]

Studies on vulnerable children explore the significant role of key influences upon positive developmental outcomes. A protective triad – consisting of personal characteristics, close family ties and external support systems – effectively lies at the heart of adaptation.[17]

The quality of the social environment, including family, friends, school and neighbourhood, can help cushion the impact of low income and other risks. The evidence calls for family-enabling environments, which encourage positive parenting and opportunities for learning the skills involved in effective problem-solving and conflict resolution. Communities must open up possibilities for participation.

Whether viewed from an ecological, mental health or child development perspective, there are several major themes embedded in the concept of resilience. Resilient individuals, families and communities are able to *survive* in the face of ongoing change or imminent threat because of internal strength and their capacity to *adapt* effectively to those changes – be they modest or sudden and life-threatening.

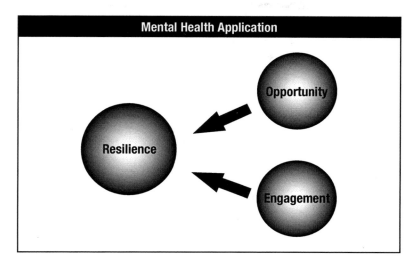

But beyond mere survival and adaptation, resilient individuals, families and communities typically emerge even
stronger as a result of the challenge. They *engage actively* in
the world around them. They *seek opportunities* to improve
their well-being and the quality of their lives. They *thrive.*

Resilience implies a state of wellness characterized
by the ability to survive, the ability to adapt or cope with
change, and the ability to thrive – to participate and to seek
opportunities – as a result of this adaptation. *Resilience is the
capacity to thrive in a changing context.*

The broad-ranging literature on resilience points to
four groups of independent but linked activity – related to
sustenance, adaptation, engagement and opportunity – that
contribute to resilience. Actions in all four areas together
comprise the resilience equation.

While these four groups include a focus on both basic
physical needs and 'higher' social and psychological needs,
they are not intended to be understood as a hierarchy or a
set of linear interventions. Resilience is the result of the combined interventions in all areas. All are important – though

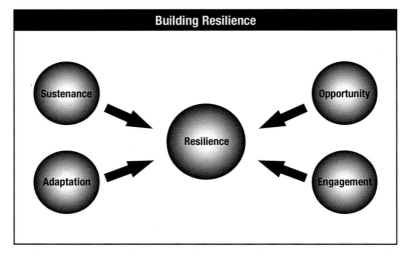

a given community may choose to focus upon a certain cluster more actively than the others at any given time.

The communities agenda seeks to ensure that there is sufficient and effective action in all four groups of activity and that they are linked both in planning and in practice. In effect, the communities agenda is not a single agenda. It looks for progress in all dimensions of resilience and must ensure that the core clusters are working well – both individually and together.

The challenge is to determine which actions help achieve this coherence. How to get from four major streams of intervention to the broader holistic communities agenda? Recent research and practice around *innovation* provide a conceptual bridge. This framing of the communities agenda was developed by applying the concept of innovation employed in the economic analysis of local regions.

Innovation is the bridging concept

The research on innovation understands local economies as the sum total of several independent but related clusters. Taken together, they act as primary economic drivers and effectively comprise the substance of the local economy. The major economic clusters are supported, in turn, by a set of foundations that ensure their healthy functioning.

This framework for the communities agenda argues that the concept of economic clusters can apply equally well to the social dimension of communities. The communities agenda is the social application of the concept of innovation. Here's the basis for this argument.

Innovation typically is considered to be the creation or generation of novel ideas, products or processes. But this conceptualization is actually too narrow. While innovation *can* involve the formulation of new ideas, it also entails the application of existing ideas in unique ways or to new fields. The concept of innovation and its social application was explored in research commissioned by the Community Economic Development Technical Assistance Program (CEDTAP) housed at Carleton University.[18]

In the knowledge economy, the creative use of current knowledge is as important as its production. Innovation typically thrives in regions and, more specifically, in communities. The regional level is critical because the factors of space and proximity contribute to knowledge development and the capacity for learning that support innovation.

The creation, storage, transmission, application and exchange of knowledge are best managed through strategic groupings known as clusters. A healthy local economy is composed of major clusters with close interactions and links. Activity within the clusters acts as the driver of economic prosperity and growth.[19]

major clusters close interactions & links

The concept of clusters is rooted in research and practice on sector strategies, which originated in the 1960s. In the 1990s, Harvard business professor Michael Porter introduced a modified form of sector-based strategy that stressed the importance of geography, informal relationships and supporting institutions. The focus of economic development shifted to clusters of industries that could gain advantage through co-location and interdependence – in which local firms exchange components and services along with flows of information and knowledge.[20]

From an economic perspective, clusters can be understood as geographic concentrations of interconnected companies, service providers, suppliers of resources, customers and manufacturers of related products. Clusters also include governments and other organizations such as laboratories, training institutes, universities and trade associations that provide specialized training, education, information, research and technical support.[21]

Clusters are geographically bounded concentrations of *interdependent* firms that exchange raw materials, common technology and knowledge. It is the relations between and among firms, and not their mere co-location, which comprise the decisive factor in defining a regional cluster. Collaboration is at the heart of clustering and of innovation.

There is an active dimension implicit in the notion of clusters – diverse interactions and links within and among various streams of activity. Synergies or multiple benefits arise from these exchanges involving knowledge, skills, human resources, ideas and financing. Clusters represent networks of activity. They embody a common domain – and effectively comprise a shared space.

Organizations within a cluster can take advantage, for example, of economies of scale by further specializing the production within firms, joint purchase of common raw materials to attract bulk discounts or common marketing.

Companies can expand the expertise available to them if they locate within a cluster of firms. They can draw upon those with complementary skills to bid for larger contracts for which individual firms would be unable to complete.

> In the first decade of the twenty-first century, the focus of many organizational change efforts is between – between organizations and their partners, be they suppliers and vendors, customers, or other organizations producing similar products and services. … We're living in a networked, organic world, and we're starting to understand the new skills, roles, and concepts needed to succeed on this different and dynamic playing field.[22]

In major urban centres throughout the world, the theory of innovation has been applied through a practice known as cluster-based economic development. This approach is rooted in the recognition that healthy regional economies are composed of two independent but interrelated parts: key clusters of economic activity and a set of supportive foundations or enabling infrastructure.[23]

Clusters do not function independently from one another. Neither do they operate in a vacuum. They must be supported and sustained by an appropriate infrastructure. Within the model of cluster-based economic development, this supportive infrastructure is referred to as 'quality foundations.' These include amenities such as roads and sewers, an appropriate regulatory framework, access to financial capital and a pool of skilled workers.

The notion of cluster-based development and its application to economic health has been adapted here to the communities agenda. This agenda effectively consists of four main clusters of activity to promote resilience – the capacity to thrive in a changing context. Resilience means *sustenance* in the face of challenge or ongoing change. It involves *adaptation* to a complex and shifting environment as well as active *engagement* with that environment. Resilience involves both a capacity and desire to thrive in response to *opportunity*.

The key clusters that comprise the resilience function are analogous to the economic clusters that act as the drivers of local economies. The actors within the clusters include citizens, groups, voluntary organizations, the private sector and all orders of government. The resilience clusters together comprise the *substance* of the communities agenda.

Each cluster is composed, in turn, of a wide-ranging set of actions that fall into one of two streams: personal capacity and community infrastructure. Investments in personal capacity refer to activities that enhance the skills, abilities and assets of individuals or households. Investments in community infrastructure represent an infusion of resources in the supply of amenities and supports that contribute to well-being.

Cluster-based economic development seeks to ensure the health of the main clusters that comprise a given economy. They are guided by relevant knowledge and supported through dense interactions and collaborative relationships.

The economic clusters together are sustained by quality foundations, which include a skilled and adaptable workforce, access to technology and technological know-how, financial capital and advanced physical infrastructure like communications, roads and sewers. The communities agenda requires an equally solid set of foundations including a supportive context in which governments, the private sector, and community and private funders act as exemplars, investors and enablers of community practice.

The work within and between clusters as well as around policy comprises the process of the communities agenda. It is discussed later along with the context that both enables and sustains this work.

The substance of the communities agenda

The *sustenance* cluster is concerned with wide-ranging conditions related to physical and emotional well-being. It focuses upon basic needs that comprise the foundation for human security. While broad in scope, the primary components of this cluster from a social perspective are decent affordable housing and adequate income.

Sustenance also focuses upon population health and basic health protections, such as immunization against communicable disease, and with actions that ensure clean air and water. The burgeoning literature on the social determinants of health makes clear the impact upon health of a wide range of social and economic factors. There is also a strong link between the sustenance cluster and the environmental dimension of sustainable development, both of which support good health.

Decent affordable housing is of interest to all nations, though the responses to this need vary widely. Recent work has seen a range of collaborative innovations involving the private sector, community groups and citizens. But investment by governments at all levels remains crucial for meeting the needs of low-income households in particular. Local governments play a unique enabling role through their zoning and associated regulations.

The concern with decent shelter reflects the very essence of well-being: accommodation comprises the largest proportion of household expenditure. Housing stability is linked closely to health and emotional wellness. Income security helps ensure that families actually can pay for housing and other basics. Income security derives both from wages and self-employment, and from programs that either supplement or replace work-related earnings.

Higher wages and direct payments to households that increase their overall income enhance their capacity to acquire basic necessities. So are measures that lower costs for essentials, such as food or fuel. Rental subsidies are another example of bolstering individual capability – in this case, the ability to pay for accommodation.

Investment in community infrastructure, by contrast, involves direct support for the supply of affordable housing. Many possible interventions help achieve this objective. The end result is more decent accommodation available in the community. It may take the form of new housing units, the conversion from former dwellings into affordable space, regional housing authorities or nonprofit housing developers. In still other cases, existing housing is retrofit to make it both livable and more reasonably priced.

Clearly, the two streams of intervention are intrinsically linked. The cost of housing depends upon local supply relative to demand. The capacity to pay for housing, in turn, affects the price of housing in any given community and thereby directly influences its affordability. Skyrocketing salaries and high demand in Calgary, for example, have had a dramatic impact upon the price of housing in that city. Rising prices have created hardship for low-income households in particular. It is essential to explore in tandem both streams of actions – related to supply and to capacity to pay.

The *adaptation* cluster consists of the group of actions concerned primarily with basic coping skills and capacities. It would be unrealistic to assume that all personal and societal problems – such as separation and divorce, unexpected job loss, economic recession, personal illness or widespread pandemic – can be avoided entirely. The challenge is to find ways to cope with these stresses and to build in the protective factors that help individuals and households face the odds that invariably will come their way – whether through family circumstance or broader social and economic factors.

The fostering of skills related to empathy, problem-solving and literacy proficiency comprises the essence of adaptive capacity. Investment in community infrastructure includes, for example, support for child care, school hubs and settlement assistance for newcomers.

On the personal capacity side of the equation, a foundational building block in the adaptation cluster relates to early childhood development. It is concerned with screening, early stimulation and supports for quality parenting. The literature on child development is rich with evidence on the importance of nurturing resilience – self-esteem, empathy and positive coping mechanisms – at the very earliest stages of life.

Another set of actions in the adaptation cluster relates to social capital interventions that help build strong families and neighbourhoods. There is clear evidence that links social capital to physical well-being, mental health and economic security. Social capital also acts as the foundation for learning. It plays an especially important role in the lives of newcomers and persons with disabilities in that it provides essential networks of support. But additional settlement assistance is required to address specific needs related to language; access to legal, health and social services; links to education, training and employment; and recognition of skills acquired offshore.

The final grouping within the adaptation cluster has to do with core proficiencies in the knowledge economy: literacy, numeracy, basic communications and problem-solving skills. Literacy proficiency, in particular, is essential not just for getting along in the world. It also creates a foundation for the engagement cluster.

The resilience cluster related to *engagement* is concerned with active participation in society. It entails more than simply adapting to social and economic pressures. Engagement reflects a sense of agency – the notion that individuals and communities can take control of circumstances that affect them. Involvement in public discourse, community decision-making processes, volunteering and recreation – all are expressions of agency. The voices and views of citizens actually count for something. Their social footprint is meaningful and significant.

Engagement is a function not only of programs and opportunities for active participation. It requires the removal of barriers that make it difficult for some individuals and groups to participate in communities and in society, more generally. Engagement is also influenced by the availability of public space. It is difficult to contribute in an authentic way to communities in the absence of places that enable shared activity and dialogue.

The links between individual capacity and community infrastructure are evident. Participation in recreational activities or sports clearly is made possible by amenities that allow this engagement – paths, hiking trails, parks and pools. Public space facilitates many forms of engagement. Neutral shared space provides a venue, for example, for members of diverse ethnic groups to exchange views around common concerns. It also enables them to work through tensions rooted in racial difference or religious intolerance. The notion of shared space, in this case, takes on true physical meaning.

Opportunity comprises the fourth resilience cluster. One stream of work in this cluster involves direct investment in work-related skills. Recent efforts have sought ways to make training more relevant to the needs and demands of the labour market. Customized training is an example of this trend. It creates bridges among voluntary organizations, the private sector, educational institutions and governments in an effort to find employment for marginalized workers.

Another group of actions in the opportunities cluster entails the creation of economic opportunities within the context of community economic development – the set of activities and organizations stemming from collective entrepreneurship and guided by principles of democratic engagement and shared profit. These actions represent investments in community infrastructure.

The opportunities cluster is also concerned with the creation of assets, through measures such as individual development accounts, learning bonds and homeownership. Building financial assets is considered a significant intervention not only for improving sustenance and the capacity to engage in society. Equally important, it fosters independence and choice, and again creates a sense of agency and hope for a better future.

Taken together, the core resilience clusters comprise the substance of the communities agenda. Resilience is the result of substantial and diverse activity in all four clusters, both individually and together. Each cluster itself must be healthy and robust.

Links between and among clusters must then be fostered in order to create a coherent agenda overall. Each resilience cluster is a complex system in itself. Each is composed of a wide set of actors and actions. Each has a set of parts that contribute to the overarching objective of resilience.

The examples of interventions in all four clusters show how investments in personal capacity and community infrastructure are closely linked within every domain. In fact, in some cases, they are inseparable. The school as hub acts as the venue within which to organize activities, such as family-based literacy programs. Investment in community infrastructure in the form of school hub provides the foundation for the focus upon individual capacity – in this case, literacy proficiency.

Despite their innate links, the two streams of intervention within each cluster typically act as though support for one domain has nothing to do with actions in the other. They operate like parallel tracks instead of being intrinsically joined.

Most of the activities within a given cluster remain as separate entities within that cluster. The component parts rarely function as a system. They are a set of disjointed pieces in which the left hand is often unaware of what the right hand is doing. This complexity makes it difficult to understand, let alone navigate, the systems within any given cluster. The parts often work at cross-purposes.

In sustenance, for example, activity concerned with affordable housing generally is not carried out with reference to policies linked to income security. In adaptation, early childhood development workers rarely engage with those involved in literacy proficiency – even though their efforts may focus upon the same people. In the engagement cluster, those concerned with marginalized youth or newcomers who feel excluded from the mainstream of society are just beginning to build bridges with those in the cultural and arts worlds. In the opportunity realm, activity concerned with skills development typically is separate from the creation of employment opportunities.

Most individuals, groups, organizations and even policies whose interests fall within the same cluster act like ships that pass in the night. There are far too few links among the wide-ranging interventions within the core resilience clusters. The links that do exist are often minimal or sub-critical – in that they do not create substantive shifts as a result of their exchange. The impact of individual efforts typically is diminished as a result. Moreover, the lack of collaboration can even create negative effects when the impact of one intervention actually works at cross-purposes to another.

Community challenges generally are addressed as distinct factors despite the fact that they are intrinsically linked and require a set of interwoven strategies for effective intervention. Comprehensive local efforts seek to forge links between and among these key factors.

These strategies recognize, for example, that a training program to help social assistance recipients move from welfare to paid employment will likely not succeed unless prospective workers who are parents have access to affordable child care. Programs to encourage the workforce participation of persons with disabilities must pay attention to their need for disability supports and workplace accommodation. Most children are unable to concentrate or learn if they go to school hungry. It is difficult to focus on studies or training if a household faces eviction at the end of the month.

Every individual piece within a given resilience cluster is significant. Each is an essential building block in the spectrum of actions that foster resilience. But the parts are rarely understood as a set of strategic interventions. They operate most often as one-off programs that may not even survive the limits of their funding arrangement.

Moreover, there are not enough points of interface to create genuine joined-up solutions. The core clusters have not bred the innovation that potentially is possible because they consist of isolated pockets of intervention focused upon their own concerns. The task of the communities agenda is figure out how to harness these clusters of activity in unique ways. Collaboration, explored later, is a core method.

There is a distinct shared space in which activities seeking the same or similar outcomes are not linked. There are also efforts in pursuit of the same or related outcomes that are working against each other. One of the major challenges of the communities agenda is to ensure that the strategic interventions within the resilience clusters work effectively as a system. While these four clusters comprise the resilience function, they themselves are constantly changing in response to new information as well as new policies and programs. Although it is possible to capture the system at any given point in time, it is essential to understand that the ground is always shifting and that new pressures, threats and opportunities are ever-present.

A core task of the communities agenda is to create healthy resilience clusters by improving the links among actors within each of the clusters. Its goal is to ensure that the sum total within the cluster is greater than the individual parts. There is a clear need for bridging mechanisms that can join up the various components into more cohesive processes.

Sometimes this bridging role is made more difficult, if not impossible, by the fact that key components of the system are missing. At times it is necessary to fill those gaps prior to playing the bridging function. Affordable housing and sufficient high-quality employment opportunities are prime examples. The main focus of the community efforts is to shore up these weaknesses. But it is equally important to ensure that the component parts – even though there might be undeveloped or missing pieces – are cooperating effectively in this task.

The communities agenda involves another type of bridging. Imagine the individual parts of a bicycle. Even if all the parts were present in one room – tires, chains, seat, brakes and handle bars – they would not go very far if they were not all working together. The individual parts are simply that. A bicycle, by contrast, is more than the sum of its parts. Put together, it can go a long way. Pulled apart, it goes nowhere. In fact, it is not even recognizable as a bike. In this case, the bicycle is the community and the resilience clusters are the component parts.

There are currently few links between and among the four resilience clusters to create a coherent whole. *A second core task of the communities agenda is to improve the links among the core resilience clusters.* Examples of this type of bridging currently are the exception rather than the rule. But the exceptions show the vast potential of making the links in the shared space between clusters.

A co-operative housing initiative, for instance, has built in a training component in which residents learn the skills of housing repair and management. They learn how to take care of their property and also acquire a marketable skill. This particular initiative is working in the shared space between the sustenance and opportunity clusters.

Another illustration of the bridging function can be seen in the affordable housing project that promotes literacy proficiency and leadership training for youth. This work links the sustenance cluster with the adaptation and engagement clusters, respectively. School programs initiated as supports for immigrant families often provide a venue for volunteering or cultural expression. These types of actions bridge the adaptation and engagement clusters.

A third core task of the communities agenda is to improve the links among communities and governments. It seeks to narrow the gap that currently exists between community needs and government policy at all levels.

Perhaps the most significant intervention in this area of shared space is to ensure that the interventions and actions undertaken by communities are accompanied by relevant policy work that enhances or supports the program and relationship changes that they are building. In BC's Capital Region, for example, people have worked hard to create a housing trust fund in which most of the 13 municipalities have come together to combine into one common fund their investments for affordable housing.

The advantage of this integrated approach is that the region will be able to plan more strategically if it is working as one rather than multiple and diverse sources of funds. The region can ensure that this pool of capital grows. It then determines collectively where to allocate those resources in order to leverage more affordable housing units.

Equally important, the initiative has made an effort to influence a series of changes to municipal bylaws that support the development of affordable housing over the long term. The establishment of a regional housing trust fund is part of the Regional Housing Affordability Strategy, which enables future work in this area.

Another example of community-government bridging arises around recreation – identified in both theory and practice as an important means of promoting engagement.[24] Community initiatives can work with local governments to secure various policy measures that support this involvement. These include subsidies for recreational programs, equipment or supplies; lower prices for use of facilities at certain times; and secondment of recreational staff to work with designated groups or neighbourhoods.

Yet another area for bridging: Comprehensive initiatives seeking to develop assets for low-income households have found that their efforts actually have harmed welfare recipients in some jurisdictions. The positive measures inadvertently have resulted in reductions in assistance or loss of eligibility. In this case, work in the shared space involves engaging provincial governments to reform their respective social assistance laws and practices. Ideally, government officials would be approached at the earliest stages of a community effort in order to anticipate and avoid potential negative consequences.

In some instances, provinces and municipalities have changed their legislation to accommodate various improvements rooted in community efforts. In other cases, the governments did not introduce legislative or policy changes but agreed to protect the initiative by designating it as an exception or pilot that was studying the behavioural impact of a certain intervention.

These are just a few examples of how the communities agenda can help connect communities and governments. Communities are in a unique position to create strategic links in the areas of shared space – within clusters, between clusters and around policy. The communities agenda provides an essential relational function. Collaborative relationships are at the core of this bridging work.

All this to say...

Four resilience clusters – sustenance, adaptation, engagement and opportunity – comprise the substantive focus of the communities agenda. Cluster-based economic development, earlier described, pointed out that it is not possible for clusters to survive on their own. They need to be sustained through quality foundations which ensure their health. The process elements of the communities agenda are as important as its substantive focus.

The process of working in these areas of shared space is neither simple nor simplistic. This preliminary discussion of the communities agenda makes clear that it is a multi-faceted agenda within the complex setting of communities. The first step in the process of the communities agenda is to organize for complexity – the subject to which we now turn.

Endnotes

[1] Putnam, R. (2000). *Bowling Alone: The Collapse and Revival of American Community*. New York: Simon and Shuster.

[2] Florida, R. (2002). *The Rise of the Creative Class*. New York: Basic Books.

[3] World Commission on Environment and Development. (1987). *Our Common Future*. Oxford: Oxford University Press (Brundtland Commission).

[4] Torjman, S. (2001). *Reclaiming Our Humanity*. Ottawa: Caledon Institute of Social Policy, Coalition of National Voluntary Organizations, United Way of Canada and the Canadian Council on Social Development, December.

[5] Jackson, A. (2000). *Why We Don't Have to Choose Between Social Justice and Economic Growth: The Myth of the Equity/Efficiency Trade-off*. Ottawa: Canadian Council on Social Development, October.

[6] For a description of the work of the Resilience Alliance and the ecological interpretation of resilience, see *www.resalliance.org*

[7] Gunderson, L., C. Holling, L. Pritchard and G. Petersen. (2001). "Resilience." In H.A. Mooney and J. Canadell eds. *The Earth System: Biological, and Ecological Dimensions of Global Environmental Change*. Encyclopedia of Global Environmental Change. Scientific Committee on Problems of the Environment. Vol. 2: 530-531.

[8] Gunderson et al. *Ibid*.

[9] Westley, F., B. Zimmerman and M. Quinn Patten. (2006). *Getting to Maybe: How the World is Changed*. Toronto: Random House Canada, p. 5.

[10] See, for example, Frankel, V. (1959). *Man's Search for Meaning*. Boston: Beacon. See also V. Frankel and B. Benard. (1993). *Turning the Corner from Risk to Resiliency*. Portland, OR: Northwest Regional Educational Library.

[11] Lash, R. (2004). "Want health and happiness? Be resilient." *The Globe and Mail*, November 5, C6.

[12] For a description of Project Resilience, see *www.projectresilience.com*

[13] Wolin, S.J. and S. Wolin. (1992). "The Challenge Model: How Children Rise Above Adversity." *Family Dynamics of Addiction Quarterly*, 2(2).

[14] Kretzmann, J. and J. McKnight. (1993). *Building Communities from the Inside Out: A Path toward Finding and Mobilizing a Community's Assets*. Evanston, Ill: Center for Urban Affairs and Policy Research, Neighbourhood Innovations Network, Northwestern University.

[15] Steinhauer, P. (1996). *Methods for Developing Resiliency in Children from Disadvantaged Populations*. Paper prepared for the National Forum on Health. Ottawa, March.

[16] Willms, JD. ed. (2002). *Vulnerable Children: Findings from Canada's National Longitudinal Survey of Children and Youth*. Edmonton: University of Alberta Press.

[17] Steinhauer, P. (1996). *The Primary Needs of Children: A Blueprint for Effective Health Promotion at the Community Level*. Ottawa: Caledon Institute of Social Policy, April.

[18] Torjman, S. and E. Leviten-Reid. (2003). *Innovation and CED: What They Can Learn from Each Other*. Research paper commissioned by the Community Economic Development Technical Assistance Program (CEDTAP) housed at Carleton University. Ottawa: Caledon Institute of Social Policy, January.

[19] Jarboe, K. and A. Alliance. (2001). *Knowledge Management as an Economic Development Strategy*. Washington, DC: Economic Development Administration, US Department of Commerce.

[20] Porter, M. (1990). *The Competitive Advantage of Nations*. New York: Free Press.

[21] Den Hertog, P., E. Bergman and D. Charles eds. (2001). *Innovative Clusters: Drivers of Innovation Systems*. Paris: Organisation for Economic Co-operation and Development.

[22] Linden, R. (2002). *Working across Boundaries: Making Collaboration Work in Government and Nonprofit Organizations*. San Francisco: Jossey-Bass, p. 4.

[23] Economic Development Administration (EDA). (1997). *Cluster-Based Economic Development: A Key to Regional Competitiveness*. Washington, DC: US Department of Commerce.

Chapter 2
Organizing for Complexity

In summary

Communities must organize themselves strategically in order to embark upon and sustain work in the four resilience clusters. The decision-making processes currently in place in communities typically are not able to effectively address the complexity of the challenges they face.

The primary step in working in the shared space is to establish a local decision-making process that ideally is multisectoral in representation. Its purpose is to develop a strategic plan that is both comprehensive and long term. Despite the focus upon problems, the plan must build first and foremost upon community strengths. An emerging style of leadership, sometimes referred to as 'leading between,' is required to steer the collaborative process involved in organizing for complexity.

Communities are complex systems

The goal of the communities agenda is to foster resilience in order to build strong and vibrant communities. Resilience is the result of actions in four independent but related clusters: sustenance, adaptation, engagement and opportunity. These dimensions of resilience comprise the *substance* of the communities agenda.

The main task of the communities agenda is to work in the shared space – within the resilience clusters, between clusters and around policy. That is the *process* of the communities agenda.

The core clusters that comprise the substance of the communities agenda derive from research on the concept and practice of resilience. The literature on resilience is important not only for identifying the substance of the communities agenda. It is also instructive for its process – how to work in the shared space. Resilience involves the capacity to cope with, adapt to and thrive in the face of ongoing change, complex challenge or sudden threat. Adaptive capacity is a core theme.

The notion of adaptive capacity, which is a defining characteristic of resilience, has been the focus of considerable interest in recent years. The ecological interpretation of resilience, in particular, lies at the heart of a body of scientific study concerned with complex adaptive systems. This emerging science explores the functioning of living ecosystems in order to apply the lessons embedded in their adaptive capacity.[1]

The concept of complexity has also been the subject of extensive research rooted in complexity science, which represents a growing body of interdisciplinary knowledge about the dynamics of change. The development of a complex systems view emerged in response to the fact that the important questions about a given field tend to be too big for any one discipline alone to answer.

Complexity science essentially can be understood as the study of complex adaptive systems and the patterns of relationships within and between them. Networks with multiple interacting parts are a key feature of these adaptive systems. Their structure and very existence depend upon the constant flow of new information and resources.

Complexity science is rooted in the study of living organisms – with all their messiness, unpredictability and emergence.[2] This body of work is based on the assumption that neither a given system nor its environment will ever be constant. Uncertainty and paradox are inherent features; continual change and natural creativity are the norm. As decision-makers, individuals within a system are highly interdependent. *Problems can be solved only by understanding the patterns of relationship and resulting activity.*

Organizations traditionally were analyzed – and portrayed in schools of management – as machines with discrete parts that could be drawn clearly on an organizational chart. The lines of communication and relationships within these organizations were viewed as straight and vertical. Linear systems that follow clear and predictable patterns effectively become the sum of their parts.

The work on complex adaptive systems, by contrast, draws its conclusions from the study of ecosystem response to changing environments. It applies these lessons to the challenges facing organizations and communities. Complex adaptive systems involve many components which are linked in nonlinear fashion. They are more than the sum of their respective parts because of their multiple connections at many levels. While this diversity creates unpredictability, it can also give rise to creativity and innovation.

Communities can be seen as complex adaptive systems that are alive and continually evolving. They are far from a static set of organizations and sectors with clear lines of accountability. They face constant challenge and change. They are messy and unpredictable. That is their strength.

The 21st century world of complex systems and turbulence is no place for disabling and dispiriting mechanistic thinking. We are confronted daily by events and outcomes that shock us and for which we have no answers. The complexity of modern systems cannot be understood by our old ways of separating problems, or scapegoating individuals, or rearranging the boxes on an org chart. In a complex system, it is impossible to find simple causes that explain our problems or to know who to blame. A messy tangle of relationships has given rise to these unending crises. To understand this new world of continuous change and intimately connected systems, we need new ways of understanding. Fortunately, life and living systems offer us great teachings in how to work with a world of continuous change and boundless creativity. [3]

In applying complexity science to organizations and communities, adaptive capacity appears rooted in the ability to engage in various forms of creative problem-solving and to learn through the application of new knowledge. The test for communities as evolving ecosystems is to anticipate change, enhance their capacity to manage challenge and harness opportunity. They undertake these tasks within a context that is both evolving and unpredictable.

The social and economic context is complex

In addition to being complex systems, communities themselves are rooted in a difficult social and economic context.[4] Major urban centres struggle with tough challenges related to complex social problems – racial tensions, social exclusion, unstable housing tenure, homelessness, drug abuse and domestic violence – though these problems are not unique to large cities.

Despite an improved economy overall, far too many communities still grapple with high rates of unemployment and poverty. Immigration and population shifts within the country – from rural to urban and from reserve to city – have created tensions rooted in racism and exclusion. The shifts have also given rise to new social needs, such as settlement assistance, affordable housing, language training and the recognition of credentials acquired offshore. Many neighbourhoods face additional stresses related to the marginalization of certain populations.

While the overall unemployment rate in Canada has improved since the difficult mid-1990s, the jobless rate for some groups remains higher than average. They include young people who drop out of school, women who leave the workforce for extended periods to care for young children or aging family members, displaced older workers, Aboriginal Canadians, recent immigrants, visible minorities and persons with disabilities.

Neither does the aggregate unemployment rate take into account the extent of underemployment – i.e., the numbers working fewer hours than they would like or at jobs that fall below their capabilities. While there are no official figures, underemployment is known to be especially high among young people and new Canadians whose skills acquired offshore are often not recognized in this country.

Over the past decade, there has also been growth of nonstandard employment – including self-employment, contract work and part-time work. Many of these jobs offer little more than a low wage and insecurity. There is no pension coverage or supplementary health provision. There are few opportunities for training to upgrade skills or act as a steppingstone to better employment.

Even for those working full time, minimum wages and above-minimum but below-average earnings do not usually provide a living wage. The money is simply not sufficient to cover decent affordable housing and adequate food for a family. The working poor comprise about half of Canada's low-income population and are typically not eligible for benefits, such as supplementary health and dental care, which most welfare programs make available, however inadequately.

Our system of social programs has not, as a whole, met its full potential. The wartime proposal for a federal program for unemployed workers who do not qualify for or who exhaust their unemployment insurance benefits never came to pass. Many jobless Canadians end up on provincial or territorial welfare or may not even qualify for the social safety net altogether.

The rapid postwar expansion of Canada's social security system began to slow in the mid-1970s as it struggled to cope with pressures imposed by significant economic, social, demographic and political changes that continue today. Marriage breakdown and single motherhood are key causes of poverty and inequality, and create demands on welfare and social services.

The mass movement of women into Canada's workforce in the past few decades has had profound and continuing implications for social and economic policy. These include the need for family policies such as child benefits, early learning and child care services, parental leave and family-friendly workplace practices. More than half of all working-age women are now employed in the paid labour market.

Medicare never expanded beyond doctors and hospitals to provide the full range of mental and physical health care for all Canadians, including preventive care, home care, prescription drugs and dental care services, envisaged by its architects. Canada also failed to build a comprehensive system of income security, and social and employment services for persons with disabilities – many of whom must rely on social assistance for income support and disability services.

Taken together, the economic, social and demographic factors create a tough mix. Marriage breakdown, underemployment and low earnings threaten to condemn, in their old age, a growing number of Canadians to poverty. Child poverty brings a higher risk of health challenges and poor school performance. These problems can limit opportunities in adulthood, resulting in greater likelihood of unemployment and low wages, increased demand for social programs and lost tax revenue.

In addition to the changing content, the very nature of work itself – the basis for livelihoods – has shifted dramatically with machines replacing human heads and hands in many areas of production and life, more generally. This substitution is by no means a new phenomenon. Continual technological change is one of the defining characteristics of market economies. But upgraded technologies – especially those that are information-based – are transforming work-places and are demanding ever-renewed and higher levels of knowledge, skill and education.[5]

The liberalization of trade has also had a major impact upon the structure of economies. International trade agreements have modified substantially the way that many industries, in both Canada and abroad, do business. Most local economies throughout the country, and indeed the world, are still adjusting to these structural changes. Communities that once thrived on traditional manufacturing jobs experience similar difficulties. As these industries have relocated, closed or downsized, their laid-off workers have been thrust into a precarious labour market.

Again, the shift toward the globalization of economies is not new. The movement of people and goods across borders has taken place for thousands of years. What *is* different is the speed of change, hastened by technological innovation, and the rapid and explicit expansion of markets opened up through liberalized trade.

From an economic, social and environmental perspective, globalization is a two-edged sword. On the one hand, it has generated additional wealth in many countries, which have seen an overall rise in living standards. It has also made clear the deep connections among nations.

At the same time, globalization has given rise to unprecedented disparities. Some say that it encourages a 'race to the bottom' in which the relentless corporate search for cheaper and leaner modes of production has resulted in the loss throughout the industrialized world of millions of decent jobs. It has created social dislocation in response to widespread unemployment and glaring inequalities of wealth, which have led in turn to concerns about social cohesion and marginalization.

Lack of funds to support the range of required interventions has long been a stumbling block in progress against complex problems. The current property tax base, on which local governments must rely for the bulk of their revenues, is too limited to tackle the scope of challenges with which all communities grapple. An even deeper structural weakness results from their lack of fiscal levers to raise, on a sustained basis, the revenues they need.[6]

But revenue gap, while substantial, is only one obstacle. The sheer sweep of issues that communities must address has shed light upon an equally serious problem. There is a significant governance gap – or mismatch between the complexity of local challenges and the corresponding problem-solving capacity. Governance refers to the structures and processes by which decisions are made and power is shared. Communities must put in place, first and foremost, decision-making mechanisms that enable them to grapple with complexity.

Communities need new structures to tackle complex challenges

If communities are to promote resilience, they need to move from narrow and hierarchical forms of decision-making to more sophisticated processes. Municipal governments generally have assumed responsibility for tackling local challenges. While they are on the front lines of decision-making, they are effectively constrained in this capacity.

Municipalities deal mainly with issues that fall within their mandate – though these vary by province. They may need a broader set of community voices if they seek changes in areas beyond their political jurisdiction that have significant local impact, such as provincial health policy or federal transportation policy. While democratic by definition, electoral representation may not reflect the richness of the community in terms of its racial, age or sectoral profile.

Municipal governments are also bound by electoral clocks and are thereby inherently limited in their actions.

Local governance bodies differ from municipal governments in several important respects. While local governance bodies are not elected structures, they seek explicitly to identify and harness the range of assets embedded in communities, no matter how impoverished or 'distressed.' Local governance structures make a deliberate and conscious effort to capture the diversity of community in both demographic profile and composition by sector. Nor are they hampered by the rhythms and constraints of the political process. They can develop plans which are longer term in vision and scope than can municipal strategies that are limited by electoral mandates.

It is of interest that the emergence of local governance structures actually embodies, at a community level, a major transformation under way throughout the world. The shift *from government to governance* reflects a move away from governing by detailed rules and regulations set out in acts of parliament to decision-making by frame-setting legislation. The formulation of more thorough regulation and policies is left to local institutions and actors.[7]

The importance of local governance is also embedded in the notion of sustainable development. A move to more sustainable forms of development requires significant changes in decision-making. Creating an appropriate governance framework and the necessary tools to assist local efforts are critical to the goal of achieving sustainable communities.

Local governance bodies play a pivotal role in the communities agenda. They provide the focal point for its unique expression and act as its champion. They help set a guiding vision for the local effort and its associated strategic plan. They determine the resilience clusters and specific areas of shared space upon which to focus. They identify and bring together diverse players to make these decisions.

Local governance structures also harness resources, including appropriate financing. They link the comprehensive initiative with relevant organizations, projects and resources in the broader community. They provide opportunities for learning and monitor results on an ongoing basis.

Of course, local governance bodies do not simply emerge on their own. They must be convened by an individual, group or organization able to act in this capacity. An effective convener must be a local actor with the ability to bring together many different parties with diverse interests.

The convener usually has a designated role in the community – political position such as mayor or city official, local funder like a United Way or representative of a certain interest, such as robust economy or active social services. Conveners must be, and must be perceived to be, both balanced and fair in their words and actions. The leadership challenges embedded in the convening role are discussed below.

Comprehensive initiatives are emerging

Local governance structures in many communities throughout the country, and indeed the world, have been responsible for spearheading a promising new form of community practice known to as 'comprehensive community initiatives.' This broad approach to local intervention typically engages a wide range of sectors and citizens in the resolution of complex problems.[8]

Comprehensive initiatives have emerged in recent years both in response to practices that have proven ineffective and as a reformulation of actions that have been tried in the past. While there is significant activity under way in most communities to meet social and economic needs, the interventions currently in place work like independent parts of a machine that have no links to each other. They tend to be discrete entities with their own missions, values, mandate, objectives and funds. They adhere to their unique mandate.

The new approach draws on practical evidence that actions meant to improve life prospects are often ineffective – at least in part because they are so piecemeal. Fragmented responses cannot possibly work well in a world in which all the components are intrinsically linked.

The weakness of the compartmentalized approach is that the parts of the system, when not integrated, are not simply benign. That would be good news. The reality is that the parts frequently work against each other in ways that make life more difficult. Eligibility for one form of assistance, for example, may cancel qualification for another. A benefit provided through one program may reduce the level of support delivered by another. Governments often play this trade-off game because it helps them reduce costs – though the 'savings' are usually false.

The practice of segmentation, or "hardening of the categories," creates significant blockage in the ability to accomplish anything effective.[9] Traditional methods have been unsuccessful because they do not take into account the wide-ranging factors at play or the joined-up interventions that ideally are required to make a significant difference.

> What we've learned in building community initiatives, is that because these little pots of money and resources flow into the community around categorical ideas, they create sub-constituencies or mini-constituencies in the community that have to compete with each other to survive. So in effect, what we've done with our resources from the outside source is we've disorganized the community, contributing to its dysfunction and downfall.[10]

Comprehensive initiatives, by contrast, seek to break down the artificial boundaries of compartmentalization that characterize the way that both governments and communities generally tackle social and economic issues. These initiatives draw on the "accumulating evidence that services meant to improve the life prospects of the poor were often proving ineffective – at least in part because they were so fragmented."[11]

Traditional solutions are also inappropriate because they often assume that government alone can solve problems without appreciating or harnessing the substantive contributions that can be made by others, including business, voluntary organizations and citizens. Governments typically are organized to deal with human problems as if these can be segregated into distinct social, health, education and economic needs. Most public spending is directed toward one component of a particular issue or remedial intervention after a crisis has occurred. Current government structures and community agencies appear to have limited capacity to address problems in holistic and preventive ways.

Comprehensive initiatives embody new perspectives on the changing role of government and the place of communities in promoting resilience. An approach shaped by the community is distinct from government practice, which usually identifies the desired goals of a project, activities deemed acceptable and associated time frame for their achievement. Comprehensive community initiatives, by contrast, place local actors and citizens at the heart of this definition.

Perhaps most important about the emerging comprehensive approaches is that complexity is written into their very blueprints, embedded in both their substance and process. They recognize the various components of tough problems and their related parts. Comprehensive efforts know that a complex set of 'joined up' actions is required to promote resilience. They are a positive response to the fact that traditional methods of dealing with issues – single programs to tackle identified problems – are inappropriate.

The new synthesis rejects addressing poverty, welfare, employment, education, child development, housing and crime one at a time. It endorses the idea that the multiple and interrelated problems of so-called 'vulnerable' neighbourhoods require multiple and interrelated solutions. [Its proponents] insist on combining physical and economic development with service and education reform, and all of these with a commitment to building community institutions and social networks.[12]

Comprehensive initiatives are creating a new weave of promising practices. These efforts seek to be broad-ranging not only from the perspective of the issues they choose to address. They are also inclusive from the vantage of the individuals they engage.

Fostering inclusion and diversity

The shift from government to governance has seen citizens assume an increasingly active role in decisions that affect their lives. Their occasional vote is not enough to make most feel that they are truly part of a democratic society in which their concerns are heard – let alone addressed. While governments are the primary formulators of policy, there is growing recognition of the need to engage the potential targets of any measure and citizens, more generally, in articulating policy questions and developing feasible options.

Clearly, comprehensive initiatives must take a flexible approach to citizen engagement. A diverse mix of citizen roles is possible, including serving on the local governance body or its working groups, providing a staffing function such as outreach work or community organizing, interpreting community data and attending public meetings.

Comprehensive initiatives must create opportunities for a wide array of these members, especially people living in poverty, racialized youth and Aboriginal Canadians who often are marginalized from these processes and community life more generally. Groups that are usually targeted for special consideration need to participate actively in local decision-making.

It is of interest that the diversity theme is embedded deeply in the concept of resilience. Studies of resilient eco-systems have shown that the ability to thrive in a changing context is greatly enhanced through diversity. Adaptive capacity in ecological systems is a function of genetic, bio-logical and landscape variety.[13]

From the perspective of the communities agenda, this diversity must be reflected not only through demographics. The sharing of decision-making responsibility may involve multiple linkages among citizens, government departments, the private sector and voluntary organizations. It also re-quires the collaboration of diverse stakeholders operating at local, regional, provincial, national and international levels.

Vibrant Communities is an example of a major initiative that embodies this multisectoral approach. At its core are 15 centres throughout the country seeking local solutions to reduce poverty. Because the poverty reduction strategy in each of the cities varies widely, they are joined in their re-spective efforts through a structured learning circle called the Pan-Canadian Learning Community.

Of the total group, six communities known as Trail Builders receive extensive funding to develop multi-year comprehensive strategies to reduce poverty.[14] While each plan is unique, all Trail Builders share an important feature. A local governance body assumes responsibility for the initiative and presides over its activity. In order to partici-pate in Vibrant Communities, each centre *must* involve di-verse representation in this governance structure: business, government, voluntary organizations and people living in poverty.

The governance body formulates, implements and evaluates all aspects of the local poverty reduction strategy.

Its work is guided by the principle of inclusion. People living in poverty are seen not simply as targets or subjects of the proposed interventions but as participants in the formulation and application of these actions. Their involvement helps ensure the relevance of the work.

Not surprisingly, this engagement is easier said than done. It is impossible for any group – let alone a local project with modest funding – to be entirely representative of the community. All it can do is try to move toward greater inclusion and monitor continually how well it is doing in this regard.

As a first step, each community must understand its face. Some of the collaborating cities have developed a formal poverty profile to identify more precisely their marginalized members, such as racialized youth, persons with disabilities or Aboriginal Canadians living off reserve. In other cases, entire neighbourhoods have been designated as high risk or 'vulnerable.'

Another challenge around inclusion relates to the logistics of participation. Many low-income individuals have not participated in these kinds of local initiatives. The processes can be intimidating – or at least not welcoming. Sometimes meetings are convened in venues like boardrooms or city council chambers, which are unfamiliar to many in the community. Both the formal procedures of such meetings and the language may be foreign, creating barriers to participation.

There are other practical issues. Meetings may be held in the evening to accommodate employed members of the local governance body. The result is that even those with low or modest incomes must pay for child care to enable their participation outside of school hours. Transportation is another problem not only with respect to cost. Many women feel vulnerable travelling alone in the evening.

Lessons from the ground include the fact that it is important to hold meetings in places like community centres and libraries where all members feel welcome and comfortable. It is also helpful to provide practical assistance, like child care subsidies or services to ensure that parents can participate. Ideally, meetings are combined with a nutritious meal for participants – and for their children if child care is made available on site.

Some communities have created advisory groups of low-income residents who serve as a sounding board for local initiatives. These groups can give feedback on priority issues, how the initiative presents the poor in its public communication and the most helpful ways to undertake identified strategies.[15]

Despite acknowledging the need for citizen engagement, the actual practice lags behind the intent. Sufficient progress has not yet been made around the inclusion of certain groups, such as Aboriginal Canadians and persons with disabilities – most of whom live in poverty. A conscious and deliberate effort must be made to involve these individuals as well as young people, particularly from diverse racial backgrounds.

Understanding the complexities

The creation of a local governance structure, diverse in both demography and sectoral representation, is the starting point for complexity. It is the body in which shared minds and perspectives can view the world through a complexity lens. At the heart of the communities agenda is the ability to see and appreciate the messiness of both the local context and its unique challenges.

The factors that comprise a given problem are often so intrinsically linked that it is difficult to pinpoint a single trigger or sole cause. In fact, communities typically face a cluster of interrelated complexities rather than a single problem. It is not surprising that the UK refers to these tough challenges as "wicked problems."[16]

Take, for example, the question of poverty concentration in urban centres. While less acute than in American cities, there has been growing income polarization and geographic concentration of low income in many Canadian neighbourhoods. In 2004, Statistics Canada reported that poverty had become increasingly concentrated in low-income neighbourhoods in the nine largest urban centres in the country. The number of high-poverty neighbourhoods jumped from 190 in 1980 to 291 by the year 2000.[17]

But these so-called distressed neighbourhoods are defined by more than the concentration of poverty. The data show that they are characterized as well by a constellation of factors, which include teenage pregnancy and high proportion of lone-parent families, low levels of full-time school attendance, poor literacy skills, higher rates of chronic and mental illness, housing instability, substance abuse and crime, greater numbers of working age adults without market income and disproportionate reliance on government income security programs.

It is not possible within this confluence of characteristics to say that one single dimension is the primary root cause of the 'distress' and that the other factors ensue as a result. The problem at hand – in this case high rates of inner-city poverty – could have been triggered by any one or several of these elements. A range of possible drivers, either singly or in combination, may be responsible. Sorting out causes and effects is difficult.

For some households, poverty may result from poor literacy skills, which made it difficult for the family head to find decent employment. Teenage pregnancy may prevent young women from completing their high school education and finding suitable employment. In other households, illness or disability may have significantly interrupted or even prevented participation in the paid labour market. In short, multiple starting points can lead to the same result – in this case, low income.

This example is meant to illustrate a general point: *The presence of multiple factors at play in a given set of circumstances means that there are many possible starting gates for taking action to tackle the problem. The challenge is to find the appropriate levers or points of intervention.*

The framework put forward in this book argues the need to intervene in all core resilience clusters – sustenance, adaptation, engagement and opportunity. Granted, it may not be possible to work in all clusters at the same time. But it is at least feasible to think in four domains and to explore the links among their constituent parts. It is also possible to devise a strategic plan that ultimately involves intervention in all four clusters.

The process of tackling complex work must start with a clear statement of objectives. International research on the social indicators of well-being is helpful in this regard.

The Organisation for Economic Co-operation and Development (OECD) is an international body that monitors trends in economic and social well-being, primarily in developed countries. Its publication *Society at a Glance: OECD Social Indicators* presents an overview of social trends and policy developments using indicators from OECD studies and other sources. The indicators include information on the numbers of asylum seekers and suicides, divorce and fertility rates, low-paid employment, joblessness, days lost to strikes, prison populations, gender wage gaps, longevity, health infrastructure, and educational and poverty levels.[18]

To help understand the links among these seemingly disparate indicators, the OECD has grouped them into four broad objectives of social policy: improved human health, enhanced self-sufficiency, greater social inclusion and great-er equity of outcome. Each major societal objective can be seen to correspond, respectively, to the four resilience clus-ters – sustenance, adaptation, engagement and opportunity. The work in each cluster effectively is driven by an overall objective, which is rooted in international thinking but ex-pressed through local action.

Because different routes may be taken to achieve a de-sired objective, there is growing recognition of the need to state clearly the rationale for the pathway that communities have chosen to pursue. The challenge for the local initiative lies in the articulation of its intended strategy. In fact, evalu-ation models currently being developed around complex themes refer to this formulation as the 'theory of change' that underlies the specific actions.

Theory of change implies an intended pathway – or linked sequence of steps that lead to a set of desired goals.[19] The community may assume that certain residents are poor primarily because they lack access to affordable housing. It may decide to launch a series of actions to deal first with the accommodation problem. Another community may deter-mine, by contrast, that the poverty experienced by designat-ed groups results largely from lack of access to training and employment opportunities. It may choose to embark upon an entirely different approach to the problem.

> A theory of change statement is a brief description of the con-
> text in which the initiative is taking place, the goals and tar-
> gets it is pursuing and the strategies it has adopted. It presents
> the ideas and assumptions guiding the initiative and explains
> the unfolding pathway it anticipates following to achieve its
> intended results. The theory of change serves as a conceptual
> baseline against which progress and lessons learned can be
> identified as the initiative evolves.[20]

Once the community has identified its desired object-ive, it then engages in a process of 'backwards mapping' to determine how to reach that goal. It starts at the end and works back to spell out the steps to be taken in respect of that objective. Part of the effort involves an identification of community assets.

From problems to assets

Traditional approaches to local intervention generally have assessed communities from the perspective of their weaknesses. Emerging approaches, by contrast, view communities as the sum of their strengths – capacities that can be harnessed to tackle their problems. Comprehensive initiatives start with the premise that, in order to be successful, development must have its roots planted firmly in the community and must harness its key assets in the form of local talent, commitment, skills and resources.

The asset-based approach to community development clearly acknowledges the deep-rooted problems with which communities must grapple. It does not gloss them over or pretend that these have no impact upon local psychology. It recognizes, for example, that economic production has changed dramatically with a loss in manufacturing and outsourcing of employment beyond the borders not only of communities but also the country. Shifting economic sands have been linked to poverty, crime and substance abuse.

Large urban centres, as noted, face stresses arising from immigration with insufficient resources to aid the settlement of diverse communities. Other communities are losing population – especially their young people, who are finding greener pastures in oil fields and tar sands. But dwelling on these problems is not the solution.

In response to this desperate situation, well-intentioned people are seeking solutions by taking one of two divergent paths. The first, which begins by focusing on a community's needs, deficiencies and problems, is still by far the most traveled, and commands the vast majority of our financial and human resources. By comparison with the second path, which insists on beginning with a clear commitment to discovering a community's capacities and assets, and which is the direction this guide recommends, the first and more traditional path is more like an eight-lane superhighway. [21]

Asset-based community development sees the conventional needs-driven path as a dead end. The alternative route focuses upon capacities and strengths. It opens up a range of possible interventions not previously considered. A capacity framework leads to the development of policies and activities based on abilities, skills and assets – especially of low-income people and their neighbourhoods – as a way to move constructively toward solutions.

An important body of literature on asset-based community development refers to the strengths of individuals not so much as resiliences but rather as gifts or talents. Every person, regardless of family circumstances or so-called special needs, brings to the world a unique set of gifts and talents. It is these gifts that need to be recognized and harnessed in order to improve the quality of life in communities – regardless of the identified problem.

The *Our Millennium* project was essentially about giving gifts – but not in the traditional sense of the concept. *Our Millennium* was a special project initiated in the late 1990s by the Community Foundations of Canada to mark the new century. Designed as a nationwide public engagement program, its purpose was to use the occasion of the millennium as an opportunity to strengthen and celebrate community.[22]

The project invited Canadians to make lasting gifts – group projects or activities that make their communities better places. They were encouraged to contribute their gift within one of 11 theme areas: youth and children; arts and culture; environment; heritage; connections; recreation; learning; safety and crime prevention; care and support;

global citizenship; and other. More than 6,500 projects were registered involving an estimated 4.6 million participants.

The type of giving encouraged by the project was entirely voluntary and non-commercial. Its purpose was to foster a sense of community in which people came together and felt that they had made an important contribution and had connected with others by virtue of their small, but significant, action.

The resource manual *Building Communities from the Inside Out* sets out a framework and practical advice for finding and mobilizing a community's assets. It outlines the potential gifts – especially of community members such as young people, persons with disabilities and seniors – typically considered to have little to offer in the way of positive contributions.[23]

Of course, identifying assets can be a major challenge in itself. The glass-half-empty mindset is not trained to recognize strengths. It is often difficult to identify capacity when the siren call is the morass of problems around which the community has rallied. *Building Communities from the Inside Out* sets out a proposed inventory to map both individual capacities and the assets of communities.

The inventory of personal skills, in particular, is wide-ranging and substantial. Virtually every aspect of household management, including window washing, household cleaning, lawn mowing, catering, bartending, dishwashing and driving a car or van, is considered a valuable skill. To that is added the list of community skills such as organizing church dinners, doing yard work and participating in parent-teacher associations.

Together these lists of capacities carry a strong message: Most people have a wide range of abilities that are rarely recognized as strengths or exceptional qualities. Many of these skills can form the basis of a business or enterprise.

It is of interest that this asset-based approach is consistent with the notion of capacities put forward in the Nobel prize-winning book *Development as Freedom*.[24] The central thesis of this book is that healthy human development is a function not only of what individuals *have* in the form of concrete assets but also of what they can *do* in terms of their abilities. Human development must be concerned with both poverty and capability – the capacity to cope, adapt, grow and thrive through mobilizing often unrecognized skills and opportunities.

This notion of innate strengths applies equally well to communities. Every locality – no matter how poor or impoverished – is rich in resources. Communities also have innate resiliences or assets that provide a strong foundation upon which to build. Every community can start from a position of strength despite the fact that it typically is viewed from the perspective of its weaknesses.

In its *Community Resilience Manual,* the Centre for Community Enterprise identifies 23 local assets that are associated with resilience, including such factors as the outlook of citizens, quality of their relations and availability of financial and organizational resources.[25] The manual describes how a local area can assess its vitality in respect of these features and take intentional action to meet the challenge of change on an ongoing basis.

The concept of assets also figures prominently in a body of literature on sustainable livelihoods. This work is concerned with the ways in which communities self-organize to ensure that all members have access to the basics of life. It identifies the major pools of capital – natural, built (sometimes referred to as produced capital), social, human and financial – upon which communities can draw to create sustainable livelihoods.[26]

Natural capital refers to land, stocks of natural resources and ecosystems. It is essential to survival and comprises the basis of life. Built capital includes buildings, equipment, machinery and physical infrastructure, such as water and waste systems, community centres and playgrounds that do not occur naturally. Social capital refers to relationships, networks and norms that enable collective action. Human capital comprises the knowledge, skills, competencies and other attributes embodied in individuals that facilitate the creation of personal, social and economic well-being. Financial capital involves stocks of available wealth in the form of cash and other liquid assets as well as capital held as stocks, bonds and other securities.

Another significant asset is cultural capital, which links members of a group through bonds rooted in common values, language, customs, traditions, beliefs and arts. The United Nations *Convention for the Safeguarding of Intangible Cultural Heritage*, which took effect in 2002, defines intangible cultural heritage as the practices, representations, expressions, and knowledge and skills that communities and groups recognize as part of their cultural heritage.[27]

Intangible heritage is expressed through language, performing arts, rituals and festive events, knowledge and practices concerning nature and the universe, and traditional craftsmanship. It is seen as distinct from tangible cultural heritage and its derivative cultural industries – which include publishing, music, audiovisual technology, electronics, video games and the Internet.

Growing interest in pools of capital has helped shift attention from a sole focus upon traditional measures of economic activity, such as gross domestic product (GDP), to investment in different forms of wealth that underpin development. The capital model is being employed in the formulation of indicators by national and international bodies, such as the wealth of nations work being undertaken by the World Bank.

In Canada, the approach has been incorporated in several contexts, such as the efforts of the National Roundtable on the Environment and the Economy, the genuine progress indicators (GPI) devised by the Pembina Institute for Appropriate Development and GPI Atlantic, and the Canadian Index of Well-being formulated by the Atkinson Charitable Foundation in association with several partner organizations.

The mapping of assets has emerged as a key methodology to help identify obvious and latent strengths embedded in individuals, groups, organizations, institutions, and natural and built space. All communities can build from a position of strength despite their struggle with tough problems. The asset-based approach sees abundance – and in this sense is consistent with the mental health notion of resilience as a set of inner strengths. The challenge lies in finding the leaders who bring with them, and can draw out, the glass-half-full philosophy.

New leadership style is required

With comprehensive community initiatives as a new breed of local intervention, it should come as no surprise that they require a different style of leadership in order to function effectively. Articulate champions are needed to inspire support for these efforts and maintain commitment during difficult periods.

Leading these kinds of complex undertakings is neither easy nor straightforward. It involves careful judgment and skill in building consensus. The local governance structures that assume responsibility for the comprehensive community initiative deliberately convene representatives from sectors that typically do not speak the same language, let alone share a common world view or consider working together. It often takes considerable time and patience to ensure that all parties are on the same page.

Working on complex initiatives can be stressful, especially for the conveners of the effort. They need to blend patience for the time it takes to build vision and relationships with the pressure to achieve quick wins. They continually must seek new participants to invigorate the community process.

The multiple challenges along with the delicate balancing of diverse interests and perspectives implicit in the work mean that leaders of comprehensive efforts often need assistance, peer learning and time for renewal. Local governance structures and their respective conveners require adequate support in order to sustain their efforts over time. They can benefit from opportunities to develop their skills and expertise, especially in light of the many relationship challenges.

A new style of leadership is necessary to enable the effective work of local initiatives that involve diverse players trying to address multifaceted issues. This emerging leadership involves a focus on relationships – or 'leading between.'

> Networks challenge our conceptions of leadership, which too often are still rooted in an outmoded 'great man' theory that mistakes the formal authority of status, rank or station with the exercise of leadership. When you ask people about the leadership of an organisation, most people reach for the organigram and point to the top. When it comes to leading across networks there are no such easy answers. New network-based ways of organizing social and economic activity will only thrive if we can evolve new models of leadership that embrace the distinct 'organising logic' of networks, and do not seek to apply an old set of principles in an environment that has been dramatically altered. We must learn what it means to lead effectively not just within individual organizations, but across the networks of which they are part. 'Leading between' will be the new leadership imperative of the coming decades.[28]

This 'leading between' style differs from traditional models, which view leaders as the individuals who are vested with power and influence, and who can persuade people to follow a single or common vision. Participants in a community process effectively become the followers who look to the leaders to provide direction. Followers rarely are encouraged to recognize their own capacity to take initiative or solve problems for themselves. Collaborative relationships, built on mutual respect rather than formal authority, involve skills that have not before been required of public sector leaders.

The new leadership style required for complex initiatives appears to lie less in decision and more in deliberation. It is not so much a question of characteristics or personality traits of individuals but rather their behaviours or what they do, especially around building trust and cultivating strong working relationships among parties to a common effort. As in the complexity science earlier described, leaders must pay attention to the relationships within and between the parts of the systems with which they are engaged.

> Now more than ever, we have to fundamentally shift our ideas of what makes an effective leader. We have to shift them away from this secretive, command and control, "we know what's best." …. We need to go from the leader as hero, to the leader as host. [29]

The new leadership style requires an understanding of the dimensions of networks, which spark innovation and help address complex problems more effectively. These so-called 'smart networks' embrace diversity and encourage the development of quality relationships that foster innovation and collaboration. Those who play a pivotal role in knitting together the diverse players are referred to as 'network weavers,' who employ a unique set of skills to assist the development of quality connections.[30]

Finally, the new leadership involves the sharing of credit among the diverse players involved in a collaborative effort. This sharing is often difficult when promotion and recognition are based on individual performance appraisals that typically look at quantitative criteria, such as number of publications or projects, level of sales or contract revenue. Funders can effect change by encouraging – or even requiring – broader recognition of those involved in joint work.

Another barrier to collaboration is the age-old problem of turf war – the fact that recognition usually is accorded to an individual or department within an organization rather than to a cross-cutting team effort. This is especially true of governments, which are organized along rigid vertical lines rather than in horizontal clusters. The new leadership style taking hold within comprehensive community initiatives may go some way to address the problem. It is a style based on mutual support and shared credit for achievements among all involved parties.

One way to reduce turf war is to compel collaboration as part of the performance expectation. The UK government, for example, explicitly requires what it calls 'joined-up' work around social exclusion and neighbourhood renewal. This approach is described more fully in the chapter on *Creating an Enabling Environment*. Of course, compelling any type of behaviour will not necessarily reduce interpersonal tensions. These will always exist and their mediation requires a different form of relationship building.

It is also of interest that a new type of turf war actually has appeared on the horizon. In some communities, several different organizations have taken it upon themselves to assume the role of convener. They have created their own comprehensive initiative. In fact, one city recently counted 17 of these processes.

The good news is the recognition of the need for local governance structures to address complex issues. The bad news is the time and resources that can go into planning, possibly at the expense of local action. In fact, multiple structures inadvertently may be creating a new form of fragmentation and duplication – albeit a more sophisticated and complex one than in the past. Relationship tensions quickly bubble to the surface under these circumstances.

There are other challenges inherent in comprehensive initiatives that leaders must address. A real constraint, for example, is the demand on time, energy and resources. The supports required for multifaceted, community-based initiatives – even though they may be relatively abundant when assets are broadly included in the mix – are always stretched to the limit. Local efforts realistically can achieve only so much. They struggle continually to find a balance between broad definition of the issue and relatively targeted strategies to tackle its various elements.

Comprehensive initiatives typically articulate overall goals within a long-term vision. While these objectives are crucial for charting the scope of the work, they must be balanced by shorter-term targets and concrete actions that provide tangible evidence of progress. Interim goals can help generate the momentum to sustain participation and attract additional partners. The challenge for communities is to find the right combination of strategic vision and specific action.

It is possible that a community already has rallied around a concern, such as child poverty, early childhood development, settlement of new Canadians or racial tolerance. In this case, the community may decide to work on the broader set of issues one step at a time – by focusing first upon areas around which it can claim some victory. The importance of achieving quick and early wins as part of long-term comprehensive processes should not be underestimated. The successes help keep people at and around the table when they see that their efforts have borne fruit.

In a study conducted with leaders of comprehensive community initiatives in the US, for example, most interviewees warned against initial wide-ranging planning without quick tangible results.[31] In order to maintain momentum, comprehensive initiatives must pursue issues and concerns that resonate with the lived reality of local residents. At the same time, these efforts must be guided by a longer-term, strategic vision so as not to be overwhelmed by the multiple facets of the concerns that brought them together in the first place.

All this to say…

One way to keep going in the face of wicked problems is to recognize, celebrate and harness the assets that comprise the wealth of every community. But harnessing assets moves beyond their mere recognition. It involves unleashing their potential by enabling new combinations that lead to innovative solutions. The challenge is to determine how to capture this rich set of assets – whether singly or in combination through novel forms of collaboration. The range of collaborative possibilities lies at the heart of *Working in the Shared Space*, to which we now turn.

Endnotes

[1] Zimmerman, B. (2005). "Generative Inquiry and Relationships: Complexity and Applied Dissemination." Presentation to the Applied Dissemination Workshop, J.W. McConnell Family Foundation, Montreal, April 14-15.

[2] Westley, F., B. Zimmerman and M. Quinn Patton. (2006). *Getting to Maybe: How the World is Changed*. Toronto: Random House Canada.

[3] Wheatley, M. (2001). "Innovation Means Relying on Everyone's Creativity." *Leader to Leader*. The Peter F. Drucker Foundation for Nonprofit Management. Spring, 20: 2.

[4] Battle, K., M. Mendelson and S. Torjman. (2006). *Towards a New Architecture for Canada's Adult Benefits*. Ottawa: Caledon Institute of Social Policy, June.

[5] Torjman, S. and K. Battle. (1999). *Good Work: Getting It and Keeping It*. Ottawa: Caledon Institute of Social Policy, February.

[6] Torjman, S. and E. Leviten-Reid. (2003). *The Social Role of Local Government*. Ottawa: Caledon Institute of Social Policy, May.

[7] Torjman, S. (2002). *From Trade-Off to Trade-Up*. Ottawa: Caledon Institute of Social Policy, February.

[8] These are described in Torjman, S. and E. Leviten-Reid. (2003). *Comprehensive Community Initiatives*. Ottawa: Caledon Institute of Social Policy, March.

[9] Charles Pascal, Executive Director of the Atkinson Charitable Foundation.

[10] Yates, G. (2004). "Rebuilding Communities." *Ideas That Matter*. 3(2): 16.

[11] Schorr, L. (1997). *Common Purpose: Strengthening Families and Neighborhoods to Rebuild America*. New York: Anchor Books: 306-315.

[12] Schorr, L. (1997). *Ibid*, p. 319.

[13] Folke, C., J. Colding and F. Berkes. (2002). "Building resilience for adaptive capacity in social-ecological systems. In F. Berkes, J. Colding and C. Folke eds. *Navigating Social-Ecological Systems: Building Resilience for Complexity and Change*. Cambridge, UK: Cambridge University Press.

[14] Torjman, S. (2005). *The Group of Six*. Ottawa: Caledon Institute of Social Policy, April.

[15] Torjman, S. (2004). *Engaging Disenfranchised Groups in Urban Health*. Ottawa: Caledon Institute of Social Policy, October.

[16] See discussion of "wicked problems" in V. Bogdanor ed. (2005). *Joined-Up Government*. Oxford: Oxford University Press, p. 6.

[17] Heisz, A. and L. McLeod. (2004). *Low-income in Census Metropolitan Areas, 1980-2000*. Ottawa: Statistics Canada, April.

[18] Organisation for Economic Co-operation and Development (OECD). (2005). *Society at a Glance: OECD Social Indicators*. Paris.

[19] Fulbright-Anderson, K. A. Kubisch and P. Connell. (1998). *New Approaches to Evaluating Communities. Volume 2: Theory, Measurement and Analysis*. Washington, DC: Aspen Institute.

[20] Leviten-Reid, E. (2005). *Learning and Evaluation for Trail Builder Initiatives in Vibrant Communities*. Ottawa: Caledon Institute of Social Policy, February, p. 4.

[21] Kretzmann, J and J. McKnight. (1993). *Building Communities from the Inside Out: A Path toward Finding and Mobilizing a Community's Assets*. Evanston: Center for Urban Affairs and Policy Research, Neighbourhood Innovations Network, Northwestern University.

[22] Torjman, S. and E. Leviten-Reid. (2001). *Social Capital and the 'Our Millennium' National Project*. Ottawa: Caledon Institute of Social Policy, April.

[23] Kretzmann, J. and J. McKnight. (1993). *Building Communities from the Inside Out: A Path toward Finding and Mobilizing a Community's Assets*. Evanston, Ill: Center for Urban Affairs and Policy Research, Neighbourhood Innovations Network, Northwestern University.

[24] Sen, A. (1999). *Development as Freedom*. London: Oxford University Press.

[25] Colussi, M., M. Lewis and P. Rowcliffe. (2000). *The Community Resilience Manual: A Resource for Rural Recovery and Renewal*. Port Alberni, BC: Centre for Community Enterprise.

[26] See, for example, the Sustainable Livelihoods Framework formulated by the UK Department for International Development at *www.dfid.gov.uk*

[27] Torjman, S. and D. Minns. (2005). *Sustainable Development Framework for Science and Technology: Social and Cultural Dimensions*. Ottawa: Caledon Institute of Social Policy, February.

[28] Skidmore, P. (2004). "Leading Between." *Demos Collection*. 20: 89-102.

[29] Wheatley, M. (2002). "The Servant-Leader: From Hero to Host: An Interview with Margaret Wheatley." *www.margaretwheatley.com/articles/herotohost.html*

[30] See, for example, *www.networkweaving.com*

Chapter 3
Working in the Shared Space

In summary

Each of the four resilience clusters can be understood as an area of shared space. Work in the shared space involves three main tasks. An evidence base to support the selected intervention must be developed. Collaborative relationships must be formed, where possible and appropriate. Progress toward identified goals must be monitored on an ongoing basis with results fed back into the process for course correction as required. Knowing, doing and reviewing comprise the three components of work in the shared space.

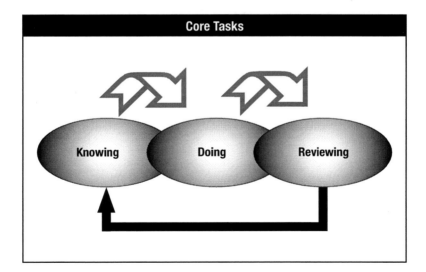

The context

The goal of the communities agenda is to foster resilience in order to build strong and vibrant communities. Resilience is the result of actions taken in four interdependent clusters related to sustenance, adaptation, engagement and opportunity. Work in the shared space ensures that the clusters, both individually and together, are performing to their greatest potential. The communities agenda seeks both rigour and excellence in local initiatives.

The chapter on *Organizing for Complexity* noted that a core leadership challenge lies in guiding the work in the shared space. This activity involves the creation of healthy resilience clusters in which the component pieces function well together – in which the sum of joined-up efforts is greater than the contribution of the individual parts. This relational work derives from the application of the concept of innovation and, more specifically, the practice of cluster-based economic development.

As described, economic clusters can be understood as geographic concentrations of connected companies, service providers, suppliers, customers and manufacturers of related products. Clusters can also include governments and other organizations such as laboratories, policy institutes, colleges and universities, standard setting agencies, and trade and professional associations that provide specialized research and information, education and training, and technical support.

Members of a given cluster basically form an ecosystem. *Clusters represent networks of activity within a shared space.* It is the relations between and among firms – not their mere co-location – which are the key drivers of success.[1] There is an active dimension implicit in clusters in that they involve diverse interactions and links within and among various streams of activity. These exchanges create multiple benefits related to ideas, knowledge, skills, human resources and financing.

From an economic perspective, companies expand the expertise available to them when they locate within a cluster of firms. They can draw upon organizations with complementary skills to bid for larger contracts for which individual companies are unable to compete. They can exchange information and knowledge as well as goods and services. Organizations within a cluster can also take advantage of economies of scale by specializing production within individual firms, joint purchase and common marketing.

In order to succeed, the firms that comprise various clusters seek to understand their potential client group or target market. They work from the most up-to-date scientific, technological and financial information. They keep abreast of, and often try to change, the regulatory environment in which they operate. They monitor and track the activity of firms in related fields ("the competition" in business terms) – all the while looking for opportunities for collaboration and joint venture.

In applying the practice of cluster-based economic development to the communities agenda, the four clusters that comprise the resilience function can be seen as equivalent to economic clusters. The task of the communities agenda is to spark and support multiple exchanges within and between clusters.

Several core elements of work are involved in ensuring these linkages. They relate to gathering information, creating collaborative relationships and monitoring progress: knowing, doing and reviewing. These dimensions of work in the shared space are considered here in general terms. Subsequent chapters apply these dimensions to each resilience cluster.

Studies of the knowledge economy have found that the creation, storage, application and exchange of knowledge are best managed through clusters.[2] As in its economic application, these strategic groupings require a solid knowledge base. Information must be updated regularly and fed back into the cluster to reinforce its current efforts or to change direction as needed. Healthy clusters are composed of interactions that both reinforce existing relationships and create new links. It is these multiple exchanges that spark innovation – the application of ideas in novel ways. Collaborations give rise to new combinations of ideas and action.

The previous chapter described how work in the shared space starts with the creation of a local governance mechanism, diverse in both demography and sectoral composition. A core task of this governance mechanism is to assess the wicked problems that have drawn them together in the first place and the scope of work they will undertake to tackle these concerns. It sets out a pathway of intervention by articulating the theory of change that underpins the challenges they intend to address. It develops an associated logic model with a clear statement of objectives.

This statement helps determine how widely the initiative will cast its net. The process involves the identification of community assets and possible ways to harness them in new combinations. The community is ready to start working in the shared space.

Knowing:

Building the evidence base

Working in the shared space requires a clear understanding of the dimensions of the identified cluster that the community has selected as the primary focus of its interventions. If it has decided to work on affordable housing, homelessness or income security, for example, then its efforts will situate mainly within the sustenance cluster. If it is concerned with child care, social networks or literacy, then the adaptation cluster is its principal arena. Work on recreation, cultural expression or local decision-making is rooted in the engagement cluster. Intervention in the areas of skills training, employment and asset creation falls within the opportunities cluster.

Once the point of entry for community intervention is identified, the context must be understood from several perspectives. A clear contextual and conceptual knowledge base comprising various types of information is required. Knowledge is more than just information – it is data combined with experience, context, interpretation and reflection.

While the term 'knowledge' often is used generically, the International Organisation for Economic Co-operation and Development (OECD) breaks down the concept into several component parts.[3] *Know-what* refers to basic factual information and effectively presents the profile of a given problem. *Know-why* provides the causal or correlative explanation that underlies the know-what. Correlation means that certain factors generally are found together, though there may be no proof that one actually causes the other. *Know-how* is concerned with the requisite skills or ability to do something. Know-how is linked closely to *know-who* – the relevant people or groups considered to be the key actors around a given issue.

Why is it important to know about these 'knows'? It is not sufficient to understand only the know-what or know-why of a given situation. It is the know-how that typically makes things happen. This know-how often is transmitted through or undertaken by the know-who part of the equation – members of the community. Local people "know where the ice is thin" – crucial knowledge when skating through complex problems.

The OECD literature uses the terms standard and codified knowledge, which generally represent know-what and know-why, respectively.[4] Codified knowledge does not become alive or applied until it is tempered by tacit knowledge reflected in the know-how and know-who. This combination often means that quantitative objective data must be blended with qualitative subjective information in order to get a complete picture of a specific issue.

Know-what

Know-what refers to the current state of the designated cluster. An initiative focused upon poverty, job creation or child development, for example, will need to collect data pertinent to these issues. Know-what often takes the form of statistical data that present a picture of local circumstances.

Know-what may include, for example, basic demographics such as population size, age and racial profile. It may involve an economic snapshot such as average income, rate of unemployment or reliance on income security programs. Its social dimensions – as indicated by educational attainment, marital status, average cost of housing and percentage of households in core housing need – may also be of interest.

But relevant statistical data are often difficult to obtain at the local level. National data generally are not easily disaggregated and many communities are now putting in place systems and processes to help draw the home picture.

The Waterloo-based poverty reduction initiative called Opportunities 2000, for example, developed a poverty profile that formed the basis of its work.[5] The profile included data on the rate and depth of poverty as well as a breakdown of low income by group, such as youth and persons with disabilities. The data were gathered from local statistics and the disaggregation of national data to that region.

As part of the national Action for Neighbourhood Change initiative, a working draft of a Neighbourhood Vitality Index was created.[6] The Index provides a framework for establishing baseline profiles of designated neighbourhoods from a potential pool of 180 indicators. It also includes indicators that track progress on the change process itself. United Way of Canada-*Centraide Canada* is working with the Centre on Governance at the University of Ottawa and the City of Ottawa to create a network of organizations and individuals that will enable the sharing of practice and comparison of research findings on place-based work, including further development of the Neighbourhood Vitality Index.

The Community Foundations of Canada has launched a civic indicator initiative based on the Toronto Community Foundation's Vital Signs effort.[7] Vital Signs is an annual community check-up that measures the vitality of the community, identifies significant trends and assigns grades in at least 10 areas critical to the quality of life. While each community will choose its own indicators, every year there will be a set of common issues and core indicators that all foundations will include in their reports and upon which the Community Foundations of Canada will base its national report.

The J.W. McConnell Family Foundation has provided support for the pilot phase of the Vital Signs program in which the Community Foundations of Canada will develop tools to support the application of this work throughout the country. Community foundations in Toronto, Ottawa, Montreal, Vancouver, Victoria, Calgary, Red Deer, Medicine Hat and Waterloo Region will pilot the instrument.

In response to the need for local data, the statistical agency of Newfoundland and Labrador developed, in association with Memorial University and the provincial Strategic Social Plan, a set of Community Accounts.[8] These accounts are compiled from a variety of statistical databases and sources of information that are then translated into a uniform template for every community across the province. The profiles are posted to a Community Accounts website to which all government departments, community organizations and individuals have access. While the information enables each locality to understand its unique profile, the province-wide consistency helps communities assess their progress relative to other regions. Nova Scotia is involved in a similar effort known as Community Counts.

In 2006, Agriculture and Agri-Food Canada's Rural Secretariat followed the examples provided by Newfoundland and Labrador and by Nova Scotia, and launched a national statistical website. Communities across the country may now access, free of charge, economic and demographic information that can be used as the basis for planning and revitalization work.

In order to construct a comprehensive picture of the know-what, communities may need to work with a range of organizations within the cluster. These include core voluntary organizations such as social planning councils, early childhood development centres, arts councils and economic development agencies for information related to sustenance, adaptation, engagement and opportunity, respectively.

Local governments and universities may also have relevant data and research capacity to contribute to the effort. In the absence of data, they can provide advice as to the most appropriate methodology to collect the information. Part of working in the shared space involves developing relationships with the organizations able to interpret the relevance of data and its implications for action.

Know-why

The know-why component of the evidence base takes the form of the theory of change that provides an anchor – both destination and direction – to the relationship building which ultimately must be carried out within and between clusters. While different routes may be selected to tackle an identified problem, there is growing recognition of the need to state clearly the rationale for the pathway – or linked sequence of steps – that individual communities have chosen to pursue.

The community may assume, for example, that residents in certain neighbourhoods are unable to break out of poverty. Because they cannot afford decent accommodation, they may live in unstable, poor quality housing that affects their physical and mental health. The community may choose to launch a series of actions to tackle the lack of adequate housing.

Another neighbourhood may decide, by contrast, that the poverty challenge would be better addressed by focusing upon appropriate training and employment. If the problem has been compounded by racial discrimination or workplaces that are inaccessible to persons with disabilities, it may embark upon a broad educational approach in which citizens actively engage in dialogue on the key issues.

A theory of change, described in the chapter on *Organizing for Complexity*, involves the formulation of a logic model that spells out a series of linked actions. This articulation is founded upon research evidence derived from theory and practice in relevant areas, such as poverty reduction, child development and neighbourhood renewal.

Once the community has identified its desired objectives, it then engages in a process, sometimes referred to as 'backwards mapping,' in order to determine how it will reach that goal. It starts at the desired objective and spells out the steps that must be taken to arrive at that point. It sets out the map for the journey upon which community members have agreed to embark.

The theory of change developed by the community effectively comprises its unique know-why. The details of the journey are delivered by the relevant know-how.

Know-how

Know-how refers to information about specific interventions – or various ways to reach the desired destination. In the case of poverty reduction, for instance, there are many possible interventions, which ideally are combined in unique ways.

These options include providing high-quality child care to assist working parents; enhancing literacy, numeracy and basic computer skills; and making available opportunities for training and upgrading in various market-relevant fields. Other possible interventions link prospective workers to job vacancies; support community economic development; make available grants and loans for entrepreneurship; ensure an adequate supply of affordable housing; and remove barriers experienced by certain groups, such as racialized youth and persons with disabilities.

At the public policy level, measures that help reduce poverty include higher child benefits to provide more money to lower-income families; an adequate minimum wage, indexed to inflation; and a 'living wage' paying better than minimum wages that cannot provide an adequate income, especially to families.[9] An associated set of actions can be taken by local governments to decrease or offset costs such as lower bus fares and fees for recreational and cultural programs; financial assistance with recreational equipment and clothing; and child care subsidies in Ontario municipalities.

Additional measures to tackle poverty can be delivered through the income tax system. The taxpaying threshold can be raised so that workers with low earnings can pay less income tax and retain more of their take-home pay. Employment Insurance and Canada/Quebec Pension Plan payroll taxes can be reduced – again to enable workers to keep more of their earnings. The value of nonrefundable and refundable tax credits can be increased to ease the taxpaying burden for lower-income households.

Unlike traditional medicine in which certain problems typically require specific responses, complex social and economic problems with many components involve a range of diverse interventions focused upon individuals, households and groups. Another set of interventions is concerned with trying to influence the broader social and economic context – such as the availability of quality child care or affordable housing. Individual and community interventions are described in subsequent chapters on the core resilience clusters.

Know-who

Know-who is a question of knowing who is involved, both in the community and beyond its borders, in related initiatives. This information helps in the application of lessons from similar work. Equally important, it may be possible to link in some way with existing efforts in order to share resources or even to create new forms of intervention.

The information base for the cluster should include a map of key players in the cluster and current interventions. As discussed in the chapter on *Organizing for Complexity*, a technique known as asset mapping has emerged as a core tool to surface both the obvious and latent strengths of communities embedded in individual members, groups, organizations, institutions, and natural and built space.

Understanding the Early Years is an example of a major national child development initiative whose interventions are shaped by the extensive inventory of local data in each community.[10] Assets are plotted on a map so that their geographic location and dispersion can be clearly identified. These patterns are juxtaposed with statistical data on key child development outcomes in order to create better links among problems and resources, and to see where improvements can be made. The project is an example of how the information base – the know-what, know-why, know-how and know-who – comprises the foundation for the doing component of the work.

Vibrant Surrey, a partner in the national Vibrant Communities initiative, is developing a geographic informational system (GIS) mapping tool. The Economic Security

Mapping Project will help provide a clearer picture of the community by breaking down information to the street level. It can combine the location of child care services and providers, for example, with existing demographic information to identify strengths and gaps in resources.

Know-who also involves understanding what orders of government and, more specifically, which departments have authority for certain domains. Under the *Constitution Act* of 1982 that replaced the *British North America (BNA) Act* of 1867, the federal government is responsible for the peace, order and good government of the country. The Act confers a spending power that allows Ottawa to make payments to individuals, institutions or other governments for purposes that Parliament does not necessarily have the power to regulate. The federal government has jurisdiction over areas that affect the well-being of the nation, including the armed forces, communications and international trade.[11]

More complex is the field of income security in which both federal and provincial governments share an interest. From virtual provincial authority in the 1860s, income security has evolved over time as an area of federal dominance. Ottawa pays for and administers the Canada Child Tax Benefit and the Universal Child Care Benefit. It is responsible for delivering and financing three elderly benefits – Old Age Security, the Guaranteed Income Supplement and the Allowance – as well as veterans' benefits.

The federal government has authority for the programs deemed to be social insurances – namely Employment Insurance and the Canada Pension Plan. Even here, the issue is not absolutely clear cut; Quebec runs the parallel Quebec Pension Plan and significant changes to the Canada Pension Plan require the agreement of a majority of provinces. Provincial governments administer last-resort social assistance, commonly known as 'welfare,' and deliver various tax credits. They also operate workers' compensation.

The federal government effects significant redistribution of income through a progressive income tax system. It collects revenues and distributes social benefits through refundable credits, nonrefundable credits and deductions.

Constitutional responsibility for health and welfare, by contrast, was accorded to the provinces. They operate a wide-ranging set of programs and services related to education, health care, home supports, early childhood development and child care, social assistance, housing, training and employment, transportation, and culture and citizenship.

Municipalities have emerged in recent years as pivotal players in the search for sustainable development – solutions that seek simultaneously to advance economic, social, cultural and environmental well-being. Local governments are an especially important focal point for social intervention, given their crucial role in housing and homelessness, public health, transportation, and culture and recreation.[12]

Municipalities in Ontario, in particular, have had to assume a leading role in the social arena, primarily as a result of the so-called disentanglement exercise in 1998. The province announced at the time that it was assuming responsibility for education but turned over to local governments the authority and associated costs for social assistance and social services, including child care and home supports – though without adequate compensating revenues.[13]

Doing:

Creating links

The 'doing' component of the communities agenda involves the creation of links among existing players within the cluster or forging new relationships within and between clusters. Most of the doing in the shared space involves some form of collaborative work.

Collaboration is a broad concept that refers to a wide range of engagement possibilities – from the simple exchange of information to deeply entangled joint ventures. Included in the collaboration continuum are information exchange, shared learning and training, integrated development plans and initiatives, consolidated application procedures and protocols, joint procurement and common evaluation. It should be noted that groups in Québec have longed worked in various collaborative forums. Their *'tables de concertaction'* are just one example of how they have tried to organize strategically within and between sectors.

Some would argue that collaboration involves the production of a common good or service. It results when people from different organizations or units within the same organization produce something together through joint effort, resources and decision-making, and share ownership of the final product or service.[14] Collaboration is not an end in itself but is merely the means to an end – whether it be improved service delivery or a bigger objective like reducing poverty.

Despite diverse definitions and forms of collaboration, these relationships are linked by a common foundational principle: The whole is generally greater than the sum of its parts. There is an underlying assumption that the results of a collaborative effort typically are larger and deeper than what any single person, group or organization alone can achieve. The creation of links within and between clusters lies at the heart of joined-up communities.

The trend toward joined-up interventions is a world-wide phenomenon. The move has been promoted through the power of new communications technologies. Open source programming and knowledge-based collaborations, such as Wikipedia, are breaking down traditional boundaries and are pushing the bounds of the possible. In fact, the exchange of knowledge is the most common form of collaboration.

Information exchange

Information exchange can take many different forms and involves minimal entanglement. But even the most basic collaboration – the simple but deliberate sharing of information – is important for the health of any single initiative and, indeed, for the cluster.

One example of a sustained form of information exchange was the 18-month policy dialogue in 2004 linked to the Vibrant Communities initiative, earlier described. Representatives from 10 federal departments – (the former) Human Resources Development, Health, Heritage, Justice, Status of Women, Industry, Citizenship and Immigration, Privy Council Office (Urban Aboriginal Strategy), Indian and Northern Affairs, and the Canada Mortgage and Housing Corporation – were invited to a monthly discussion convened by the Caledon Institute of Social Policy.[15]

The purpose of the dialogue was to deepen awareness among government officials about comprehensive strategies for poverty reduction. It provided a forum for government and community participants to reflect on how they might work together to tackle poverty.

Although government officials generally recognize the significant role that communities play in addressing complex issues, sustained opportunities to explore with practitioners the challenges involved in local work are rare. A decision was made to alternate presentations between government and community participants. Initial meetings focused on building a common language and shared understanding about comprehensive, multisectoral approaches to poverty reduction.

Throughout the process, an effort was made through telephone hook-up to encourage the participation of low-income residents in particular. Community members from Saskatoon, for example, described the 20-year plan they had developed to revitalize inner-city neighbourhoods and to strengthen the voice of low-income residents in provincial social assistance policy. In another case, representatives from the Inner City Halifax project, many of whom are African Nova Scotian, talked about their experience of racism and discrimination.

Joint research

Researchers both within and between universities are working increasingly in collaborative arrangements in order to expand the range of their knowledge and scope of their investigations. The questions that they are able to raise by virtue of this sharing and the scope of possible solutions to explore expand dramatically when different disciples combine their respective areas of knowledge and expertise.

One of the most elaborate research consortia in the country is the Human Early Learning Partnership (HELP) that integrates behavioural and social sciences with biomedical sciences to study life course development, with an emphasis on the early years of conception to age 6. HELP involves more than 200 faculty, researchers and graduate students from six BC universities: University of British Columbia, University of Victoria, Simon Fraser University, University of Northern British Columbia, Thompson Rivers University and University of British Columbia Okanagan Region. Since its inception in 2002, it has been building a collaborative research infrastructure involving seven major research units.

One of those research units is known as The Consortium for Health, Intervention, Learning and Development (The CHILD Project). CHILD is a team of academic researchers and community professionals from across British Columbia whose goal is "to study early childhood development through a series of linked, interdisciplinary research projects."

Ten research studies within The CHILD Project address this overall goal through distinct philosophical and

disciplinary lenses. Studies include a focus on income assistance, outdoor play spaces, home instruction for parents
in Aboriginal communities and infant neuromotor screening. Every study is made up of a partnership between an
academic team of researchers and at least one community
agency; most teams include researchers from more than one
discipline. The use of different, but complementary, methodologies was designed to provide, within one coherent
program of research, information on the contexts and pre-
dictors of early child development.

Joint learning

Joint learning is another form of collaboration that goes beyond the exchange of information. It refers to explicit and
focused efforts to ensure that participants working toward
a common goal understand the scope of the issues and keep
current in their respective fields of interest.

Communities of practice represent one form of collaborative learning, which involves sustained meetings with representatives from diverse organizations to promote learning
in ways not easily produced by other arrangements, such
as one-time training sessions. This joint learning seeks to
develop a shared repertoire of methods, tools, techniques,
language, stories and procedures. Communities of practice
achieve this goal by building a sense of trust and comfort in
asking questions and exploring various methods around a
given intervention.

Representatives from diverse federal departments recently formed their own community of practice around the
communities agenda. They meet regularly to explore topics
of common interest, such as improving collaboration within
the federal 'family' and finding ways to line up their work
more closely with local efforts.

Another example of shared learning is the Pan-Canadian Learning Community embedded within Vibrant

Communities. The 15 participating sites meet on a month-ly basis, typically by teleconference, to develop and share practice around their respective areas of work. The learning structure has helped individual communities attain a higher profile, both at home and throughout the country, than had they worked on their own. This profile raises public aware-ness and promotes a broader understanding of poverty and possible interventions. It is significant as well when seeking support from funders.

The fact that the communities are linked together is also empowering. Participants have stated that the national con-nection gives them a voice beyond their own community.

Equally important is the quality factor. In theory, shar-ing lessons helps ensure that groups need not start from scratch every time they embark upon a particular course of action. They can learn from each other, effectively raising the bar of practice for all. The topics explored through this learning initiative include business engagement in poverty reduction, strategies for sustainable incomes, fundraising for social change, living wage campaigns, gender and pov-erty, community involvement in policy change, and learn-ing and evaluation.

Shared planning and intervention

Shared planning and intervention lie at the core of the com-munities agenda. Many communities have begun to forge links among groups and organizations involved in specific policy areas, such as affordable housing.

A Housing Affordability Partnership grew out of an earlier collaborative initiative and included representatives from the Community Council, BC Housing, Canada Mort-gage and Housing Corporation, Canadian Homebuilders Association, Urban Development Institute, Rental Owners and Managers' Association, nonprofit housing providers, Vancouver Island Health Authority, financial institutions, municipal planners and community associations. Several other cities have similar coordinating mechanisms. The Housing Affordability Partnership actively supported the creation of a regional housing trust fund, described in the next chapter on *Supporting Sustenance,* to coordinate the flow of capital into various housing projects and subsidies.

The Safe Communities Foundation is another example of shared planning and intervention. It is a unique partnership between the private and public sectors with a mission to make Canada the safest place in the world in which to live, learn, work and play. In a safe community, all sectors work together to reduce injuries and ensure the safety of members. The concept is rooted in an official World Health Organization international safe community movement. Because the term 'safe community' is not legally owned or controlled by any one group, it is used and interpreted in many different ways throughout the world.[16]

Collaboration can also take place within government – though it should happen more often than it does. There is extensive literature on the need for increased collaboration, often referred to in government circles as 'horizontal management.' The development of federal councils is an example of how federal departments within a geographic locale can work together on common issues. Horizontality in government is discussed at greater length in Chapter 8 on *Creating an Enabling Environment.*

Service integration

Service integration is a form of collaboration that brings together two or more service providers for more comprehensive and coordinated delivery. There is growing interest in shared service delivery as a way to overcome the artificial segregation that creates gaps, redundancies and problems, described earlier in *Organizing for Complexity.* At the federal level, efforts are under way within the newly created

Service Canada to rationalize and ease entry to federal programs and services. The approach largely follows the lead of other orders of government that have long tested various forms of service integration.

Perhaps the most advanced in this respect is Québec, which for several decades has consolidated its provision of health and social services in local community service centres (known as CLSCs or *Centres locaux de services communautaires*). It recently has taken additional steps toward service integration by establishing 95 local service networks. Their role is to ensure that services within each geographic region are accessible and delivered in an integrated fashion.

Integration of services is a key policy thrust in Saskatchewan led by the Human Services Integration Forum, a group of senior officials from across provincial human services departments. With the support of Regional Intersectoral Committees, its mandate is to strengthen interagency planning and service delivery across the province.

School[PLUS], an initiative of the Government of Saskatchewan launched in 2002, is a model for schools and communities to work together toward learning success and well-being for every child and young person in the province. The goal of the program is to ensure that schools provide relevant and responsive learning programs that develop the 'whole child,' with support from networks of community members, families, social, health, justice, and culture and recreation.

The Children's Treatment Network of Simcoe York is another interesting example of collaboration. It was created in response to the barriers faced by many families with children with severe disabilities. The Network is a nonprofit delivery model that serves the needs of children with multiple disabilities. It is an integrated network involving numerous service providers, including health care, education, recreation, social and community resources. Its purpose is to create a single point of contact for families and a cohesive plan of care for children and youth from birth to age 19 who have a wide range of multiple disabilities and complex conditions.

Many local governments throughout the country have consolidated their housing, social services and recreational programs within a single department. The City of Hamilton, for example, has achieved this integration through its Department of Community Services. York Region is another example of service integration. After extensive consultation with stakeholders and community members, Regional Council approved a Human Services Strategy that recommended the creation of a coordinating body dedicated to the long-term and integrated planning for and funding of human services.

The City of Edmonton has joined up programs within the Community Services Department. Its report *Towards 2010 – A New Perspective: An Integrated Service Strategy* describes how the Community Services Department coordinates its range of programs and services. The Edmonton plan is discussed at greater length in the chapter on *Creating an Enabling Environment.*

Joint ventures

In some cases, governments have moved from service integration within their own sphere to joint ventures that involve other orders of government. Collaborative arrangements, such as tripartite agreements, have emerged in response to the fact that certain organizations – including governments – do not have sufficient fiscal or jurisdictional levers to do the job. Only by combining their respective mandates, resources, skills and plans can they achieve common objectives.

Under the Vancouver Agreement, for example, the federal, provincial and municipal governments developed a strategic plan for the Downtown Lower East Side. The March 2000 agreement commits these governments to work together, along with communities and local business, on a coordinated strategy to promote sustainable economic and social development in that area.

The Canada-Manitoba-Winnipeg Agreement for Community and Economic Development is a similar joint venture. Its purpose is to provide a mechanism for coordinating and implementing a community and economic development strategy for Winnipeg. The parties to the Agreement are expected to work with the voluntary and private sectors to identify methods for increasing community capacity, renewing downtown and older residential neighbourhoods, improving opportunities for urban Aboriginal peoples, and encouraging sustainable economic development through innovation and technology.

Another example of multi-government collaboration at the local level is the seven-city arrangement in Alberta. Exceptional growth in Central Alberta prompted municipalities located along a shared band of highways to work together to promote their region as a well-planned, coordinated and attractive place to visit and do business. Mayors, reeves and senior staff from four counties and seven cities and towns met to create standards to guide development along a common corridor. Discussions centered on a joint approach for landscaping, signage and design for building facades and orientation, screened storage and other development. The participating communities have formulated a joint business plan to be financed through a shared-cost agreement.

Joint problem-solving

Other collaborative efforts involve communities and governments working together to solve complex problems. The Trail Builders in the Vibrant Communities initiative are engaging increasingly in solving problems in association with various orders of government. The United Way of Calgary, for example, organized a series of meetings involving community organizations and representatives from the Alberta government to discuss the Assured Income for the Severely Handicapped program, which pays monthly benefits to persons with severe and prolonged impairments.[17]

The intent of the structured problem-solving process was to address, through dialogue rather than confrontation, the weaknesses embedded in that income security program. The rationale was that if government officials understood the presenting problems, they would be in a better position to resolve them or at least consider solutions. The provincial government responded positively to the process and announced several important improvements, including an increase in benefits as well as their indexation to inflation.

This type of approach exemplifies the collaborative work between communities and government. It illustrates how positive results can be achieved by turning private troubles into public issues. Ideally, every intervention within the communities agenda will seek ways to effect broader shifts by incorporating, where possible and appropriate, a policy dimension that helps scale up its local actions. The intent is to create larger systemic change by taking on bigger leverage points – that have an impact on tens, hundreds and possibly thousands of households.

Most collaborative efforts are self-organizing. But sometimes groups and organizations are instructed to work this way – the choice is not theirs and they are responding to a clear requirement set by the leader. In this case, the leadership is far more directive and prescriptive than the emerging style discussed in Chapter 2 on *Organizing for Complexity*.

The UK experience in joined-up solutions to joined-up problems, described in the chapter on *Creating an Enabling Environment*, is probably the most sophisticated example in the world of government involvement in joint ventures. The disadvantage to this approach is that the agenda is not entirely community-driven and generally needs ongoing government direction and support to sustain it. The advantage is that this enforced collaboration usually achieves measurable results – the third key dimension of work in the shared space.

Reviewing:

Monitoring progress

Evaluation typically is undertaken to determine whether selected interventions worked or not – whether they were positive or negative, strong or weak, relative to their intended results. While this information is important, it may not be the most critical. It is clearly not sufficient. The purpose of monitoring progress is not only to measure results. Equally crucial is the need to learn from the intervention and to adjust direction as the innovation develops.

Evaluations typically begin *after* the foundations of an initiative have been laid and the work is already under way. It would be more helpful to have feedback about performance on an early and ongoing basis so that interventions which appear to be less than effective might be identified and altered.

Traditional learning and evaluation generally look back and assess the difference between then and now. Emerging work within complex community initiatives moves beyond a simplistic retrospective. It is important to know this information sooner than later – which may be too late.

Perhaps the central question in the review process is not so much which interventions worked effectively but rather what was learned from a given effort. Both the 'what' and 'why' are important. Which interventions were considered positive and why? What factors contributed to their success?

Why did certain actions not work well? What could have been done differently to ensure a better result?

Evaluation that values learning shifts the focus of the review from one of judgment to continual improvement. It views the world not in after-the-fact black and white but in varying and changing shades of gray. It assumes that mistakes may be made because the course being pursued is virtually uncharted. At any point, a shift in direction from the original work plan may be required and should not be considered a failure. In fact, no change in direction may be a sign that there has been little self-critique – or even fear to take bold steps.

This focus upon learning presents a challenge. In the past, most community initiatives were not really encouraged to learn. They were supported to do whatever it takes to succeed in meeting identified targets and measurable results. Sometimes the only way to *know* what might be appropriate is to *do* and then *review*. The doing and reviewing lead to new knowledge, which is then fed back into the comprehensive local initiative as it progresses. A continual virtuous circle.

As described in the chapter *Organizing for Complexity*, new governance mechanisms have emerged in response to the fact that traditional decision-making processes were not sophisticated enough to address the complex problems that communities typically face. Similarly, new evaluation techniques are evolving because conventional methods are not sufficiently multidimensional to capture the scope of work being undertaken by different players within diverse sectors.

The review processes themselves are complex and messy – as they should be. They require a new and more sophisticated form of assessment, known as developmental evaluation, to capture the scope of the work and its impacts.[18] This type of review sends back information into the effort on an ongoing basis as a feedback loop to allow continual course correction. It is an evaluation process that values learning as much as it seeks results.

Developmental evaluation is rooted in the theory of change that guides the community work. Theory of change is a statement of intended pathway – a linked sequence of steps that lead to desired goals. The process involves clear identification, at the planning and design stages, of designated outcomes in pursuit of specified objectives. It involves regular monitoring of progress toward these results with continual benchmarking against itself or similar efforts, where possible. Organizers then reflect on the information attained through monitoring in order to make required adjustments to the work.

> The theory of change articulates the key ideas guiding the initiative in its work: its conceptualization of the issue; the goals it seeks to achieve around community capacity building; household outcomes and system changes; the specific strategies to be pursued; and the role of the collaborative relative to that strategy. This type of evaluation requires the continual flow of information within and between all stages of work in comprehensive local efforts. This feedback is important not just for the individual initiatives. Ideally, their lessons are documented and disseminated to ensure that others can benefit. This sharing helps raise the bar of practice so that reflections on what works effectively, and not so well, can be incorporated in similar or future efforts.[19]

But there are challenges in this richness. Different types of data are needed to capture the various process and outcome results that these comprehensive efforts can achieve. Some elements, such as higher incomes or numbers of households that have gained access to affordable housing, lend themselves to quantification. Other qualitative results are conveyed only by capturing perceptions such as improved self-esteem, enhanced sense of belonging or improved community relationships. Communities may find that in order to demonstrate progress, they must employ a range of data collection methods, which can be time-consuming and resource intensive.

Another challenge arises from the implication of a logical and consistent sequence of events. A rise in educational attainment, for example, typically leads to a better job. Wage increases improve a household's standard of living. The availability of quality affordable child care helps ensure that working parents can seek and maintain employment. While these sequences are probable, they are not always guaranteed. Sometimes the route is not always direct. Other intervening or unexpected variables, such as marriage breakdown, illness or death of a family member, sudden layoff, plant closure or environmental disaster such as toxic spill or poisoned water supply, can affect the trajectory of a designated set of actions.

A related caution is the fact that the consistent presence of two variables together does not necessarily imply a causal link. These factors may be correlated – or generally found together. With complex social issues, in particular, it is not easy to prove causality. In many cases, two factors that frequently are linked actually influence each other in multiple ways. It is not possible to draw a straight line between cause and effect. Certain factors may be present in combination but the what-caused-what part of the story is often unclear. Clear attribution is not immediately apparent.

> Outcomes are also difficult to measure because causal relationships are hard to attribute. This is partially because the mechanisms of change are not obvious and it is hard to legitimately claim that events that follow interventions are caused by those interventions without a clear causal chain of events.[20]

The problem is evident, for example, in the relationship between poverty and health. There is a vast body of evidence which links poverty and ill health. Persons with lower incomes tend, on average, to have poorer health.[21]

But while poverty is clearly related to – or correlated with negative health outcomes – low income does not necessarily cause poor health. The fact that people living in poverty face an above-average risk of a wide range of illnesses does not mean that they are all certain or even likely to get sick. But they do happen to run a greater risk than those with higher incomes.

For some people, the relationship between poverty and illness may work in the opposite direction. Individuals in poor health may have to seek less strenuous employment or work fewer hours, thereby reducing their earnings capacity. A disabling illness or accident can force an employee out of the labour force and result in a drastic reduction in income.

In addition to causality, other factors make it difficult to gauge the impact of specific interventions even with a clear logic model in place. A program may be initiated, for instance, in which high-quality child care is made available at no cost to a group of teen mothers to enable them to complete high school. In this example, successful school completion likely was due to the intervention – additional supports that allowed these women to focus upon their education.

It is possible, however, that other factors were also significant. The families of some teens may have provided assistance to ensure their success. The attention that the young women received by virtue of being involved in the program – known as the 'placebo effect' – may also have played a role.

Possible measures

Any desired pathway requires an associated set of indicators to determine progress toward a defined objective. Say, for instance, that the goal of the community initiative is to reduce poverty. There are many possible ways to get there.

The desired outcome may be achieved, for example, by enhancing the education and skills of an identified group in an effort to promote their employability. While the immediate result is not necessarily reduced poverty, the intervention typically improves employability potential. Evidence points to a strong positive link between educational attainment, occupational status and income. Higher levels of education are clearly associated with better jobs and higher income.

Based on this information, a focus upon knowledge and skills development is considered a powerful poverty reduction strategy – though that may take some time to occur. If this route is selected, then a desirable short-term result in respect of this objective might be the number of participants who increased their level of education or acquired new or upgraded skills.

A project that targets vulnerable individuals such as high school dropouts, the long-term unemployed or homeless persons might consider improved literacy proficiency as the relevant measure of success. If, by contrast, the effort seeks to upgrade the skills of those who become unemployed because of technological change, then the desired results might involve retraining options.

Alternatively or in addition, a poverty reduction effort might create jobs or link jobless workers to employment opportunities. In this case, the measurable outputs of the effort would be the number of new jobs or work placements. These various possible actions in respect of a specified policy objective are intended to illustrate a general point: The desired outcome – reduced poverty in this case – can be achieved in different ways including education and training, employment and increases to wages and/or benefits. Specific results and their associated measures will vary depending upon the selected route.

Because comprehensive community initiatives involve a broader scope of actions, they also seek to achieve wide-ranging impact. In fact, outcomes at three levels – households, organizations and larger systems – typically are tracked.[22]

At the every least, comprehensive community initiatives seek changes in the social and economic well-being of households. Social results at the household level include, for example, access to affordable accommodation and improved quality in terms of security, space, cleanliness and repair. Meaningful and committed support networks around individuals may have been nurtured. Members of groups typically marginalized, such as racialized youth, persons with disabilities or people living in poverty, may participate more actively in local decision-making or in community activities and events.

Economic measures for households relate to employability, employment status, and level of income and assets. Employability indicators are concerned with the knowledge and skills of prospective workers and include upgraded training and education. Employment measures, by contrast, pertain to the availability and quality of jobs.

Other economic indicators involve longer periods of earned income and reduced reliance on social assistance, Employment Insurance or other programs of income support. A change in source of income – such as a shift from social assistance to paid employment – is as important as a change in level. Actual earnings may not increase substantially in the near term because the initial move often involves low-paying, unstable employment. Nonetheless, the change in income source represents an important step on the pathway to economic independence.

In addition to improvements for households, comprehensive initiatives are concerned with organizational shifts that enhance community capacity to effect fundamental change. The local effort may decide to track the number and type of collaborative arrangements that it has helped create.

Another relevant category worth monitoring involves the use of resources, such as mobilization of additional financial or technical assistance. Easier access to stable funding enables effective organizational development. There may be higher volunteer participation in community activities – a major contributor to social capital, earlier described. The effort may enhance the capacity for organizational learning, which in turn releases creative energy around new ways of thinking and acting.

Finally, these wide-ranging local efforts seek broader systemic changes such as greater availability of quality affordable child care, increased access to recreation amenities and programs, reduced out-migration and additional welcoming public space. There may be substantial improvements in employment practices or workplace accommodation to reduce barriers to employment for persons with disabilities, recent immigrants or street youth.

Procedural changes in public policy include removal of disincentives or provision of appropriate supports, such as home visiting programs for parents of newborns and young children. As a result of the local effort, there may be improved coordination of policies across departments and orders of government, and better collaboration between government and communities.

Data collection

The broad scope of work involved in comprehensive community initiatives requires a variety of data collection methods and sources. At the same time, it is essential to choose carefully the types of information and associated measures considered most relevant. Excessive requirements can overwhelm organizations and divert limited resources from their substantive work and primary purpose – to improve social and economic conditions.

Basic organizational record keeping is often sufficient to document immediate results including numbers of people receiving services or achieving specific objectives, such as employment or affordable accommodation. Surveys and interviews can help determine the value of a certain project or the progress resulting from designated interventions. Deeper impacts, such as higher household income over an extended period or improvements in the quality of life, generally require more specialized and sophisticated types of data collection and analysis.

Communities must develop systems for both gathering and storing data. Some types of information, like changes in source and level of household income, are inherently difficult to collect. They also raise serious privacy issues related to confidentiality. Appropriate protocols must be in place to protect personal information.

Changes in income are especially difficult to track due to personal concerns about divulging financial information. There are also technical challenges involved in measuring these kinds of changes.

In tracking income changes, for example, households must report their overall income derived from both employment and government benefits and not just their work earnings. It is sometimes difficult for households to know precisely this amount. Families generally do not count as part of their overall income certain benefits, such as the federal GST credit and Canada Child Tax Benefit, and other refundable provincial child benefits and tax credits, which are delivered through the income tax system. Moreover, workers who recently moved from welfare to the paid labour market are often reluctant to report their earnings for fear that they could lose related assistance, such as rent supplements or disability supports.

Reflection

In addition to tracking changes in household well-being, opportunities should be created for all stakeholders in local initiatives to reflect on their work and document the lessons learned. Reflection sessions are structured processes in which participants consider whether the ideas guiding their initiatives are being borne out in practice.[23]

Typically, these sessions begin with a review of the initiative's goals and strategies. Progress is assessed along with how the key lessons might influence subsequent stages of the work in order to enhance future performance.

Reflection sessions are valuable for capturing the insights of participants about the strengths and limitations of their work. The sessions serve to document current actions and to build capacity for future efforts. Reflection sessions can be organized for a single comprehensive effort or conducted with a cluster of initiatives engaged in similar work, such as employment development or affordable housing.

Trail Builders within Vibrant Communities, for example, are required to hold annual half-day reflection sessions in order to assess their progress toward objectives. Participants include the convener organization, members of the local governance structure, key working groups, funders and people living in poverty.

All projects must go back to the original theory of change developed when they first came on board the pan-Canadian initiative in order to assess progress relative to established goals and benchmarks; identify positive and limiting factors; and discern key lessons. On the basis of this reflection, the theory of change subsequently is updated and modified if required.

Finally, while comprehensive initiatives may claim success in their work, they often face tough challenges in trying to express, in a compelling way, its significance. Sometimes the real power of an initiative can be conveyed only by telling its story – the social and historical context, relationships among its component parts and perceived impact of the local effort. Story-telling is now being acknowledged as a valid and powerful source of evidence, even though it has always been deeply embedded in Aboriginal culture.

More specifically, 'credible performance stories' are being recognized increasingly as a way to capture the experience of complex initiatives and draw attention to their most significant elements.[24] These stories are not intended to prove and explain the causal impact of the initiatives in question. Rather, their purpose is to make a reasonable case, based on multiple lines of evidence, for the value of the program or initiative.

> Resident wisdom is the intentional process of validating people's experience and credentialing them prudentially as valuable, credible information for planning, and as evidence of the achievement of results. Traditional practice would rely solely on community indicator data. However this is typically in relation to numbers, and resident wisdom tends to add depth to understanding what numbers alone cannot achieve.[25]

The emerging experience with the story methodology has found that stories serve many purposes. They help summarize data relevant to the initiative and point to factors that contribute to its effectiveness and limitations. They can make concrete, like no other methodology, the scope of possible interventions. Stories enable the sharing of practices and insights with others engaged in similar work. They support reflection and learning – in order to apply lessons and alter the work plan as required.

All this to say...

Work in the shared space involves knowing, doing and reviewing. Relevant information must be gathered to understand the dimensions of the cluster and possible interventions. Multiple links both within and between clusters are created through various collaborative relationships. Reviewing involves monitoring progress and correcting course as required.

The chapters that follow apply these dimensions of work in the shared space to each resilience cluster. The discussion starts with sustenance – beginning with the basics.

Endnotes

1   den Hertog, P., E. Bergman and D. Charles eds. (2001). *Innovative Clusters: Drivers of Innovation Systems*. Paris: Organisation for Economic Co-operation and Development.

2   Jarboe, K. and A. Alliance. (2001). *Knowledge Management as an Economic Development Strategy*. Washington, DC: Economic Development Administration, US Department of Commerce.

3   Organisation for Economic Co-operation and Development (OECD). (2000). *Knowledge Management in the Learning Society*. Paris.

4   OECD. (2000). *Ibid.*

5   Hodgson, D. (1998). *A Community-Based Program to Reduce Poverty*. Ottawa: Caledon Institute of Social Policy, May.

6   See Action for Neighbourhood Change. (2007). *Rebuilding Neighbourhoods: A Neighbourhood Vitality Framework*. Ottawa: United Way of Canada-Centraide Canada at *www.anccommunity.ca*

7   See *www.vitalsignscanada.ca*

8   See *www.communityaccounts.ca*

9   Battle, K. and S. Torjman. (2001). *The Post-Welfare State in Canada: Income-Testing and Inclusion*. Ottawa: Caledon Institute of Social Policy, May.

10   See *www.hrsdc.gc.ca/en/hip/sd/300_UEYInfo.shtml*

11   Battle, K. and S. Torjman. (2001). *The Post-Welfare State in Canada: Income-Testing and Inclusion*. Ottawa: Caledon Institute of Social Policy, May.

12   Torjman, S. (2003). *The Social Role of Local Government*. Ottawa: Caledon Institute of Social Policy, May.

13   Torjman, S. (1997). *Disentanglement – or Disengagement?* Ottawa: Caledon Institute of Social Policy, January.

14   Linden, R. (2002). *Working Across Boundaries: Making Collaboration Work in Government and Nonprofit Organizations*. San Francisco: Jossey-Bass.

15   Torjman, S. (2005). *Policy Dialogue*. Ottawa: Caledon Institute of Social Policy, June.

16   See *www.safecommunities.ca*

17   Makhoul, A. (2005). *Assured Income for the Severely Handicapped Public Policy Initiative*. Ottawa: Caledon Institute of Social Policy, May.

18   Quinn Patton, M. (1997). *Utilization-Focused Evaluation: The New Century Text*. 3rd ed. New York: Sage Publications.

[19] Leviten-Reid, E. (2007). *Reflecting on Vibrant Communities (2002-2006)*. Ottawa: Caledon Institute of Social Policy, January.

[20] Meager, S. (2006). *A Neighbourhood Vitality Index: An Approach to Measuring Neighbourhood Well-Being*. Toronto: United Way of Greater Toronto, p. 10.

[21] Raphael, D. ed. (2004). *Social Determinants of Health: Canadian Perspectives*. Toronto: Canadian Scholars' Press Inc.

[22] Leviten-Reid, E. and S. Torjman. (2006). *Evaluation Framework for Federal Investment in the Social Economy: A Discussion Paper*. Ottawa: Caledon Institute of Social Policy, January.

[23] Leviten-Reid, E. (2007). *Reflecting on Vibrant Communities (2002-2006)*. Ottawa: Caledon Institute of Social Policy, January.

[24] Mayne, J. (2003). *Reporting on Outcomes: Setting Performance Expectations and Telling Performance Stories*. Ottawa: Office of the Auditor General of Canada, April.

[25] Yates, G. (2004). "Rebuilding Communities." *Ideas That Matter*. 3(2): 15.

Chapter 4

Supporting Sustenance

In summary

The goal of the communities agenda is to build resilience in communities in order to ensure their strength and vibrancy. Resilience is the result of actions taken in four independent but related clusters – or areas of shared space. The sustenance cluster is concerned primarily with basic needs, discussed here primarily from the perspective of income security and housing. While actions in support of sustenance are essential to overall well-being, they are not sufficient. Ideally, actions in this cluster link to the other domains that comprise the resilience equation.

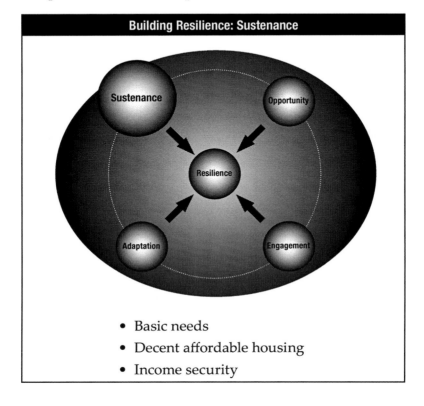

Building Resilience: Sustenance

- Basic needs
- Decent affordable housing
- Income security

The context

The concept of resilience – whether interpreted from an ecological or mental health perspective – speaks clearly to the ability to survive. An individual, family, organization or community that is resilient has managed to withstand sudden change, external pressure and even shock. The survival imperative is as true for natural ecosystems as it is for social systems, such as organizations and communities. The capacity to adapt, engage or thrive is impossible if basic survival is seriously threatened.

Work in the shared space – in this case the sustenance cluster – begins with establishing a clear knowledge base. It next involves a set of actions that seek to create collaborative relationships within the cluster, between clusters and around policy. Finally, work in the shared space involves monitoring progress against identified outcomes. *Knowing, doing and reviewing are core elements of work in the shared space.*

Knowing:

Creating the evidence base

Basic survival is a concern throughout the world. It is a daily struggle for billions who are far from adapting, engaging or thriving – the other core components of resilience. A veritable sea of humanity lives in extreme poverty. The global Make Poverty History campaign currently under way calls attention to the plight of more than half the world's population who subsist on less than $1 a day. They struggle daily simply to be, let alone become something better or stronger.

In fact, the United Nations had identified poverty as the "greatest threat to political stability, social cohesion and the environmental health of the planet."[1] In order to translate this overriding concern into a practicable plan of action, the United Nations Development Programme crafted in the year

2000 a set of Millennium Development Goals for a concerted attack on poverty and illiteracy, hunger, discrimination against women, unsafe drinking water and a degraded environment. Five of the eight Development Goals deal directly with issues related to basic survival – eradicating extreme poverty and hunger; reducing child mortality; improving maternal health; combating HIV/AIDS, malaria and other diseases; and ensuring environmental sustainability.[2]

The Millennium Development Goals make clear that actions within the sustenance cluster link intrinsically to the environmental dimension of sustainable development – clean air, water and soil – though these core elements of survival are not considered here. Access to primary health care is also a major concern, especially with respect to immunization and disease prevention.

This chapter explores the social and economic components of sustenance and, more specifically, access to decent affordable housing and basic income. The primary focus on shelter and income is rooted in the recognition that safe and clean human habitats comprise the foundation of well-being. The World Summit on Sustainable Development (2002), the *Istanbul Declaration on Human Settlements* (1996) and Agenda 21, the *Rio Declaration on Environment and Development* (1992) all identified access to decent human habitats as a fundamental social objective.

Despite these global pronouncements, millions throughout the world live in precarious circumstances. Even in a wealthy country like Canada, hundreds of thousands of families and individuals can barely make ends meet because their rent consumes most of their budget. They often go without food and other essentials, such as warm clothing, because their slim pay cheques or welfare payments hardly cover even the basics. Many live in unsafe, infested or cramped quarters.

At last count in 2001, 14 percent of households in Canada lived in core housing need. This means that their housing was lacking in the number of bedrooms per family size, the dwelling was unsafe or the household paid more than 30 percent of its income on accommodation. Of course, national averages hide the wide variability by region. The percentage living in core housing need ranged from 11 percent in Alberta to a staggering 39 percent in Nunavut.[3]

The figures are troubling in light of the evidence on the health, social and economic benefits of decent affordable housing. Dozens of studies corroborate the profound and wide-reaching connections between poor housing and a range of risks. Badly maintained housing is responsible for many childhood injuries.[4] Damp, moldy interiors are linked to higher risk of respiratory disease and asthma. Unstable living arrangements, made worse by parents' inability to pay the rent, have a negative impact upon the emotional, behavioural and cognitive development of children.

There are significant psychological dimensions to housing as well. Families that lack access to secure and affordable accommodation may have to move frequently, interrupting children's schooling and making it difficult for adults to retain employment.[5] Neighbourhood conditions are another important factor. These include the safety and quality of the neighbourhood in which the housing is located and the access it provides to schools, parks and playgrounds, employment and affordable accessible transportation.

In theory, there should be no need to talk about sustenance in a developed nation. It should be a given in a rich country, such as Canada. Unfortunately, that wealth is very unequally distributed. It is often a struggle to direct attention to the deep divisions between the have's and the have-almost-nothings. Despite persistently high rates and deep levels of poverty, access to basics is still not generally considered a pressing problem. In countries of plenty, households and even communities that are poor are often considered responsible for their own misfortune. But the large numbers and the complexity of poverty's causes and effects clearly challenge this assumption.

At last count in 2004, there were 3.5 million Canadians with low incomes, which translates into a poverty rate of 11 percent of the population.[6] Among children under 18, 13 percent lived in low-income families. Even Canadians employed full time may not earn enough to lift them out of poverty. Among working-age Canadians ages 18 to 64, 2.4 million or 12 percent had low incomes in 2004. The working poor typically are employed in jobs that pay low wages or do not work sufficient hours.

Another important measure of low income is depth of poverty, which refers to how far poor Canadians fall on average below the low income cut-offs. (These represent the measure of poverty generally employed in this country, though they are not an official standard.) In 2004, the average low-income family fell $7,200 below the poverty line. While the trends over the years mirror the ups and downs of the economy, there has been little long-term progress overall.

Low income is a heavy and stubborn millstone that imposes severe social, economic and personal costs. It means lost opportunities for individuals, the economy and society. It brings greater risk of a wide range of health, social and educational problems.

Certain groups – including single-parent families led by women, Aboriginal Canadians, young single people, recent immigrants and persons with disabilities – face a higher threat of poverty than the national averages would indicate, and are more likely to remain poor for longer periods.[7] They experience greater odds not only of falling below the low income line in any given year, but also of chronic, deep and long-term poverty that can exclude them from the benefits of participating in work and contributing to the broader community. Many become marginalized from society – living on the streets, seeking comfort in alcohol or drugs, or expressing anger at a world that makes no place for them.

Growing up in a low-income household also carries risks down the road. Childhood poverty is associated with lower educational attainment, a greater likelihood of involvement in criminal behaviour, a range of psychological problems and lower earnings in adulthood. Parental poverty effectively starts a chain of social vulnerability leading to reduced readiness for school, poor behaviour and attendance, higher risk of unemployment, perceived marginality and low-status jobs.[8]

Children who live in poverty for sustained periods are more likely to be vulnerable than children who experience poverty for relatively short periods. The duration of poverty has negative effects on their measured IQ, verbal ability and achievement scores. Children who live in persistently poor families have been found to score 6 to 9 points lower on various assessments than children who were never poor. Moreover, the negative effects of persistent poverty seem to grow stronger as children get older. Severity of poverty is another key factor. Children in the very low family income group (below 50 percent of the poverty line) scored 7 to 12 points lower on various developmental scores than did children in the near-poor group.[9]

While very low income is serious, it is not the only concern from a sustenance perspective. Relative inequality is an equally troubling problem.[10] A growing volume of research evidence makes clear that inequality matters. Across the income spectrum, lower income and reduced opportunity relative to others in a given neighbourhood or nation have been found to have a negative effect on health. Access to basics is essential in order to decrease 'absolute poverty.' But so are redistributive programs and tax policies that seek to reduce relative poverty by narrowing the gap between rich and poor.

A recent report looked at the earnings and after-tax incomes of Canadian families raising children under 18, comparing families in the late 1970s and those in the early 2000s. The study found that Canada's income gap is growing. In 2004, the richest 10 percent of families earned 82 times more than the poorest 10 percent – almost triple the ratio of 1976, when they earned 31 times more. In after-tax terms, the gap has reached a 30-year high.[11]

Several recent studies have been exploring the rate and depth of poverty not just on a national basis. They are drilling down into the data to determine the extent of the problem in designated geographic areas such as provinces, cities and even neighbourhoods. A national study entitled *Urban Poverty in Canada* explored the rate of poverty in major urban centres. The study found that a disproportionate number of the poor live in metropolitan areas. While the poverty rate varied widely across the country, inner-city areas on the whole had substantially higher poverty rates than suburban communities.

Building on this 'poverty by geography' approach, a comprehensive report entitled *Poverty by Postal Code*, was published in 2004 as part of research into social issues being undertaken by the United Way of Greater Toronto. The study found a substantial rise in the poverty rate among Toronto families over the last two decades, with almost one in five families living in poverty in 2001.

The report also geographically mapped the growing concentration of poverty in certain neighbourhoods. It found, for instance, that one in three lone parents and one-third of the visible minority population now live and raise their families in high-poverty neighbourhoods. Between 1991 and 2001, the number of children growing up in high-poverty neighbourhoods doubled and their numbers were disproportionately higher than the city as a whole.[12]

Unemployment in these areas, not surprisingly, was greater than the city as a whole. By 2001, close to one-half of the renter neighbourhoods in high-poverty neighbourhoods and 43 percent of all renter households throughout the city were in core housing need, paying more than 30 percent of their income on rent.

In addition to the dramatic rise in the concentration and incidence of low income, *Poverty by Postal Code* noted the growth in high-poverty neighbourhoods, which have almost doubled every ten years since 1981. The number rose from 30 high-poverty neighbourhoods in that year to 66 in 1991 and 120 by 2001. In 1981, there were four very high-poverty neighbourhoods. The figure more than doubled to nine in 1991 and then jumped to 23 by 2001 – nearly six times their number in 1981.[13]

The dramatic rise in neighbourhood poverty is of concern for many reasons. The multiple risks of living in a poor neighbourhood are significant – and long-lasting – for children and youth, newcomers to the country and the entire community. Poor neighbourhoods often spin into decline, leading to poor health, crime and abandonment by both residents and businesses. A recent study by the Canadian Institutes for Health Research found a clear link between quality of neighbourhood and level of health. It concluded that place does indeed matter when it comes to health and well-being.[14]

Know-how and know-who

A wide-ranging set of actions can be taken to address basic needs. These interventions effectively represent investments in two major streams: community infrastructure and individual capacity. Investments in community infrastructure involve an infusion of funds into the supply of factors essential for well-being. Investments in individual capacity, by contrast, refer in this cluster to actions that support households' ability to pay for decent food, clothing, shelter and other necessities of life.

In the developed world, the private sector plays the primary role in ensuring basic sustenance through adequate pay, associated benefits and decent working conditions. These dimensions are discussed in the chapter on *Creating an Enabling Environment*. But governments have an equally important ability and responsibility to reduce the rate and depth of poverty, if not eradicate the scourge.

The federal government in Canada has committed itself on the international stage – at least on paper – to ensuring access to basics. Protections afforded under the *International Covenant on Economic, Social and Cultural Rights* are especially relevant to social development. Article 11 recognizes the right of citizens to a decent standard of living, including adequate food, clothing and housing, and to the continuous improvement of living conditions. Article 25 of the *Universal Declaration of Human Rights* gives every person the right to a standard of living adequate for health and well-being including food, clothing, housing and medical care, and necessary social services. These articles set clear obligations on governments to ensure that basic human rights are met.

The primary role of government in reducing poverty was recognized explicitly in a 1989 House of Commons all-party resolution, which committed the federal government to move toward the eradication of child poverty by the year 2000. The start of the millennium came and went with a small dent in the problem, largely the result of an improving economy and the introduction in 1998 of the National Child Benefit. But the country remains far from its eradication objective.

The Québec Government is the only jurisdiction in the country to enact anti-poverty legislation. Bill 112 was drafted by a coalition of 22 community groups and includes a *National Strategy to Combat Poverty and Social Exclusion*. The law commits the Québec government to establish an anti-poverty action plan and to report publicly every three years on progress toward this objective.

The National Strategy identifies several key areas of intervention. School success and the social integration of young persons must be promoted. Basic education and access to continuing education must be improved to enable adults to complete and update their occupational qualifications. Volunteer and community actions that contribute to the social inclusion of persons living in poverty must be supported. For persons living in poverty, there must be greater access to culture, recreation and sports.

It is of interest that these strategies to reduce poverty focus largely upon the actions discussed in the chapters on *Advancing Adaptation* and *Ensuring Engagement*. The efforts to reduce poverty, a primary concern of sustenance, involve actions in the related resilience clusters.

Local governments also play an important role in meeting basic needs. In response to Québec's anti-poverty legislation, the City of Montréal proclaimed a *Montréal Charter of Rights and Responsibilities*. The Charter requires elected officials, employees and City-controlled agencies to protect and promote inclusive citizenship. It spells out commitments around economic and social life, cultural life, recreation, physical activities and sports, and the environment and sustainable development.

With respect to economic and social life, the City of Montréal makes seven promises, which include taking appropriate measures to ensure that housing meets public health and safety standards, and to provide relocation services if a dwelling must be closed or vacated. The Charter also obliges the City to consider the needs of vulnerable persons – especially those in low- and modest-income households – in its implementation of housing measures.

More recently in 2005, the Government of Newfoundland and Labrador announced in its Speech from the Throne a commitment to transform itself from the province with the highest rate of poverty to the jurisdiction with the lowest rate. In June 2006, it released *Reducing Poverty: An Action Plan for Newfoundland and Labrador* that calls for a long-term, comprehensive and integrated approach to tackling the problem.

As part of its commitment, the government established a Ministerial Committee with seven participating Ministers. The Government of Newfoundland and Labrador also signalled its intent to work with the federal government, other provincial governments, Aboriginal governments and organizations, business and labour, and community groups in this effort – described more fully in the chapter on *Creating an Enabling Environment*.

Basic needs can be met, as discussed, by investing directly in the supply of required amenities, like decent shelter. In recent years, all orders of government have put dollars into various forms of affordable housing – though it can be argued that the amounts are not sufficient relative to the growing problem.

The high cost of housing in some urban centres is due to many factors, including demand pressures in markets such as Toronto, Calgary, Vancouver and Victoria. It is also related to the cost of land for development, which clearly drives up the price of housing. The high cost of land in densely populated urban areas emerged as a major international concern at the UN-Habitat World Urban Forum held in Vancouver in 2006.

Governments can take steps to tackle the shortage by purchasing land for modestly priced accommodation or selling it to developers willing to build affordable housing. Provinces can ensure that municipalities have a long-term supply of affordable land for future development. Governments can direct funds toward community land trusts – nonprofit corporations that separate the ownership of land from the ownership of buildings and other improvements. Their purpose is to hold a body of land permanently in trust for the community.

Funds can also be invested in the rehabilitation and repair of existing housing stock to bring it up to standard. The federal Residential Rehabilitation Assistance Program currently supports this type of investment. Some municipalities have introduced emergency loans for low-income homeowners. To ease problems of affordability, local governments can consider the possibility of funding and administering a rent bank to help low-income households pay for short-term rent arrears.

Municipalities can provide incentives in the form of reduced or waived property taxes to developers that build affordable housing. Local governments can implement policies requiring new subdivisions to include a minimum number of affordable housing units, as determined by local market conditions. Municipalities can adopt 'housing first' policies in which priority consideration is given to constructing housing on city land deemed surplus. They can reform regulations and zoning bylaws to be more permissive of secondary suites, in which a smaller dwelling is added to a primary residence.

In addition to direct investment, governments can introduce tax credits to encourage private and voluntary sector investment in reasonably priced housing. In an effort to make homeownership more affordable and accessible, the Canada Mortgage and Housing Corporation recently introduced several new measures. It will provide mortgage insurance that allows lenders to make interest-only mortgage payments for up to the first 10 years when they purchase or refinance their home.

The second stream of interventions in the sustenance cluster is to focus on the demand side of the equation. The demand side refers to the capacity of households to pay for new or existing housing. Ability to pay can be enhanced in one of three ways: decent wages, adequate benefits and reduced costs.

Governments must set reasonable minimum wages in their respective jurisdictions. They can also act as exemplary employers by paying decent wages to employees and contractors, discussed further in *Creating an Enabling Environment*.

Another way to enhance the capacity to pay for basics is by increasing the payments delivered through income security programs, such as the federal Canada Child Tax Benefit and provincial child benefits. The adequacy principle applies to other programs as well, such as Employment Insurance for short-term interruptions of earnings, the Canada Pension Plan disability benefit in the event of severe and prolonged disability, and the Guaranteed Income Supplement paid to low-income seniors.

Finally, governments and publicly regulated bodies, such as utility companies, can ease access to basics through various measures to reduce costs. Heat and electricity are obvious housing-related examples, although some community initiatives have worked to lower the costs for other important basics, such as transportation and recreation.

It is clear that governments are at the core of meeting sustenance needs for all citizens. But communities can add significant value – by supplementing and complementing the protections that governments should provide in respect of basic needs.

Communities have long been involved in charitable activities in the form of food banks and emergency shelter. Habitat for Humanity, which combines private sector contributions of building supplies with volunteer labour to construct homes for low-income families, is just one of several hundred examples of voluntary activity in affordable housing.

The World Vision Canada Aboriginal Council is another case in point.[15] The Council worked with members in Saskatchewan, Manitoba and Northwestern Ontario to help community members construct their own housing using alternative techniques that are both affordable and energy efficient. Three First Nations communities participated in the project and built several houses using an innovative low-skill method, known as straw-bale construction. The Council also set up a housing co-operative, raising the initial capital through the construction of two homes using donations of cash, labour, materials and land. The houses were then used as equity for acquiring additional funds from financial institutions.

When communities choose to build nonprofit or social housing in order to tackle the affordability challenge, they often face the 'not-in-my-backyard' syndrome. Many residents believe that social housing will reduce the value of the neighbourhood property. However, some communities have begun to use that particular stock as the foundation for community investment. They are employing their public housing as equity to lever financial capital for community economic development and additional affordable housing.

These examples are important in that they speak to the power of community engagement. But they are clearly not sufficient. There is far more potential in community action than is represented by this work.

The challenge rooted in a strategic plan that employs a complexity lens is to seek wide-ranging and sustainable solutions that can have a significant impact over time. The purpose and value of investing in local governance mechanisms, discussed in *Organizing for Complexity*, is to move toward more complex and strategic interventions that represent broader and deeper change in both numbers affected and policy systems.

While the comprehensive plan developed by local governance structures provides the framework, communities typically select one or two areas of concern and focus upon individual projects within those designated areas. They are compelled to work in this way because of lack of resources and the pressure for quick wins, earlier described. But they must take better advantage of the power of the comprehensive governance mechanism that they have created.

One of the most important ways to support long-term change is through a coordination mechanism that encourages collaboration around the two major streams of intervention earlier identified – investment in community infrastructure and investment in individual capacity. Within the context of the communities agenda and the resilience framework in particular, communities have an opportunity to approach this work as a cluster of actions that can be taken in a more integrated way.

Comprehensive community initiatives can coordinate, both within and between clusters, the broad range of players who should be engaged in sustenance. No single body can pull together all the pieces or oversee the range of actors who need to be involved in the complex sustenance cluster. There is also a special need for coordination among various orders of government and the private sector – all of which are implicated in sustenance, and in housing and income security more specifically.

Doing:

Creating links within the cluster

New stock

The first type of collaborative work involves links within the cluster itself. There are many examples of this joining up – only a few of which are illustrated here. The Quality of Life CHALLENGE in BC's Capital Region is a multi-year effort, for instance, to improve housing and income opportunities for people living in poverty and to strengthen the social fabric of the community.[16] Affordable housing is a primary focus.

BC's Capital Region has a rental vacancy rate of 0.6 percent – among the lowest in Canada. At more than $500,000, it has one of the highest average house prices in the country. Some 22,200 households in the area are deemed to be in core housing need. They are unable to find housing that meets basic standards for adequacy, suitability and affordability. A regional government commitment to limit urban expansion in respect of environmental and agricultural sustainability has added to the pressure.

In response to the accommodation problem, a Housing Affordability Partnership was established with representatives from the Community Council, BC Housing, Canada Mortgage and Housing Corporation, Canadian Homebuilders' Association, Urban Development Institute, Rental Owners and Managers' Association, nonprofit housing providers, Vancouver Island Health Authority, financial institutions, municipal planners and community associations.

The Housing Affordability Partnership actively supported the creation of a Regional Housing Trust Fund to coordinate the flow of capital into various housing projects. Housing trust funds are set up by local governments or nonprofit agencies to increase the availability of affordable accommodation, including new construction, retrofit of older buildings and rental subsidies.

In April 2005, six of the region's 13 municipalities – which account for more than half of its population – voted to establish such a trust fund, contributing a total estimated $635,000 annually. When all 13 municipalities join the Regional Housing Trust Fund, they will contribute $1 million annually with the capacity to create up to 75 affordable housing units each year. These funds leverage 14 times that amount from provincial and federal governments and other sources.

While significant, there is no question that a trust fund must be supplemented by other measures. The Quality of Life CHALLENGE influenced bylaw changes in seven municipalities, including the use of an affordability lens in assessing new housing developments and the legalization of secondary suites. As a result of these changes, BC Capital Region was able to move from simply joining up work within the cluster to creating important linkages with government – effectively scaling up their efforts through relevant policy changes.

Retrofit of existing stock

Sometimes the solution to the affordable housing shortage lies not in the creation of new stock. The regeneration of existing housing is another route – though this too can require extensive coordination and collaboration, as evident in Saint John. The sheer quantity of older inner-city housing stock presents a unique challenge to community revitalization, as does the City's high poverty rate relative to the rest of New Brunswick.

In 2004, the federal government announced plans to develop a comprehensive Canadian Housing Framework intended to support a continuum of housing. Six representatives from the Saint John business and voluntary sectors were invited to make a 10-minute presentation to the Minister of Housing as part of his national information-gathering tour. The community requested instead to pool the individual time allocation in order to have one hour with the Minister and to put forward a common proposal rather than six separate submissions. A united leadership, which included the Mayor, business representatives, a City councillor and all nonprofit groups involved in housing development, presented the submission.

The Saint John team asked the federal Minister to assign one employee from the Canada Mortgage and Housing Corporation to formulate a strategic plan for affordable housing. A five-day planning event was organized to articulate a local vision for extensive revitalization. The process resulted in recommendations for 178 short-, medium- and long-term projects, which now comprise the community's affordable housing strategy. It includes renewal of the existing stock and securing of funds for several hundred new housing units. The scope of the strategic plan likely would not have emerged in the absence of the broad collaborative effort responsible for its development.[17]

Service coordination

Sometimes housing needs can be met by approaches other than the creation of new housing, the renewal of old stock or even home ownership. Communities can maintain current living arrangements – particularly for seniors and persons with disabilities – by ensuring the coordination of essential supports and services.

For many individuals, housing needs go beyond four walls and a roof. They require supports, such as technical aids and equipment in the form of wheelchairs, visual aids, volume control devices and prosthetic appliances, which enable the activities of daily living. Attendant services provide assistance with personal needs such as feeding, bathing and dressing. Homemaker services help with household tasks, such as meal preparation and home maintenance. These aids and services currently are provided through a patchwork of arrangements. Community initiatives can ease access to and coordinate this range of assistance, thereby ensuring that residents can remain in their homes and neighbourhoods.

Reduced costs

Comprehensive initiatives can promote access to basics through various actions that reduce costs. This type of intervention does not focus directly upon bolstering household income. But it has a significant impact upon that income by lowering the cost of essentials. Utility rates are a case in point.

Energy poverty is deemed to exist when a household must spend more than 10 percent of its income on basic heat and light. For most middle- and high-income Canadians, energy bills account for an estimated four percent of total household expenditure. In Saint John, low-income residents spend between 10 and 15 percent of their incomes to light and heat their homes. A large proportion of the low-income earners live in rented apartments constructed prior to World War II. Often draughty and usually outfitted with electric baseboard heat, these accommodations are expensive to keep warm.[18]

The provincial utility, New Brunswick Power, announced in 2005 its intention to raise utility rates by 16 percent. This rate hike threatened to put many more New Brunswick households into energy poverty.

The utility also indicated that it would hold public hearings, for the first time since 1993, on the proposed change. The comprehensive community initiative in Saint John applied for and was granted intervener status in the process. This position helped it gain access to important financial data regarding energy poverty and enabled the discussion of potential solutions in cooperation with the local utility, Saint John Energy. Never before had low-income residents in New Brunswick had a voice at these hearings.

Two significant changes have occurred as a result of this work. The utility has changed its billing structure away from a block rate that offered volume discounts to high energy users. Low-income households were never reaching the lower rate and effectively were subsidizing the power rates paid by people living in larger, more expensive houses. In future, that billing practice will be replaced by one that rewards energy conservation.

The second key shift was the utility's agreement that energy is an essential service. Its monthly charge of $19 was the second highest in the country and the utility was proposing to raise it to $21. The recognition of energy as an essential service has opened the door to discussing the impact of rate design on low-income households throughout the province. The Saint John comprehensive community initiative is now working with the public utility to find longer-term neighbourhood solutions to energy poverty. These include possible savings through reduced energy use and technology upgrades.

Between clusters
Sustenance and adaptation

Household incomes can also be stretched through access to basics like food, thereby enabling payment for other essentials, such as adequate housing. The Agincourt Community Services Association in Scarborough, Ontario, for example, works with a range of partners on its Food Security Programs initiative.[19]

A Cooking Healthy Together workshop, which focuses upon good nutrition, safe food handling and multicultural cooking, is offered to parents with children up to age 6.

Similar workshops are organized for English as a Second Language students and for community members who are homeless. Monthly cooking clubs are held for isolated seniors, new Canadians and stay-at-home parents.

The Association partners with FoodShare on the Fresh Food Market initiative, which makes available quality, locally grown produce at low cost. FoodShare is a nonprofit organization which works on the entire system that puts food on the table: from the growing, processing and distribution of food to its purchase, cooking and consumption.

Community gardens and pick-your-own field trips are also part of the food security objective. While these individual projects do not eradicate poverty, they help low-income households maintain their health and become food self-sufficient. Equally important, they provide opportunities for ongoing social support. The wide-ranging value of social networks is discussed in *Advancing Adaptation*.

Sustenance and engagement

The Toronto Housing Corporation, the not-for-profit housing corporation owned by the City of Toronto, is another example of work between clusters. It provides housing to an estimated 164,000 tenants in communities throughout the city.[20]

The Corporation seeks to be the preeminent social housing provider in North America and to set the standards and benchmarks by which other nonprofit housing providers measure their performance. It intends to meet this ambitious mission by investing not only in bricks and mortar but also by enhancing the health of the neighbourhoods in which its homes are located.

To this end, the Corporation invested $100 million to improve older buildings and increase energy efficiency. It completed 62 community safety plans and 110 safety audits in partnership with police and other local agencies. The Corporation partnered with Carpenter's Local 27 and George Brown College on pre-apprenticeship programs for youth. It offered the Tomorrow's Leaders' program to 200 young people in 16 communities.

In the summer of 2006, the Three Communities Mask Mosaic Project brought together youth, children and seniors to work with the community's artist in residence. Participants created more than 80 masks that captured events, emotions or significant milestones in their lives. The masks were showcased in a community parade and were later displayed across the city.

These initiatives are selected examples of the broad scope of interventions in which the Toronto Housing Corporation is involved. It explicitly links its primary focus with other clusters – moving beyond housing to interventions that seek the engagement of young people, teach leadership skills and rebuild a sense of neighbourhood.

Sustenance and opportunity

The nonprofit Quint Development Corporation in Saskatoon is an example of innovative action for affordable housing that creates links between clusters. Its primary focus is co-operative home ownership, which has attracted growing attention as an important asset. Benefits include stability for children, enhanced mental well-being, higher wealth and savings, increased social participation and improved neighbourhood stability.

Quint Development Corporation survives as a result of the many partnerships it has created. It relies on the support of several departments in both the Saskatchewan Housing Corporation and the City of Saskatoon. Quint also involves credit unions and local businesses including contractors, architects, a real estate agent, lawyers and insurance coops that offer technical support and preferred rates on their goods and services.

But the focus of the work moves beyond home ownership by incorporating an economic development component. Quint set up a home renovation program funded in part by the Canada Saskatchewan Career and Employment Services Community Works Program, with additional funding in the first three years of its operation from the Co-operators insurance company. The renovation crew ensures that the homes are attractive and that they meet minimum health and safety standards. The on-site repair work, coupled with training sessions, afford the crew several months of on-the-job experience, which has improved their skills and associated opportunities for paid employment.

The five older core neighbourhoods of Saskatoon participated in another important example of joined-up activity.[21] They have not fared well in recent years, with an aging housing stock, high rates of poverty and a loss of business and service providers that have moved to other areas. A study undertaken by the nonprofit Quint Development Corporation and CHEP Good Food Inc. found a doughnut-shaped distribution of food stores across the city – with core neighbourhoods as the empty centre. After unsuccessfully trying to attract a food retailer to the core neighbourhoods, the two organizations formulated a business plan to establish a community-owned food store. This effort has evolved into what is now referred to as the Station 20 West Community Enterprise Centre.

Through the Urban Development Agreement, the City of Saskatoon helped purchase and remediate the land and sold it at relatively low cost for the development of the site. The Saskatoon Library became interested in joining the project; their studies had shown the importance of co-locating with other business and community activities when moving into areas of low literacy. The Saskatoon Housing Corporation is joining the partnership with plans to build 50 to 60 affordable housing units.

In addition, various health providers are collaborating to create an integrated community health centre at Station 20 West. The Westside Community Clinic is interested in co-locating in the Community Enterprise Centre and the College of Dentistry is exploring the establishment of a clinic in the complex for residents who currently must take a bus to the campus for dental services. The College of Medicine is looking to establish a pediatrics clinic, and the Saskatoon Health Region wants to set up clinics to provide both public health and primary care.

The complex will also be used to house the Quint Development Corporation. CHEP plans to use some of the space for its Good Food Box operations, an incubator to develop community food businesses and a good food café. The cluster-based dynamic evident in this example has sparked hope for a more positive future for the neighbourhood.

Around policy

Higher wages

Expanding the supply of affordable housing, not surprisingly, takes time. In the meantime, subsidies to low-income households can alleviate much of the burden in finding decent affordable accommodation. Comprehensive community initiatives can coordinate the wide range of efforts which seek to ensure that households will be better off working than they are on programs of income support.

In fact, several communities are involved in collaborative initiatives to make work pay. Actions include encouraging employers to provide decent wages and improving government programs that supplement income or replace earnings in the event of temporary or permanent interruption of work. Communities can also seek to ensure, through coordinated efforts, that eligible recipients have access to various income security and tax-delivered benefits to which they are entitled.

Comprehensive community initiatives in Edmonton, Calgary, Niagara and Waterloo have embarked upon living wage campaigns to convince both public and private sector employers to improve their wages and associated employment practices. 'Living wage' refers to the fact that statutory minimum wages set by governments are not high enough to adequately support families.[22] The issue of living wage is discussed more fully in Chapter 8 on *Creating an Enabling Environment*.

These initiatives require extensive coordination among governments, private sector employers and voluntary organizations. A broad community strategy is desirable in that major wage changes can have a significant impact upon certain firms or sectors that comprise the local labour market. But these community efforts, while important, should be understood as supplements to adequate minimum wages and other employment standards as well as earnings supplements and employment expense credits.

Access to benefits

A major problem around sustenance arises from the fact that potential beneficiaries of programs are often not aware of these benefits. Several communities have taken steps to facilitate access to measures intended for low- and modest-income households. As part of a *Make Tax Time Pay* initiative, for example, Vibrant Communities Edmonton set out to find effective ways to inform low-income Edmonton residents about the Alberta Child Health Benefit. This provincial measure provides an average $265 a year per child for prescription drugs, dental and optical care, and emergency ambulance services.[23]

While the Alberta government had developed strategies to publicize the benefit, take-up levels were relatively low – at just 36 percent of the eligible population for the Edmonton area, for example. An estimated 14,900 eligible residents of the city were not collecting the benefit. In order to redress this gap, the conveners of Vibrant Communities Edmonton fostered relationships with three orders of government – the Canada Revenue Agency, the Alberta government and the City of Edmonton.

The partners subsequently identified six other benefit and subsidy programs of which low-income families likely were unaware. The collaborative planned a publicity and education campaign, designated and secured tax assistance locations accessible to low-income families, provided the required training and support materials for volunteers, and prepared the infrastructure to handle the higher number of applications.

The Guaranteed Income Supplement campaign in Waterloo Region is another example of how communities can work with government to enhance access to income benefits.[24] Old Age Security provides almost all senior citizens with modest monthly taxable benefits. In order to improve living standards for lower-income seniors, the Guaranteed Income Supplement (GIS) was introduced in 1967 as a monthly benefit to Canadians who receive full or partial Old Age Security pensions and who have little or no other income. Receipt of the Guaranteed Income Supplement also qualifies low-income seniors in a number of jurisdictions for provincial top-ups to the federal GIS.

New recipients of the Guaranteed Income Supplement must apply and current beneficiaries must re-apply every year because the payment takes into account any changes in income. But some seniors fail to file a tax return each year because they do not have taxable income or have health problems, mental and physical limitations, or literacy and language barriers. Identifying these individuals is a difficult task if they do not submit a tax return, receive no Old Age Security payment or are homeless.

The (former) Department of Human Resources Development Canada had been aware of a problem with take-up rates for the Guaranteed Income Supplement since 1993 and had responded by producing printed program materials, contacting seniors and service providers, and making presentations to financial planners. (A successful court challenge against the federal government had expedited this outreach.) Starting in 2001, all Canadians who file tax returns are sent notification to apply for the Guaranteed Income Supplement. This improvement still leaves unresolved the question of how best to reach seniors who were unaware of the supplement.

Representatives from Opportunities Waterloo Region, the conveners of the local comprehensive initiative, formed a strategy group with Human Resources Development Canada and other organizations to determine how to reach eligible seniors who are not receiving the Guaranteed Income Supplement. One group was struck to prepare and distribute materials. The other set up training sessions for social service employees in regular contact with low-income seniors. Both the information and education processes were meant to complement the federal communications strategies. The initiative has helped more than 600 low-income seniors secure this benefit. Similar efforts have been undertaken in other communities.

Improved benefits

Comprehensive community initiatives can also improve income security programs. Vibrant Communities Calgary, for example, spearheaded a policy roundtable that brought together persons with disabilities, representatives from various community agencies and provincial government officials.

Participants were asked to identify problems with the benefits and delivery of the provincial Assured Income for the Severely Handicapped program. The group believed that if government officials understood the difficulties with the program, they would be better able to resolve the issues or at least propose compromise solutions. The Government of Alberta responded positively to the process and introduced several important changes, including a rise in benefits, an increase in the employment earnings exemption and a decrease in the employment earnings clawback rate.

The group built on the goodwill that had been created to work in a related area of policy interest. When the Alberta government was assessing the Assured Income for the Severely Handicapped (AISH) program, members of the Calgary Committee for Discounted Transit Passes had made submissions to the review committee. The Committee asked the province not only to increase the program's income payments (then $855 per month), but also to share with municipalities the cost of providing affordable transportation for all low-income Albertans. An estimated 8,500 Calgary residents receive AISH benefits, 5,000 of whom use public transit.[25]

The successful effort to establish the reduced fare transit pass program was not easily implemented. Calgary City Council finally took the step of making the passes a reality after a decade of negotiating with the Government of Alberta to contribute funds in support of low-income residents. The "Fair Fares" initiative has become a model for other communities interested in reducing high transportation costs.

Reviewing:

Monitoring progress

A veritable explosion of work is under way throughout the country, and indeed the world, on monitoring progress along the various dimensions of the quality of life. There are scores of indicator initiatives, ranging from national government work in the form of 15 Headline Sustainability Indicators in the UK to local community efforts, such as Sustainable Seattle. There are even reports that attempt to capture the range and scope of available indicators to determine the respective strengths and limitations of the various measures currently in use.

For the purposes of this discussion, one example has been selected as illustrative of the kinds of work that are possible and, indeed, under way in many communities. The review efforts in BC Capital Region have been chosen for this purpose.

Through its Quality of Life CHALLENGE, information and associated interpretations are made available to the community through the use of carefully selected indicators.[26] Where possible, the data have been made consistent with the Quality of Life Monitoring System developed by the Federation of Canadian Municipalities. The value of this approach is that it enables the community to compare its progress not only against its own targets but also in relation to other municipalities engaged in a similar process.

The first Quality of Life Indicators report, published in 1999, provided the baseline information on key indicators in six domains – population, community affordability, housing, workforce, health and community safety, and participation. The second report, issued in 2005, charts changes over that period and includes additional indicators to expand the scope of reporting.

In the area of housing, six key dimensions were monitored: housing tenure, rental vacancy rate, owner and renter affordability, dwelling condition, core housing need and social housing. No discernible change was found between 1996 and 2001 in terms of housing tenure. In most municipalities in the region, more than 70 percent of people owned their homes and the percentage of owners increased by only .9 percent.

However, the rental vacancy rate took a negative turn, dropping from 1.1 percent in 2003 to .6 percent in 2004, the lowest in the country. The low rates reflect the fact that there has been almost no new private market rental housing built in BC Capital Region over the past 20 years. Tight vacancy creates serious accommodation pressures, particularly for low-income families. Landlords are often reluctant to rent to recipients of social assistance or to persons with disabilities who may have special housing needs.

The figures also found a downturn in owner and renter affordability but no discernible change in dwelling condition, which means that the overall quality of housing in the region appears to be relatively good. The Government of BC changed in 2001; the demand for social housing grew by 160 percent between 2003 and 2004.

Clearly, the community needs to assess this range of data and explore precisely what it means. The snapshots at different time intervals paint a contradictory picture – such as a reduction in core housing need just prior to a big jump in the demand for social housing. But the numbers at least give the community some sense of the current status and changing profile of the accommodation dimension of sustenance.

This ongoing review provides the foundation for revising the knowledge base and monitoring progress toward the achievement of the community's desired goal – more affordable housing. The initiative may decide, on the basis of the figures, to step up its activity in some areas and conversely, to pull back from others.

The comprehensive community initiative in BC's Capital Region also recently completed its annual reflection session on progress relative to all its goals. The results of this work will be incorporated into a revised work plan. The review becomes part of the upgraded knowledge base, which in turn guides the next stages of the doing. This process applies not only to sustenance, but equally well to the other core dimensions of resilience.

All this to say...

Work on various aspects of sustenance is concerned primarily with basics like food, clothing and shelter. While there are many ways to support sustenance, these tend to focus primarily upon 'instrumental' methods that promote access to essential goods and services. Equally important to resilience are the 'emotional' methods that seek to develop personal capacity – adaptation and the ability to cope at its very core.

Endnotes

1   United Nations Development Programme. (1994). *Human Development Report 1994*. New York: Oxford University Press, p. 20.

2   See *www.un.org/mdg/* for a description of the UN Millennium Development Goals.

3   The Canada Mortgage and Housing Corporation calculates estimates of core housing need. See *www.cmhc-schl.gc.ca*

4   Sandel, M., J. Sharfstein and R. Shaw. (1999). "There's No Place Like Home: How America's Housing Crisis Threatens Our Children." San Francisco: Housing America and Doc4Kids Project, Boston, MA, p. 25-26.

5   Schmitz, C., J. Wagner and E. Menke. (1995). "Homelessness as One Component of Housing Instability and Its Impact on the Development of Children in Poverty." *Journal of Social Distress and the Homeless*. 4(4): 301-317.

6   Figures provided by Ken Battle, Caledon Institute of Social Policy.

7   Battle, K. and S. Torjman. (2005). Background paper on poverty prepared for the Canadian Institute for Health Information. Ottawa: Caledon Institute of Social Policy, unpublished.

8   Hertzman, C. (2000). "The Case for an Early Childhood Development Strategy." *Isuma: Canadian Journal of Policy Research*. 1(2): 11-18, Autumn.

9   Smith, J., J. Brooks-Gunn and P. Klebanov. (1997). "Consequences of Living in Poverty for Young Children's Cognitive and Verbal Ability and Early School Achievement." In J. Duncan and J. Brooks-Gunn eds. *Consequences of Growing Up Poor*. New York: Russell Sage Foundation, p. 164.

10 Raphael, D. ed. (2004). *Social Determinants of Health: Canadian Perspectives*. Toronto: Canadian Scholars' Press Inc.; Raphael, D. (2002). *Poverty, Income Inequality and Health in Canada*. Toronto: CSJ Foundation for Research and Education, June; Marmot, M. and R. Wilkinson eds. (1999). *The Social Determinants of Health*. Oxford: Oxford University Press.

11 Yalnizyan, A. (2007). *The Rich and the Rest of Us: The Changing Face of Canada's Growing Gap*. Ottawa: Canadian Centre for Policy Alternatives.

12 United Way of Greater Toronto and Canadian Council on Social Development. (2004). *Poverty by Postal Code: The Geography of Neighbourhood Poverty 1981-2001*. Toronto, p. 43.

[13] United Way of Greater Toronto and Canadian Council on Social Development. (2004). Ibid., pp. 21-23.

[14] Canadian Institute for Health Information. (2006). *Improving the Health of Canadians: An Introduction to Health in Urban Places.* Ottawa.

[15] Simpson, A. (1999). *'Self-build' Housing in Aboriginal Communities.* Ottawa: Caledon Institute of Social Policy, November.

[16] See *www.qolchallenge.com*

[17] Makhoul, A. and E. Leviten-Reid. (2006). *Vibrant Communities Saint John: Dismantling the Poverty Traps.* Ottawa: Caledon Institute of Social Policy, March.

[18] Makhoul, A. and E. Leviten-Reid. *Ibid.*

[19] These programs are described at *www.agincourtacsa.info* and in Biglar, F. (1998). *Alternatives to Food Banks.* Ottawa: Caledon Institute of Social Policy, August.

[20] See *www.torontohousing.ca*

[21] Cabaj, M., A. Makhoul and E. Leviten-Reid. (2006). "New Service in Inner-City Saskatoon – Station 20 West." *In from the Field: Exploring the First Poverty Reduction Strategies Undertaken by Trail Builders in the Vibrant Communities Initiative.* Waterloo: Tamarack – An Institute for Community Engagement, May.

[22] See living wage guide and references at the website of the Economic Policy Institute at *www.epi.org*

[23] Makhoul, A. (2006). *Vibrant Communities' Edmonton Make Tax Time Pay Campaign.* Ottawa: Caledon Institute of Social Policy, February.

[24] Makhoul, A. (2005). *Waterloo Region's Guaranteed Income Supplement Campaign.* Ottawa: Caledon Institute of Social Policy, January.

[25] Makhoul, A. (2005) *Assured Income for the Severely Handicapped Public Policy Initiative.* Ottawa: Caledon Institute of Social Policy, May.

[26] See *www.qolchallenge.com*

Chapter 5
Advancing Adaptation

In summary

The goal of the communities agenda is to build resilience in communities in order to ensure their strength and vibrancy. Resilience is the result of actions taken in four independent but related clusters – or areas of shared space. The adaptation cluster is concerned primarily with basic coping skills required to survive in a complex world.

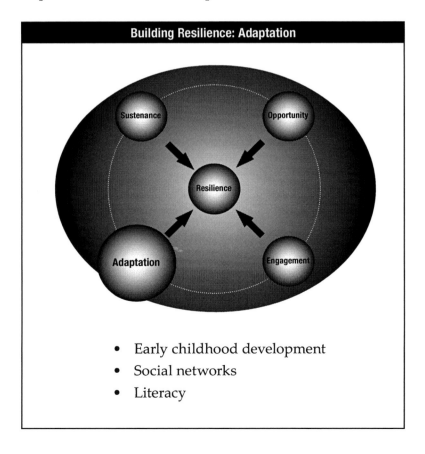

- Early childhood development
- Social networks
- Literacy

This chapter explores adaptation primarily from the perspective of early childhood development, support networks and basic literacy proficiency. Together these comprise a form of social immunity. While actions in support of adaptation are essential to well-being, they are not sufficient. Ideally, these actions link to the other domains that contribute to resilience.

The context

The concept of resilience in both its ecological and mental health applications speaks not only to basic survival. Complex systems – whether individuals, families, groups or even communities – are able to carry on because they have managed to adapt to tough pressures and changing circumstances. The practical application of resilience ranges from personal steps taken by individuals to high-level activities carried out by national governments.

Adaptation lies at the heart of resilience.[1] It refers to the ability to contend with everyday pressures, continual change and unexpected trauma or shock. It applies to natural ecosystems and their capacity to cope with environmental pollutants or emergencies. This ability to adapt applies equally well to organizations and individuals.

Because adaptive capacity is central to resilience, it has been the subject of considerable study. The ecological dimension of resilience comprises the core of a body of research that seeks to understand the nature of complex adaptive systems. This emerging science studies the functioning of living ecosystems and their adaptation to change in order to apply these lessons to individuals, organizations and communities.

Adaptation is effectively a form of social immunization that involves basic coping skills in a changing world. Physical capacity to cope with illness and disease is enhanced through vaccination and immune-bolstering factors such as adequate rest, healthy diet and clean air. Social capacity is similarly developed through actions that contribute to adaptation, including the building of self-esteem, empathy, problem-solving capacity and literacy proficiency.

Working in the shared space – in this case the adaptation cluster – involves the development of a solid evidence base. It next entails a set of actions that create collaborative relationships within the cluster, between clusters and around policy. Finally, working in the shared space requires the continual monitoring of progress against identified outcomes.

Knowing:

Creating the evidence base

The evidence base for the adaptation cluster consists of a vast literature built on studies of early childhood development, parenting, social capital and literacy. The following discussion represents only the tip of a voluminous iceberg.

Adaptation includes basic cognitive skills and a sense of emotional well-being. These are the core building blocks for participating in the world and for coping with its daily challenges. Both head and heart are drivers of adaptation.

From the perspective of individuals, the ability to adapt is linked to personal resilience – the sense of inner capacity to tackle problems. Self-esteem lies at the core of personal resilience. It involves not only self-understanding but also an ability to view the world through the eyes of others. Even the youngest children can learn to appreciate others' feelings. Their *Roots of Empathy* lie deep.[2] Adaptation involves a capacity to respect and even celebrate difference – whether rooted in race, religion or sexuality. It can be understood as a form of emotional literacy.

Basic emotional and intellectual capacities are personal attributes that are nurtured from within. But the ability to cope with the demands of life in a complex world also requires networks of supports that are nurtured from without. Family, friends, neighbours and colleagues provide respite and guidance in the face of tough challenges, offer solace and comfort when things go wrong and share in the joy when things go right.

Family members typically fill this social role – particularly for children when they are young. In fact, the quality of the parent/child relationship lies at the core of healthy child development. Secure attachment to caring and supportive families is crucial. Opportunities for well-being throughout life basically are created or denied in the critical early years, when child development is forged along multiple dimensions – physical, emotional, social, linguistic and intellectual.[3]

These conclusions derive from studies on population health, early intervention and neurological research. They show that significant brain development occurs between conception and age 1, and that stimuli before age 3 greatly influence the wiring of nerve cells and neural pathways in the brain. Children who do not receive the nutrition and stimulation necessary for healthy development in the early years may have difficulty overcoming deficits later on.[4]

Studies of children considered to be at risk because of vulnerable personal circumstances – such as poverty – have found that those with close, affectionate relationships with parents, grandparents, other adults and siblings are better able to cope with adversity and the disadvantages of low income. Positive parenting practices help build resilience in children and counter the grind of poverty. In fact, low-income children whose parents encourage, praise, play with and interact positively with them are more likely to have good relationships at home and school than children from better-off families whose parents are hostile or punish them.[5]

The factors that foster resilience within disadvantaged children have been characterized as a 'protective triad' consisting of personal characteristics, close family ties and external support systems.[6] Protective personal characteristics include social competence, problem-solving skills, autonomy and an optimistic outlook.

Social factors embedded in the quality of family and community life are equally vital determinants of child development. The evidence calls for family-enabling environments, which assist positive parenting and communities that provide support. The Annie E. Casey Foundation talks about the importance of these enabling environments.

> This framework is also based on the premise, from our own research and the research of others, that families who live in these very vulnerable neighbourhoods are basically isolated and disconnected. They are disconnected from the economic opportunities that they need to build wealth and assets and to generate income. They are disconnected from each other because of culture, because of language, because of all kinds of orientation. They live in the same spot but they don't relate to each other beyond a very small circle. They are disconnected from the kind of services and supports or institutions that provide them their well-being. So our commitment ought to be to help those communities and their families make those connections to their communities, to the kind of family supports they need and to each other through social networks and organizations that will help them become stronger.[7]

Community-based supports for families help prevent problems and encourage the positive development of children.[8] These supports include high-quality affordable child care and local resource centres that provide information about child development and programs for families. Neighbourhood play groups offer socialization for children and informal assistance for parents. Respite through formal services or informal means, such as babysitting co-operatives, afford crucial occasional relief for caregivers. Toy- and book-lending libraries make available important learning resources, particularly for low-income families.

Early childhood development programs are an important means of promoting healthy development and overcoming childhood deficits. These programs vary widely in nature and scope, and typically include combinations of health, education and social services in the form of prenatal care, nutritional supplements for pregnant mothers, home visiting for new parents, regulated child care, parenting skills programs, Head Start and preschool programs, family resource centres and regulated child care.

Quality early childhood development has been shown to improve children's performance in school, lessen the learning risks linked to low income, and enhance parents' childrearing and coping skills. Family support, parent training and early intervention programs are estimated to reduce child abuse by as much as 50 percent and thereby stave off the lifelong consequences and costs of living with abuse. Similar programs help prevent the aggressive behaviour among young children often associated with failure in school and subsequent delinquency and criminality.[9] Family supports are also associated with greater success down the road as measured by high school completion and paid employment.

Home visiting programs that target young single mothers and enriched preschool programs that focus upon the young children of these mothers have been found to produce substantial benefits. High-quality child care can compensate for some of the developmental deficits rooted in childhood deprivation. Quality schools help build resilience by providing opportunities for problem-solving and cooperation.

> Our notions are, let's focus on revitalizing the neighbourhood that children have to grow up in and then let's provide

the kind of strengthening support to families as they engage
in raising children. That's the place we've come to as a framework of the theory: children do better when families do better
and families do better when neighbourhoods are strong.[10]

In short, the family, school and communities with which
a child interacts have a powerful effect on cognitive and behavioural development and on the prevalence of childhood
vulnerability. Social networks are a vital component of the
environment. There is, in fact, a burgeoning literature on
the value of these networks – generally referred to as 'social
capital.'[11]

Social capital is created when people come together out
of a shared purpose that goes beyond individual benefits
and incorporates the idea of connectedness. Families are a
main source of social capital. It is also built through participation in associations or social structures of cooperation
such as religious organizations, political parties, neighbourhood associations, cooperatives, sports or cultural clubs,
and through participation in civic activities like volunteering or voting.

Social capital has been found to contribute substantially to the health and well-being of individuals and communities.[12] The caring and respect that occur in social relationships, and the resulting sense of satisfaction and well-being,
appear to act as buffers against health problems. People
with less emotional support are more likely to experience
a reduced sense of well-being, depression, greater risk of
pregnancy complications and higher incidence of disability
from chronic disease. Social isolation and exclusion are associated with increased rates of premature death and poorer chances of survival after a heart attack.

Individuals in communities and societies with strong
social capital have also been found to be more prosperous
and to experience less crime.[13] Connections through trust-
ing networks and common values promote the enforcement

of positive standards for youth and enable access to mentors, role models, educational sponsors and job contacts outside the neighbourhood. In fact, the decline in neighbourhood social capital (in the form of community monitoring, socializing, mentoring and organizing) has been identified as a key driver in inner-city vulnerability, in addition to purely economic factors.[14]

Some individuals may need additional supports because of disability or a heath condition. They may benefit from more formal networks of support in which a group of people is brought together to take responsibility for providing assistance when required. Sometimes, even these circles of support are not enough. Depending upon the circumstances, additional aid in the form of personal attendants, homemakers or home care workers may be necessary.[15]

Recent immigrants may need help acquiring affordable housing, locating appropriate medical care, gaining recognition of their credentials and finding opportunities for meaningful participation. Formal services enable the settlement of newcomers and their adaptation to a new country.

While important in itself, social capital has been recognized by the Organisation for Economic Co-operation and Development as a foundation for the creation of human capital.[16] Relationships and networks enable the process of skills development and learning. Literacy, in particular, is the basis for participating in a knowledge economy. It is the ability not only to read and write but also to understand and use information.

Good literacy skills are linked to better health and more active participation in communities. Literacy represents substantial currency in terms of future income as well. The International Adult and Literacy Skills Survey confirms a not-surprising fact: In a knowledge economy, the higher the literacy proficiency, the more likely that an individual will be employed and earn a reasonable income. Poor literacy skills are linked to higher unemployment and to work in occupations with lower skill requirements and associated pay.

Recent evidence on immigrant earnings finds that literacy and numeracy affect a range of labour market outcomes including employability, stability and duration of employment, and wages. "Without exception, higher average skill levels are associated with better average labour market outcomes."[17]

In fact, literacy has been found to play a vital role in ensuring a healthy democracy. While literacy itself does not create a just and egalitarian society, it does provide the means for participating in all spheres of a community and the nation. In fact, higher levels of prose literacy have been linked to greater involvement in community organizations and volunteer activities. Poor literacy skills, by contrast, tend to constrain this economic and social participation.[18] Literacy is effectively the foundation for the participation described in *Ensuring Engagement*, another core dimension of resilience.

Doing:

Creating links within the cluster

Early childhood development

In many communities, programs and services directed toward families and children are still divided into discrete categories such as public health, early childhood development, education, child care, recreation and the arts, social services, child welfare and corrections. This fragmentation seriously impedes the ability of child- and family-serving organizations to respond appropriately to household needs.

In recent years, individual programs have begun to work more closely in many communities in order to consolidate their respective contributions. No one organization is responsible for the well-being of all children. The primary role of communities is to shore up the adaptation cluster by ensuring that the wide range of existing resources is working together and pooling resources as appropriate.

One example is Success by 6, now in place in more than 200 communities throughout North America. Initiated by the United Way movement, it is not a single program and is neither funded nor owned by a sole organization. Rather, the initiative creates links among the public, private and voluntary sectors to raise awareness of the importance of early childhood and to enhance collaboration among service providers.

A similar joined-up effort is under way in nine centres throughout Québec. *L'Initiative 1,2,3 Go!* supports community mobilization around early childhood development to ensure that all children have a healthy start in life. The project engages key parties, including service providers, community organizations, community leaders from major sectors and parents, to collaborate in their efforts to support young children and their families.

Better Beginnings, Better Futures is an early example of joined-up work in the adaptation cluster. It is a multi-ministry prevention program operating in eight high-risk communities in Ontario. The objectives are to reduce the incidence of preventable serious long-term emotional and behavioural problems in children; to promote optimal social, physical and cognitive development in children at the highest risk for such problems; and to strengthen the ability of communities to respond effectively to the needs of families. The program provides home visiting to expectant and new parents, child care, in-school assistance, before- and after-school supervision, parent training and support groups.

Other collaborative efforts within the adaptation cluster focus upon basic literacy and associated social supports. The City Centre Education Project in Edmonton, for example, was launched in 2001 when seven inner-city schools came together to create a more positive learning environment for both students and teachers.[19] Schools in the inner city are struggling to deal with declining enrollment, a transient population and families grappling with poverty and substance abuse. The project seeks to ensure that students receive an excellent education and that they all complete high school.

A professional learning community was organized among the participating schools to enhance the quality of teaching. Common areas of interest include administrative issues such as budget management, teaching methods and student supports. The project is involved with the community through links to organizations and services, such as family centres and the City Centre Joint Parent Group. The schools are also playing a more active role in ensuring the availability of affordable housing and community services.

Pathways to Education© is another example of an initiative concerned with various dimensions of adaptation, with a primary focus on literacy. It was spearheaded in Regent Park by the Regent Park Community Health Centre to tackle a 56 percent drop-out rate and is now being implemented in communities in Québec, Ontario and BC.

The program is built on four pillars. Students receive *tutoring* in all subjects on a drop-in basis four nights per week. Many of the volunteers are university students, teaching candidates and Regent Park residents. The *mentoring* component provides positive role models and individualized assistance to deal with students' unique needs and their career aspirations. *Transit tickets* are made available to offset the cost of transportation to school. *Student parent support workers* act as advocates by creating links among students, their parents and school staff. A scholarship of $1,000 per year is raised so that students have $4,000 to assist with post-secondary education. This kind of personalized support is an important message: Someone cares about the students as individuals and is working actively on their behalf.

The special attention paid to literacy and to pulling together a comprehensive range of individualized supports has produced impressive results. These include a 65 percent reduction in absenteeism, a decrease from 56 to 14 percent in the drop-out rate, a 75 percent increase in the graduation rate and 90 percent jump in the acceptance rate for four-year graduates who applied to colleges and universities. The work on various dimensions of adaptation will open for these students the doors to opportunity.[20]

Governments can also join up more effectively their actions within the adaptation cluster. As noted in *Working in the Shared Space,* the integrated services approach in Saskatchewan employs collaborative processes to improve co-ordination and responsiveness.

Healthy Child Manitoba is the government's long-term cross-departmental strategy to support the healthy development of children and adolescents. Seven partner departments are working together under the Healthy Child Committee of Cabinet to ensure that all children throughout the province are physically and emotionally healthy, safe and secure, successful at learning and socially engaged to their fullest potential.[21]

Within the Healthy Child Manitoba strategy, the Families First program seeks to enhance parents' capacity to provide a nurturing and supportive environment. This home visiting program is delivered across the province through the public health system. A public health nurse meets with expectant or new parents to learn about their strengths and needs, and to develop a plan of support. The home visitor continues to work with the family for up to three years to encourage healthy parent-child relationships.

The Healthy Baby program within the cross-departmental strategy pays a prenatal nutrition financial benefit and community support programs for all pregnant women and new parents. Through eleven regional health authorities, Manitoba Health and Healthy Living promotes early childhood health through prenatal and postnatal supports offered by public health nurses. A strong immunization program is delivered through public health and local physician offices throughout the province.

The Department of Manitoba Health and Healthy Living partners with Manitoba Education, Citizenship and Youth and with Healthy Child Manitoba to support the provincial Healthy Schools initiative. Its six components include healthy eating, physical activity, safety and injury prevention, mental health promotion, health sexuality, and substance abuse and addictions.

In recognition of the importance of early childhood development, Manitoba Education Citizenship and Youth also introduced the Early Childhood Development Initiative, which funds preschool programming and services. Manitoba Aboriginal and Northern Affairs supports community-based Aboriginal organizations that encourage the healthy development of children and youth in First Nations, Métis and Aboriginal families. The Department also provides advice and guidance to the overall Healthy Child Manitoba strategy to ensure that it serves the needs of Aboriginal children, families and communities.

The Ministry of Culture, Heritage and Tourism is responsible for a range of program areas that have an impact on early childhood development including public library services, recreation and the arts. Parents, community organizations, school divisions, health authorities, cultural groups and the business community are working together in regional Parent-Child Centred Coalitions to support children and families in their communities. Interventions vary by region and include, for example, parenting workshops, family literacy programs, family resource centres and creative play groups.

Several departments, including Justice, Family Services and Housing, Health and Healthy Living, Aboriginal and Northern Affairs, and the Healthy Child Office, work together on the issue of Fetal Alcohol Spectrum Disorder. They are building a strategy that includes prevention, intervention and supports for families.

Between clusters
Adaptation and sustenance

Strong neighbourhoods are an important foundation for healthy children and families. A recent initiative in Hamilton is targeting its efforts on reducing poverty with a primary focus on the children and youth.[22] It hopes to rally the entire community around the message "Making Hamilton the Best Place to Raise a Child." The initiative is an example of how various community groups, diverse in sectoral representation, are collaborating with local government to undertake a wide range of adaptation initiatives linked to tackling poverty.

The strategy is rooted in the work of the Hamilton Roundtable on Poverty Reduction formed in May 2005. The Roundtable is co-convened by the Hamilton Community Foundation and the Community Services Department, City of Hamilton – a significant arrangement in itself. Its diverse membership includes people living in poverty, the voluntary sector including Affordable Housing Flagship, the local social planning council, business and labour, and the provincial government.

The Roundtable seeks to raise awareness about the fact that an estimated 20 percent of the local population lives on low incomes and about the need to find practicable solutions to the problem. The strategic framework developed by the Roundtable places children at the centre of a series of linked interventions related to individuals, families, neighbourhoods, communities and government policies.

The framework identifies the critical points of investment along the pathway from birth to young adulthood – quality early learning and parenting; skills through education, activity and recreation; targeted skills development at the postsecondary level; employment; and asset-building and wealth creation. The Roundtable will explore possible improvements at all these significant points.

The focus is not individual programs or projects but rather the mobilization of the community toward the achievement of common goals related to poverty reduction. The Roundtable will work with community partners to ensure that the required supports are in place to enable children and their families to thrive, and will engage citizens in all aspects of the work.

The interesting slant to this initiative is that it bills itself as a major poverty reduction effort and is concerned fundamentally with issues of sustenance. Yet it seeks to meet this objective primarily through joining up programs and services for children and ensuring appropriate supports for families. The community is effectively taking a long-term, generational approach to poverty reduction and targeting the well-being of children as its pivotal point of intervention.

Adaptation and engagement

Some community efforts that focus primarily upon child development and support for families also build in a clear engagement dimension in which students and residents are encouraged to participate actively in the community. The City of London, to name one of many examples, has worked in partnership with the federal and Ontario governments as well as school boards and local organizations to address the health and learning needs of children. KIDS COUNT was a community-wide partnership that operated between 1992 and 1999; it subsequently has merged with the London Investment Education Council to create Investing in Children.

KIDS COUNT convened parents, children, educators, businesses and voluntary agencies to identify and implement ideas to improve health and learning opportunities for children and families.[23] The initiative organized educational projects; Love of Books, for example, lent books for preschoolers, buddy bags filled with books for children and magazines for parents to encourage families to read together. It provided homework rooms, computer learning and field trips. Breakfast and nutrition programs were set up in schools. KIDS COUNT also created youth groups that carried out civic-oriented projects, such as collecting donations for local food banks, improving local parks and organizing social and recreational events. It was involved in safety issues, including Block Parents and street proofing for children.

This learning initiative illustrates how neighbourhoods can provide a natural entry – and focal point – for linking reading, writing and citizen engagement. In many neighbourhoods, the school acts as a natural family-supporting centre and is virtually the only public resource.

Schools are convenient centres for activities and programs related to adaptation because children go there every day, often accompanied by their parents. The school facilitates the delivery of services in a safe and familiar place. Services for students can be accessed during school hours with little disruption to their studies. Intervention is easier in the case of children who require special assistance.

But schools can provide more than a front-line weapon against the troubles that students – and their families – may face. Equally important, they can serve as the focal point for harnessing the community's assets. In fact, many schools throughout the country have already assumed the role of neighbourhood hub.

Parenting and family literacy programs operate in free space provided by 54 schools in Toronto alone and an additional 35 throughout Ontario as of September 2007. Literacy and parenting at the centres are also linked to the preschool Roots of Empathy program. Parenting centres offer a play-based program for infants to 4-year-olds and incorporate book- and toy-lending libraries. They are able to detect at an early stage only physical, mental or learning condition that may require intervention, and can serve as brokers for specialized services.

The model has become even more formalized in some areas. The recently developed Toronto Best Start Network is an example of joined-up work with a community hub – typically the neighbourhood school – as its foundation. The initiative involves three provincial ministries, the City of Toronto Children's Services, four district school boards, representatives from the francophone and Aboriginal communities, and the United Way. The unique contribution of this effort is that it provides an overarching framework, called *Best Start Plan – Toronto Vision for Children*, which seeks a major redesign of services and supports for young children.[24]

The Best Start initiative involves increased coordination and integration of kindergarten, child care and family support programs around the neighbourhood hub. Staff expertise is brought together at the local level to create a team of early childhood developers, teachers, educational assistants and family support workers. The school hub provides access to a range of services such as nutrition programs, public health, children's mental health, referral to speech and language resources and early identification of children with special needs. Every hub is individually designed to reflect the unique needs of each neighbourhood.

Until recently, there had been problems in many communities related to the additional costs for the use of facilities, equipment and supervision. The educational funding formula, at least in Ontario, had restricted the use of school space by community groups. Funding of school space is on a square footage per pupil formula that did not take into account alternate daytime use, such as child care centres or health clinics. Neither did it enable after-school nor weekend use deemed to cause wear and tear to facilities and equipment.

A significant step was taken to address this problem; in November 2006, the Government of Ontario announced a plan to invest $20 million a year for the Community Use of Schools Initiative. The annual funding will help school boards reduce or eliminate the fees that youth and community groups are required to pay for the utilization of schools after hours.

The hub notion makes clear that schools are important not just for their use as public space. They also provide a venue – available to all – for the creation of social networks and promotion of literacy proficiency that comprise the core of adaptation. A wealth of resources, especially volunteers, can be brought into schools to promote the educational and social well-being of children, thereby linking the adaptation objective to engagement.

While schools are well situated to act as community hubs, other neighbourhood spaces such as early childhood centres, places of worship and community centres can also be used for this purpose. Early childhood resource centres clearly play that role, for example, in several First Nations communities in British Columbia.

A research partnership between the University of Victoria and community groups throughout the province highlighted this approach. The University partnered with 10 groups of First Nations for the delivery of a two-year, community-based postsecondary diploma program. In each host community, an average 10 community members have earned credentials to operate programs for infants, young children and their families. A follow-up study asked what the graduates and their communities had developed after this successful expansion of community capacity.

The study noted that most communities in Canada maintain an individual-centred and non-integrated approach to services for children and families. The First Nations that participated in the community capacity follow-up study believed that this practice was inappropriate because of its focus on problems, crises and special needs rather than the promotion of wellness of the whole person, family and community as a cultural and social entity.

The communities in the study are demonstrating how to move away from an individually centred, problem focus. Instead, they are creating links among home-based and centre-based infant and child care programs and other health, cultural and social programs intended for families. These include parenting supports, health education, fitness, alcohol and drug treatment services, and job training. All the communities share a vision of intersectoral service delivery and two First Nations in particular – Tl'azt'en Nation and Lil'wat Nation – have made significant strides toward implementing a long-term plan for co-located and integrated services.[25]

The co-located facilities and programs allow early childhood care and development to act as both "hook" and "hub." They act as a hook by attracting community members to the quality child care that many families need. These resources provide easy access to other "laddered" family development and health services that exist as spokes around the central core of quality child care and development programs.

The laddered system makes it possible to quickly and discretely increase services and case management where required. As a result, the hook and hub model is able to support, within their own cultural communities, children and families that are beginning to experience difficulties, require protective services or have special needs.

> By setting up child care centres as the focal point or hub of a larger system of community programs and meeting spaces, these First Nations communities have created a service delivery model that is not only multidimensional and accessible, but also culturally 'safe,' appropriate and holistic. This approach allows the communities to achieve two important goals: to promote cultural knowledge, identity and pride; and to strengthen parental involvement and parenting skills.[26]

But in order for the hub model to be successful, agencies and jurisdictions must collaborate to reduce the burden on communities of different funding application and accountability requirements. They must enable the construction of facilities that house multiple services. Finally, they must support integrated case management that combines the expertise of practitioners across diverse disciplines and works with families in their own communities. In short, the model requires an enabling environment that supports joined-up work.

Around Policy
Adaptation and opportunity

The work of the Planned Lifetime Advocacy Network (PLAN) is an example both of links between the adaptation and opportunity clusters, and of links to policy. As part of its core mission, PLAN puts into practice on a daily basis the meaning of adaptation. It builds circles of supports around persons with disabilities to ensure that they have loving people who care about them and can provide assistance, if required.[27]

At the core of PLAN is the belief that all the elements of a good life – a home, family and friends, choice and even security – involve the cultivation of meaningful relationships.

These did simply not *lead to* quality of life; they *were* quality of life.[28]

> We want our family members to have a good life. A good life for our family members with disabilities means: enjoying friends and families; having a place to call home; having adequate resources to live with dignity and becoming a contributing citizen.[29]

For the first time in history, because of medical and technological advances, persons with disabilities are outliving their parents. PLAN points out that the assumptions underlying the development of traditional policies for persons with disabilities – such as being dependent upon and predeceasing parents – no longer hold.

One of the most important concerns for parents caring for sons and daughters with severe disabilities is to provide properly for their needs. But they also seek to ensure a good quality of life for their family member after their death. The creation of support networks is crucial but not sufficient. PLAN members want to provide assurance of economic security to their relatives with severe disabilities. They want to build personal financial assets to ensure independence – a core component of the opportunity cluster.

In order to achieve this objective, PLAN recognized the need for a major policy innovation that would assist families to achieve this financial security on behalf of their relatives. The group had been proposing the development of a tax-deferred savings vehicle called a Registered Disability Savings Plan, modelled on the current Registered Retirement Savings Plan. It would encourage the financial contributions of family members toward the future support and enhanced independence of their relatives with disabilities.[30]

The group held a preliminary meeting with selected representatives from the financial and venture capital worlds to help them think through the options. Participants recommended that research be carried out to determine the 'quantum' of the proposal. How many families potentially would take advantage of this assistance? What would be a reasonable amount of savings to allow per family? How much would the proposal cost federal and provincial treasuries? What pool of capital might accrue from this tax-assisted savings measure that could be reinvested?

In order to answer these questions, PLAN received support from two participants at the exploratory meeting to carry out the required research. Two papers subsequently were commissioned, one of which dealt with possible design considerations and the scope of the quantum issues.[31] The second paper examined the interface of the proposed measure with provincial social assistance programs to ensure that these would not offset the benefit of any newly introduced federal measure.[32]

The proposal for tax-assisted savings subsequently was considered and written up in the report of the Technical Advisory Committee on Tax Measures for Persons with Disabilities that had been appointed by the Minister of Finance and Minister of Revenue in 2004 to examine the scope of tax measures for persons with disabilities. The idea of the Registered Disability Savings Plan is discussed in its *Disability Tax Fairness* report.[33]

As a follow-up to the tax report, the 2006 federal Budget announced the formation of an expert group to advise the Minister of Finance on possible designs for such a savings scheme. In December 2006, the expert group issued *A New Beginning*, which recommended the introduction of a Registered Disability Savings Plan modelled on the current Registered Education Savings Plan.[34]

In fact, the panel went beyond endorsing a disability savings plan to recommend a new Disability Savings Grant and Disability Bond. These measures would enable the participation in the scheme of low- and modest-income earners who have minimal capacity to save. The report proposed that the design of these initiatives be modelled on the learn$ave program, described in the chapter on *Optimizing Opportunity*. The work was successful: The 2007 federal Budget introduced a new Registered Disability Savings Plan along with a Canada Disability Savings Grant and a Canada Disability Savings Bond.

Reviewing:

Monitoring progress

The third crucial element of working in the shared space is to monitor progress. The information derived from the review process subsequently comprises part of the evidence base or knowing, which then modifies the implementation of the action plan.

Understanding the Early Years (UEY) is an example of a national initiative, launched by the federal government, which uses various types of quantitative and qualitative data to enable communities to work together to meet children's needs and to chart progress on an ongoing basis. Understanding the Early Years started as a pilot in North York in 1999 and grew to 12 communities by 2001. It became a national effort in 2004. Up to 50 communities will be funded by 2008.[35]

The project emerged in response to growing recognition that the quality of nurturing and attention in early childhood has a major impact later in life. Understanding the Early Years is founded on the principle that increased appreciation of the factors that foster healthy child development and community understanding of how their children are faring will help ensure the best possible start in life.

Under the program, Human Resources and Social Development Canada enters into a three-year contribution agreement with a nonprofit organization, which becomes the project sponsor for the community. The sponsoring organization hires both a community coordinator to manage the local effort and a researcher to complete an inventory of existing community programs, and to interpret and map the data.

The project provides members of participating communities with quality information on the school readiness of their kindergarten children. It identifies the family and community factors that influence child development and the availability of local resources. Parents, teachers, policymakers and others interested in the well-being of families work together on the basis of the information they collectively have gathered from several major sources.

The Early Development Instrument measures the school readiness of kindergarten children prior to Grade One and is completed by the kindergarten teachers for each child in their classes. It assesses the core domains of child development: physical health and mental well-being, social competence, emotional maturity, language and cognitive development, communication skills and general knowledge.

The Parent Interviews and Direct Assessments of Children Survey examines the relationships between children's development, and various family and community factors that might influence that development. The Survey also involves three direct assessment activities with kindergarten children to provide information on their receptive vocabulary, copying and symbol printing skills related to early literacy, and number knowledge. The instrument is based on the National Longitudinal Survey on Children and Youth for five-year-olds and collects information on 300 to 500 kindergarten children in a community.

Together, the Early Development Instrument and the Parent Interviews and Direct Assessments of Children Survey provide a balance between the subjective data completed by parents and teachers, and objective data through the direct assessments of children's abilities. For each community, these multiple sources of information form the basis of a Community Research Report which helps the community understand how well its children are doing, and the family and neighbourhood factors that may influence child development.

The information subsequently is mapped with other data to show the availability and distribution of community resources linked to child development. The mapping identifies gaps in the provision of services. Local socioeconomic data, such as the unemployment rate, average household income, educational level, family status and home ownership, is also collected and included within a Community Mapping Report.

The sponsoring organization and coordinator work with a coalition of parents, teachers, school representatives and others interested in the well-being of children to put together a Community Action Plan on the basis of the Community Research Report and Community Mapping Report. By proposing changes to programs and services that enhance the development of young children, the Action Plan serves as a blueprint to encourage the entire community to undertake concrete activities to address identified gap in the supports for young children and their families.

Toronto First Duty provides another example of ongoing monitoring and review.[36] In this case, qualitative measures form the base for measuring progress against objectives.

The initiative was created in 1999 by the City of Toronto, the Atkinson Charitable Foundation, Toronto District School Board and participating community agencies. The partnership sought to bridge the disconnect between child care, education and family support programs. It wanted to demonstrate to policy-makers, families and communities the advantages of comprehensive universal early childhood service provision.

One specific goal of Toronto First Duty was to develop an early childhood staff team that involves professionals from the education, early childhood education and family support sectors. Each sector traditionally has worked on the basis of different expectations, legislation and curriculum – creating barriers to an effective and coherent approach.

Under the initiative, diverse professionals are brought together as early learning teams to set common goals and strategies for children and their families. Child care, kindergarten, parenting programs, public health and community agencies pool their resources to develop a newly-blended early childhood/family support program. The partners form a single governing body to manage the efforts which comprises the foundation for the Toronto Best Start initiative, earlier described.

Of particular interest is the methodology that Toronto First Duty formulated for tracking its work. The Indicators of Change tool supports the assessment, planning and monitoring processes. Partners are able to determine their current status, agree to common goals and periodically assess their progress.

More specifically, the project has developed a guide that tracks the integration of early childhood programs and services along five core domains – local governance, seamless access to services, early learning environments, early childhood staff team and parent participation. Each of the five components is broken down even further, resulting in 19 indicators for the program as a whole.

Under *local governance*, for example, four indicators pertain to program mandate, policy and practices; service planning and monitoring; allocation of financial resources; and human resources. *Seamless access* involves review around capacity; child care provision and affordability; and intake, enrollment and attendance. Indicators of progress on *early learning environments* include curriculum framework and pedagogical approach, daily routines and schedules, children's development and progress, and program quality. Measures around *early childhood staff team* relate to program planning and implementation, behaviour guidance/child management, roles and responsibilities, and staff development. Finally, *parent participation* is assessed by parent input and participation in programs, parenting capacity and relationships with families.

But the review process goes a step further. For each program indicator, benchmarks have been designed to track progress along a continuum of collaborative action. Steps along the pathway include coexistence, coordination, collaboration, deeper collaboration and integration. Coexistence involves programs in the same building or neighbourhood. Coordination refers to the sharing of program plans and the provision of joint events for families. Collaboration entails the merging of resources, space and materials – and deeper collaboration even more so. Integration involves a single identity with common curriculum, policies and practices.

All this to say...

The wide-ranging and diverse efforts on adaptation described here add up to a powerful message. Healthy children are more likely to grow into healthy teens and adults who care about themselves; their families, friends and neighbours; and their common space. They are also more likely to care about and engage actively in the communities that nurtured them. Engagement is the other core element concerned with the 'emotional' dimension of resilience – and is the cluster to which we now turn.

Endnotes

1   See, for example, International Council for Science. (2002). *Resilience and Sustainable Development.* Science Background Paper commissioned by the Environmental Advisory Council of the Swedish Government in preparation for the World Summit on Sustainable Development, Stockholm.

2   Roots of Empathy seeks to build capacity of the next generation for caring and compassionate citizenship and parenting. At the core of the program is a neighbourhood infant and parent who visit the classroom every three weeks over the school year. With a certified Roots of Empathy Instructor, students are coached to observe the baby's development, celebrate milestones, interact with the baby and learn about the infant's needs and unique temperament. When children understand how others feel, they are less likely to hurt each other through bullying, exclusion and violence. See *www. rootsofempathy.org*

3   Hertzman, C. (2000). "The Case for an Early Childhood Development Strategy." ISUMA. 1(2): 11-18, Autumn.

4   McCain, M. and F. Mustard. (1999). *Reversing the Real Brain Drain: Early Years Study Final Report.* Toronto: Ontario Children's Secretariat.

5   Willms, J.D. (2002). "Research Findings Bearing on Canadian Social Policy." In J.D. Willms ed. *Vulnerable Children: Findings from Canada's National Longitudinal Survey of Children and Youth.* Edmonton: University of Alberta Press, pp. 331-358.

6   Steinhauer, P. (1996). *The Primary Needs of Children: A Blueprint for Effective Health Promotion at the Community Level.* Ottawa: Caledon Institute of Social Policy, April.

7   Yates, G. (2004). "Rebuilding Communities." *Ideas That Matter.* 3(2): 13.

8   Battle, K. and S. Torjman. (2002). *Architecture for National Child Care.* Ottawa: Caledon Institute of Social Policy, November.

9   Steinhauer, P. (1998). "Developing Resiliency in Children from Disadvantaged Populations. In National Forum on Health (ed.). *Determinants of Health: Children and Youth.* Sainte-Foy, Quebec: Éditions MultiMondes.

10   Yates, G. (2004). "Rebuilding Communities." *Ideas That Matter.* 3(2): 13.

11   Putnam, R. (2000). *Bowling Alone: The Collapse and Revival of American Community.* New York: Simon and Schuster.

12   Putnam, R. *Ibid*, p. 326.

13   Putnam, R. *Ibid*, p. 309.

[14] Putnam, R. *Ibid,* p. 323.

[15] Torjman, S. (2000). *Proposal for a National Personal Supports Fund.* Ottawa: Caledon Institute of Social Policy, October.

[16] Organisation for Economic Co-operation and Development (OECD). (2001). *The Well-Being of Nations: The Role of Human and Social Capital.* Paris.

[17] Statistics Canada. (2004). "Study: The Effect of Literacy on Immigrant Earnings." *The Daily,* September 7.

[18] Shalla, V. and G. Schellenberg. (1998.) *International Adult Literacy Survey: The Value of Words: Literacy and Economic Security in Canada.* Ottawa: Statistics Canada, May.

[19] For a description of the City Centre Education Program, see *www.tamarackcommunity.ca/g3s5g.html*

[20] See *www.pathwaystoeducation.ca/facts.html*

[21] For a description of Healthy Child Manitoba, see *www.gov.mb.ca/ healthychild*

[22] Hamilton Roundtable for Poverty Reduction. (2006). "Making Hamilton the Best Place to Raise a Child: A Change Framework for Poverty Reduction." Hamilton, May 9. See *www.hamiltonpoverty.ca*

[23] Lubell, J. (1999). *KIDS COUNT: Partners for Children's Health and Learning.* Ottawa: Caledon Institute of Social Policy, July.

[24] See Best Start Plan – Toronto Vision for Children at *www.toronto.ca/ children/beststart/bs/bsn_vision.pdf*

[25] Ball, J. (2004). *Early Childhood Care and Development Programs as Hook and Hub: Promising Practices in First Nations* Communities. Victoria: School of Child Care and Youth Care, October.

[26] Ball, J. *Ibid,* pp. 6-7.

[27] Etmanski, A. (2000). *A Good Life.* Vancouver: Planned Lifetime Advocacy Network (PLAN).

[28] Westley, F., B. Zimmerman and M. Quinn Patten. (2006). *Getting to Maybe: How the World is Changed.* Toronto: Random House Canada, p. 74.

[29] Planned Lifetime Advocacy Network (PLAN). (2003). "Securing a Good Life for Our Family Members with Disabilities: A Proposal for Federal Reforms." Vancouver, August 22.

[30] Torjman, S. (2003). *New Ingredients for the Fiscal Pie.* Ottawa: Caledon Institute of Social Policy, December.

[31] Horner, K. (2005). *The Disability Savings Plan: Contribution Estimates and Policy Issues.* Ottawa: Caledon Institute of Social Policy, November.

[32] Shillington, R. (2005). *The Disability Savings Plan: Policy Milieu and Model Development.* Ottawa: Caledon Institute of Social Policy, November.

[33] Technical Advisory Committee on Tax Measures for Persons with Disabilities. (2004). *Disability Tax Fairness.* Report to the Minister of Finance and the Minister of National Revenue. Ottawa: Finance Canada, December.

[34] Minister of Finance's Expert Panel on Financial Security for Children with Severe Disabilities. (2006). *A New Beginning.* Ottawa: Finance Canada, December.

[35] See Understanding the Early Years at *www.hrsdc.gc.ca/en/hip/sd/300_UEYinfo.shtml*. See also Social Research and Demonstration Corporation. (2005). "Understanding the Early Years: Using Research Data to Engage Communities." Learning What Works; Evidence from SRDC's Social Experiments and Research. 5(2), Fall.

[36] For a description of Toronto First Duty, see *www.toronto.ca/firstduty/*

Chapter 6
Ensuring Engagement

In summary
The goal of the communities agenda is to build resilience in communities in order to ensure their strength and vibrancy. Resilience is the result of actions taken in four independent but related clusters – or areas of shared space.

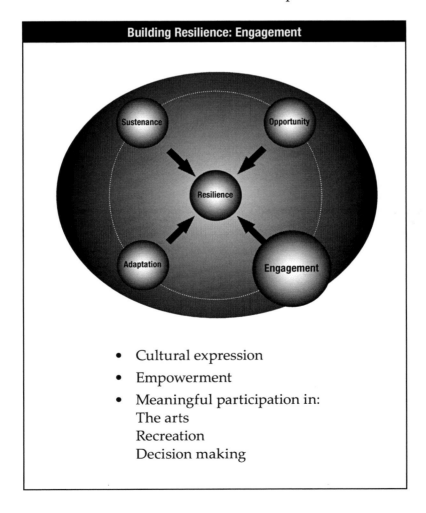

This chapter explores engagement, which is concerned with active involvement – whether through personal expression via story-telling, recreation, art or music, or participation in decision-making on the boards of organizations or in local processes.

Engagement moves beyond adaptation, which involves basic social capacity. It conveys a sense of individuals as active agents in their own life – and in society more generally. Engagement effectively represents a form of empowerment in which both individuals and groups gain a sense of pride and confidence through expression – whether it be cultural, physical, artistic or intellectual.

While actions in support of engagement are essential to overall well-being, they are not sufficient. Ideally, these actions link to the other domains that comprise resilience.

The context

Citizens who participate actively and meaningfully in their communities tend to be happier and healthier – physically, mentally, emotionally and spiritually. Those with limited access to opportunities for participating or who are excluded generally fare less well. Resilience is the result not only of meeting basic needs and bolstering the ability to adapt to and cope with change. It also involves the active engagement of citizens as shapers of their communities – and of their own future.

Engagement is a broad term that effectively can be used to refer to any kind of social activity – whether deemed positive or negative. It could be argued that those who deal in drugs or commit crimes engage in and with their communities. It could also be maintained that people are engaged just by virtue of being alive. Through their status as local resident, they basically are involved in a community whether they participate actively or not.

This passive engagement-through-being-alive approach or participation-through-crime is not the concept being considered here. Rather, the notion of engagement linked to resilience refers to the deliberate and conscious effort to take part in a non-work pursuit, such as arts or recreation. The activity may contribute to personal gain or may affect the well-being of others, through time commitment to service clubs, voluntary organizations or political associations. Engagement through cultural expression, such as story-telling, music or dance, can enhance community spirit through a sense of shared meaning and purpose.

The chapter on *Working in the Shared Space* described the knowing, doing and reviewing components of the communities agenda, which are common to all clusters. A focus on engagement – as in the other clusters – begins with establishing a clear knowledge base. It next involves a set of actions that create collaborative relationships within the cluster, between clusters and around policy. Finally, work in the shared space requires monitoring progress against identified outcomes.

Knowing:

Creating the evidence base

There is a vast literature on engagement with many component parts. It entails, first and foremost, an ability simply to partake physically in a community. It also involves a sense of belonging and embeddedness, which derives from the quality of personal networks and opportunities for expression. Finally, engagement refers to active participation in the community and society – whether in recreation or sport, service clubs or religious organizations, or decision-making processes.

There are several streams of literature in the engagement field. One category of research is largely descriptive in that it documents various types of engagement. Another body of work incorporates an evaluative dimension that explores the impact of active participation. Key findings from both streams are presented here.

Types of engagement

Engagement is fundamentally about being, belonging and participating. A sense of identity is the result both of who you are and what you do – the type and extent of contribution to the community or society.

There is no single type of engagement. Rather, it can be understood as a continuum of actions ranging from highly personal and individualized expression to participation in structured activities or organizations. A national report on the value of voluntarism describes this spectrum of possibilities – in which the benefits accrue at one end primarily to the individual, such as sport or recreation, to actions whose benefits largely affect others, such as participation on a community board or local governance process.[1]

On the other side of the coin, there is growing concern about the impact of negative engagement – typically referred to as 'social exclusion.'[2] Feelings of exclusion are not uncommon in this country, particularly among racialized youth and Aboriginal Canadians. They often experience discrimination, which bars them from decent work opportunities and lack of acceptance by the larger community. Many turn to drugs and crime as a way to earn money not available through legitimate means – and as a way to cope with their anger in a society that makes it almost impossible for them to find a meaningful place.

Appropriate responses to deep-rooted feelings of exclusion require a combination of interventions that involve both social and economic opportunities. The connections between clusters through multiple and linked interventions are crucial in tackling exclusion, particularly when racially based, with its complex social, economic and cultural dimensions.

One of the most personal and powerful ways to encourage meaningful engagement is through *story-telling and personal expression*.[3] All individuals have a story – whether it has to do with their family, cultural roots, personal challenges or hopes and dreams. Story-telling is a process in which anyone can participate regardless of age, language, level of education or disability. It helps people get to know each other; learn about their personal or community history; and share humour, emotion and life lessons.

For example, in a special school project, the students of the Southwest Regional School Board in Nova Scotia wrote history books about their local communities. The students spent several weeks identifying questions, taping interviews with community members, drafting and editing manuscripts, and selecting content and appropriate artwork. When the book was ready, they held a community celebration that began in the evening with a traditional meal. The following day involved a public gathering in which the children presented local history through drama and music. The community not only told its story but also has a legacy to leave future generations.

The tradition of story-telling is deeply embedded in Aboriginal culture in particular.

> To provide their communities with this escort made of oral stories, native elders around the world have been telling creation myths for many millennia. … The elements of this art haven't changed significantly over the centuries. In some traditions, storytellers use music, in others their voices are unaccompanied. In some traditions the storytelling experience is very participatory, with the audience involved throughout. In other places, people are happy to listen quietly for many hours and let the storyteller transport them. But the fundamental experience of storytelling hasn't changed since the beginning of human history. One person speaks to a circle of listeners, who give their attention; if the story is told well, its

words have the power to spark across the gap and take root in the listeners' souls.[4]

Story-telling provides a respectful way of helping individuals share their concerns, anger, hopes, fears and dreams and is particularly important for young people – especially those who have been emotionally hurt or abused in some way. The tradition of careful and respectful listening that is rooted in Aboriginal culture has provided a foundation for healing circles that help cope with the trauma and scarring resulting from racism, physical and sexual violence, and substance abuse.

In fact, there is a 'narrative school' of psychotherapy that focuses upon the telling of life stories to help individuals reframe their realities and begin to rebuild their lives. A US-based initiative, known as Project Resilience, engaged young people in writing personal stories in order to gain insight into their lives and begin the process of healing.

> The Project Resilience study was based on interviews with 25 adults who had grown up knowing some combination of poverty, neglect, abuse, racism, violence, addictions, and family dysfunction. All 25 had bruises that attested to their experiences. But they were also remarkably resilient, breaking out of the cycle of troubles in which they began their lives. In answer to the question, "How did you do it?," many recounted how they relied on writing to gain insight into their lives and how that insight, in turn, was central to repairing the harm they had suffered.[5]

The process of healing through writing is being taught and promoted by Youth Communication, a nonprofit youth development organization in New York City. It publishes two magazines entitled *Foster Care Youth United* and *New Youth Connections*, written by and for teens.

> By teaching the craft of writing personal essays and by publishing their work in two magazines, Youth Communication offers young people the opportunity to discover, affirm,

strengthen, and expand their resilience. In turn, thousands of teens who read the magazines are encouraged by their example.[6]

In addition to story-telling, there are other effective methods of expression rooted in cultural tradition. Drumming circles have emerged as a powerful method of teaching team-building, cooperation and discipline – particularly among youth considered vulnerable or at risk of criminal activity.

Other forms of engagement involve *participation in a formal group or organization*. Millions of Canadians are engaged in communities through volunteering time to charitable organizations and to helping others. This activity is formally tracked through the *Canada Survey of Giving, Volunteering and Participating* that was initiated in 1997 and conducted again in 2000 and 2004. Statistics Canada claims that the Survey provides the most comprehensive assessment of giving, volunteering and participating ever undertaken in the country and possibly the world.

The latest results found that 45 percent of the population volunteered during the one-year period preceding the Survey, contributing close to 2 billion hours or the equivalent of one million full-time jobs. Canadians were more likely to volunteer in the areas of sports and recreation, social services, education and research, and religious organizations.[7]

Another form of engagement involves participation by citizens in various forms of *decision-making*. The chapter on *Organizing for Complexity* described the move away from sole reliance upon government to more inclusive decision-making processes through local governance. In fact, global discussions and numerous international declarations on sustainable development have stressed the importance of engaging citizens in concerns that directly affect their lives.

For example, broad public participation in decision-making is a core component of Agenda 21, the global plan of action for sustainable development that emerged at the Earth Summit of world leaders in 1992. The plan devotes several chapters to the importance of engaging specific groups – including women, children and youth, indigenous people and farmers – in tackling challenges related to poverty reduction, conflict resolution and environmental protection.[8]

A core principle embedded in Agenda 21 speaks to the role that governments can play in encouraging and sustaining this participation.

> Environmental issues are best handled with the participation of all concerned citizens, at the relevant level. At the national level, each individual shall have appropriate access to information concerning the environment that is held by public authorities, including information on hazardous materials and activities in their communities, and the opportunity to participate in decision-making processes. States shall facilitate and encourage public awareness and participation by making information widely available. Effective access to judicial and administrative proceedings, including redress and remedy, shall be provided.[9]

The decision-making processes in which citizens participate need not be complex or overly formal. The Regent Park area of Toronto, known for its poverty, street drugs and crime, is turning itself around through various investments in its residents. The Pathways to Education© program was described in *Advancing Adaptation* as an example of its recent success. The neighbourhood has also created a series of community circles, involving tenants, staff, police, a lawyer and private security, to tackle its problems related to illegal drug trafficking.[10] The residents themselves are involved in formulating appropriate interventions.

Unfortunately, there are many thousands of citizens who wish to participate in communities but face obstacles because of an unreceptive environment. Persons with disabilities, in particular, encounter physical and attitudinal barriers that make it difficult for them to live, let alone engage actively in communities. They require special *support* in order *to enable participation.*

One way to promote this engagement is through accommodation, which involves actions to adapt the environment. The intervention may be as small as modifying a door handle or more substantial, such as redesigning a job or providing staff assistance.

Barrier-free design generally is considered the starting point for accommodation.[11] This type of design is helpful not only for persons with disabilities. It makes the world more manageable for everyone. Curb cuts, for example, are easier for young children, the elderly, parents with baby strollers and persons with mobility impairments. Plain language and large print improve clarity for all, including persons with learning, visual or intellectual disabilities.

Governments play a significant role in enabling engagement by requiring adherence to designated standards. Ontario legislation on accessibility enacted in 2005 sets benchmarks for specific industries, sectors of the economy and organizations.[12] But accessibility is only the beginning in that it enables people to be. It does not necessarily allow them to do – which is made possible by the availability of disability supports.

Disability supports refer to the range of goods and services that facilitate active participation in school, work, culture, recreation – in virtually all aspects of community life. These supports include technical aids and equipment, such as wheelchairs, walkers, hearing aids and visual aids. They also involve attendant services that help with personal grooming, homemaker services that provide assistance with essential housekeeping and interpreter services for communication.[13]

Unfortunately, in many jurisdictions throughout the country, disability supports are delivered through a maze of government departments and voluntary organizations. Their incoherent delivery has created serious problems of access. Joining-up is an important first step toward improved availability.

Benefits of engagement

A growing body of literature on social embeddedness speaks to the sense of belonging derived from various forms of engagement. Dimensions of social embeddedness include social connectivity, such as relationships and interactions with non-household family members, friends, neighbours and colleagues. Social anchoring refers to engagement through giving, volunteering and participating in religious or secular communities of faith. Social continuity is measured by such factors as duration of marriage, stability of residence and span of employment.

Statistics Canada recently reported that Canadians with a deep sense of belonging to community have more positive feelings about the state of their physical and mental health.[14] As part of a study being undertaken for the Canadian Institute for Advanced Research, UBC economist John Helliwell and colleagues are analyzing Statistics Canada data in order to identify the factors deemed to contribute to well-being.[15]

By incorporating research from the social sciences, the results have found that level of income alone is not the sole source of happiness. Factors such as trust, sense of community, time spent with family and friends, good health and good government are more important than income, especially as it rises above subsistence levels. Yet none of these elements is included in traditional economic models. The well-being approach – or happiness index – retains the standard income-oriented indicators but adds these social dimensions as separate and distinct variables.

In fact, considerable research is under way throughout the world on the emerging science of happiness.[16] Close ties to family and friends and a commitment to spending time with them were identified as strong factors in "making the human heart sing." Well-being is very much a function of social skills, close interpersonal ties, social support and a sense of belonging and contribution.

It is clear that these various forms of engagement are significant components of the well-being equation. A small sample of the wide-ranging findings is presented here in order to illustrate the growing body of results.

The substantial benefits of recreation are well documented.[17] Recreation and active living reduce significantly the risk of coronary heart disease and stroke, the leading causes of death in the developed world. They help combat osteoporosis, affecting 25 percent of menopausal women. They have been found to reduce diabetes, another major killer, and to prevent site-specific cancers, particularly in the colon, breast and lungs.

At the other end of the age spectrum, physical activity has a significant impact upon the growth and maturation of children and youth. There is also a positive correlation between physical activity and increased muscle strength, bone density and mass, motor fitness and aerobic capacity. Physical activity helps control childhood obesity, reduce elevated blood pressure, and improve overall health and growth.

In addition to building healthy bodies, involvement in recreational and cultural activities has been found to reduce or prevent emotional and social problems. Recreation and play are particularly important for healthy childhood development – promoting the acquisition of motor skills, the improvement of cognitive functions, and the growth of social skills and creativity.

Recreational programs offer safe venues for latchkey children after school. Organized sport provides children with opportunities to learn from coaches, instructors and mentors. Children who participate on teams acquire valuable leadership skills and improve their social interaction in terms of sharing and cooperation. Data from the *National Longitudinal Survey on Children and Youth* found that children who partake in organized activities outside school such as sports, music, the arts or clubs tend to have higher physical and psychological well-being and improved self-esteem; to interact more positively with friends; and to perform somewhat better in school.[18]

Recreation is emerging as crucial, not just for healthy children and families, but also for strong neighbourhoods. By building self-esteem and social skills, recreation and cultural programs encourage participation in communities. This active involvement promotes social connectedness and helps shape civic behaviour later in life.

Recreation is also being understood as a core intervention for families and children deemed to be at risk. In a significant study on the effectiveness of various methodologies, Dr. Gina Browne and colleagues found that recreational services help psychologically disordered children on social assistance maintain their social, physical and academic competence at a level equal to that of non-disordered children. Without these recreational programs, children's competence levels actually dropped.[19]

Participation by youth in recreational and cultural programs has been found to reduce boredom and delinquency.[20] Boredom is a problem for adolescents, in particular, because of its link to depression, hopelessness and loneliness. It is also associated with alcohol use among college and high school students, smoking among high school students, deviant behaviour at school and overeating.

Cultural programs in the areas of art, drama, dance, singing and music provide a different, but equally important, means of building skills in creative thinking, decision-making and problem-solving. They foster social skills including cooperative work, negotiation, conflict resolution and tolerance for difference – as well as personal skills such as individual responsibility, perseverance, self-management and integrity.

In a major longitudinal study entitled the National Arts and Youth Demonstration Project, a team of McGill-based researchers identified five community-based organizations in low-income communities across the country. As part of the study, the sites offered an after-school arts program to 183 youth, aged 9 to 15, twice a week over a nine-month period. Data were gathered through a variety of methods including pro-social and arts skills forms, questionnaires on self-esteem and emotional problems, and interview guides to help gather in-depth information. Participants showed significant gains in artistic and social skills. Comparison of results with children in matched control groups noted a significant reduction in emotional problems for participants in the program. [21]

Students have also been found to perform better academically when they are engaged with the arts. Those with more exposure to arts instruction have scored higher on average than their peers on measures of creative thinking, fluency and originality.[22] A study conducted with 25,000 students reported that those with high levels of art participation out-performed 'arts poor' students on virtually every measure.[23]

The US-based National Governors' Association spells out the value of this work in its exploration of the impact of arts education on workforce preparation.

> The arts can provide effective learning opportunities to the general student population, yielding increased academic performance, reduced absenteeism and better skill building. An even more compelling advantage is the striking success of arts-based educational programs among disadvantaged populations, especially at-risk and incarcerated youth. For at-risk youth, that segment of society most likely to suffer from limited lifetime productivity, the arts contribute to lower recidivism rates; increased self-esteem; the acquisition of job skills; and the development of much needed creative thinking, problem solving and communications skills. Involvement in the arts is one avenue by which at-risk youth can acquire the various competencies necessary to become economically self-sufficient over the long term, rather than becoming a financial strain on their state and communities.[24]

In Canada, the J.W. McConnell Family Foundation has been at the forefront of promoting the active participation of young people in the arts. Launched in 1998, *ArtsSmarts* is a national initiative that supports arts-related activities in the classroom, by encouraging the use of art as a vehicle for teaching all subjects.

There is also mounting evidence on the healing capacity of the arts. A study conducted by researchers at Northwestern Memorial Hospital in Chicago found that art therapy helped alleviate eight of nine symptoms in patients being treated for cancer, including pain, depression, poor appetite and fatigue.[25]

The arts also provide a means of community revitalization through inner-city development, building community pride and engaging ethnic minorities in civic endeavours. By creating bonds among neighbours, arts and culture promote social reconstruction and contribute to economic revitalization. Studies have found a strong arts presence to be positively correlated with reduced poverty and population growth, while areas with poor arts development have declining populations and lower incomes.[26]

Another important dimension of economic benefits involves the contribution of the arts to quality of place. There is a growing body of evidence on the role that cultural amenities play in attracting human capital – particularly for professional and technical workers. "In an era of an increasingly mobile workforce and industry, a city's urban culture and 'livability' can impact not only its existing residents and economy, but also future residents and businesses."[27]

Emerging research on the 'new geography' argues that in order to thrive in the ever-widening choices in the knowledge economy, communities must pay special attention to factors, including those relating to lifestyle and cultural choices, which appeal to a broad range of entrepreneurial companies. In this emerging framework, parks, schools and amenities replace low taxes and loose regulation as the primary tools of industrial development.[28]

Urban areas in particular are focusing on cultural and arts-related activities – museums, theatre, ballet and video production – to attract more residents to their central districts and skilled workers who are in short supply in many urban centres.[29] These developments highlight the importance of moving cultural policy to the core of urban policy and planning.[30]

Doing:

Creating links within the cluster

Community inclusion

The Community Inclusion Initiative was launched in 1997 by the Canadian Association for Community Living, People First and the federal government. Its purpose was to increase public awareness of social inclusion and develop exemplary practices to promote inclusion in a broad range of areas. The initiative operated in all 13 provinces and territories and in more than 600 communities throughout the country.

Every jurisdiction developed a unique approach with several employing arts and recreation, and cultural expression as a primary medium for promoting inclusion. New Brunswick, for example, organized around a special focus on youth. Its *Festival d'Inclusion Fest* involved more than 60 students from 15 schools across the province. They formed inclusion committees to ensure that more students with disabilities were able to participate in school activities. The *Pathways to Citizenship* effort in BC developed a handbook for youth leaders to help ensure that persons with disabilities could participate actively in recreation and other community events.[31]

Cultural expression

While cultural expression is only one of many forms of engagement, it is especially meaningful in that it speaks to the very core of personal identity. Diaspora Dialogues is an example of an effort that joins several organizations in fostering engagement through sharing cultural experience.[32] It was launched in 2005 with financial support from the Maytree Foundation and the City of Toronto through the Toronto Arts Council. Partners include PEN Canada, YMCA of Greater Toronto, Toronto Public Library and local organizations seeking to build an inclusive city that celebrates its diversity.

Diaspora Dialogues supports the creation and dissemination of fiction, poetry and drama that reflect the many dimensions of Toronto through the lens of its ethnic communities. It encourages both well-known and emerging voices from a mix of racial backgrounds to share, through various media, their personal experiences. The project combines publishing and mentoring activities with a monthly literary and artistic festival.

Decision-making

Participation in decision-making is another vital dimension of community engagement. All the local governance structures within Vibrant Communities represent a form of citizen engagement.[33] At the core of the initiative are 15 cities throughout the country seeking local solutions to reduce poverty. They are joined in their respective efforts through a structured learning circle called the Pan-Canadian Learning Community.

Of the total group, six communities known as Trail Builders receive extensive funding to develop multi-year comprehensive strategies to reduce poverty. While each plan is unique, all Trail Builders share an important feature: A local governance body assumes responsibility for the initiative and presides over its activity. In order to participate in Vibrant Communities, each centre *must* involve diverse representation in this governance structure including business, government, voluntary organizations and people living in poverty.

The governance body formulates, implements and evaluates all aspects of the local poverty reduction strategy. Its work is guided by the principle of inclusion. People living in poverty are considered not simply as targets or subjects of the proposed interventions but as core participants in the formulation and application of these actions. Their involvement helps ensure the relevance of the identified work.

Not surprisingly, this engagement is easier said than done. It is impossible for any group – let alone a local project with modest funding – to be entirely representative of the community. All it can do is try to move toward greater inclusion and review continually how well it is doing in this regard. In fact, the national sponsors of Vibrant Communities monitor closely the number of participants living in poverty and have requested on several occasions that certain Trail Builders improve their performance on this crucial measure.

Recreation

The Canadian Parks and Recreation Association is spearheading in several communities across the country a multiyear national initiative called *Everybody gets to play*.[34] The project was organized in response to the many barriers facing low-income families that wish to participate in recreational activities and programs. While program fees are a major obstacle, they are not the only one.

The Kids Recreation-Sunshine Coast pilot project in BC involves the contributions of about 40 individuals and organizations, including social workers, counsellors, teachers and principals. Several free programs were organized to determine potential interest, including fitness classes for high school students, youth dance, Instructor in Training programs for youth, the provision of fitness equipment and clothing, and volunteer training instruction for adults.

In addition to cost, a major barrier is lack of transportation to recreational areas. The region consists of eight communities spread across a 65-kilometer highway. As a result of the initiative, a major change was introduced that involved the scheduling of recreation programs at times more convenient to bus riders. Free nutritious food was also provided within the activities for children and low-cost child care was made available at fitness programs.

Culture

The Arts Network for Children and Youth links artists and organizations working with children and youth across the country.[35] It supports existing arts programs while encouraging the establishment of new ones. The Network connects the arts to diverse sectors such as justice, social services, health and education. It effectively acts as a link between arts organizations and the public and private sectors.

The Creative City Network of Canada is another example of joined-up work at a national level.[36] It was established in recognition of the fact that local governments are playing an increasingly active role in the development of arts, culture and heritage.

More than 130 local governments now comprise the Network, whose purpose is to connect individuals and organizations involved in similar cultural efforts and to serve as a knowledge-sharing, research, public education and professional development resource. Members' common interests are advanced through sharing information, experience and expertise. The Network hosts a comprehensive website related to municipal cultural policy and programs, heritage, festivals, cultural tourism, and community development and engagement.

The Learning Through The Arts collaborative is another national illustration of joined-up work around culture.[37] The initiative was set up by the Department of Canadian Heritage in association with the Government of Ontario, TD Bank Financial Group, Telus, *The Globe and Mail*, *Time* magazine, and 13 other companies and family foundations. The initiative works with 350 schools across the country. It provides professional development for thousands of teachers and hundreds of artists in order to infuse the daily educational curriculum with artistic content and process.

Disability supports

In many provinces, there is no common access point for the range of disability support programs and services that enable participation in communities. Multiple entry is a problem not just in terms of knowing about the various components of the system and meeting their respective eligibility requirements. The problem of access is compounded by the disparate ways in which information about the system is provided. Moreover, there is a serious lack of supports relative to the unmet needs for these vital goods and services.[38]

A diverse group of national disability organizations, including the Council of Canadians with Disabilities and the Canadian Association for Community Living, have called for a more coherent strategy throughout the country for the provision of these supports. Their problematic delivery, both in terms of lack of availability and difficult access, has impeded the ability of persons with disabilities to participate in all aspects of community life.

Several jurisdictions, including Québec, Prince Edward Island and New Brunswick, have moved toward joining up their access points to the disability supports system. Québec eases entry through its single door *l'Office des personnes handicapées du Québec*. Prince Edward Island recently combined its wide-ranging supports within a single Disability Support Program. Other provinces have introduced an integrated approach for technical aids and equipment, such as the Ontario Assistive Devices Program, Saskatchewan Aids to Independent Living and Alberta Aids to Daily Living.

In British Columbia, a coalition of more than 30 organizations has been working to address the Statistics Canada findings that persons with disabilities in that province have the highest level of unmet need in the country for equipment and assistive devices. The Provincial Equipment and Assistive Devices Committee (PEADC) urged the province to enter into a partnership with the community in order to improve the coordination and funding of these supports.

In response, the Minister of Employment and Immigration established in October 2005 a Personal Supports Working Group, which brings together representatives from PEADC, a crown agency (Community Living BC) and officials from five government ministries – Health, Education, Advanced Education, Children and Family Development, and Employment and Income Assistance. The Working Group has developed a common vision and shared values as first steps in its "participation model" for a disability supports program.[39]

Between clusters
Engagement and sustenance

SKETCH – *working arts for street-involved and homeless youth* is a nonprofit charitable organization that provides arts programming, and job and life-skills training for youth between the ages of 15-29 who are or are at risk of being street-involved or homeless.[40] The project offers a way for these youth to experience a sense of safe space and relief from the pressures of street life – effectively tackling sustenance through engagement.

The initiative is based on the premise that these young people can best be engaged through alternatives to traditional therapy by reaching them emotionally and through direct participation. Working in the arts has been found to enhance self-esteem, strengthen resilience and spark a desire to learn more.

SKETCH integrates job and life skills development with artistic disciplines including visual art, drama, music and new media. The project works with small groups of young people to restore their self-worth and invigorate their lives with purpose and direction. Community connections are fostered through collaborations with local artists and organizations, job placements, internships, mentoring/educational opportunities and inter-agency referrals.

Engagement and adaptation
i. Links to networks of support

The Belonging Initiative is a national collaboration to end isolation and loneliness among persons with disabilities.[41] It is being spearheaded by the PLAN (Planned Lifetime

Advocacy Network) Institute in partnership with the Canadian Abilities Foundation, Canadian Association of Independent Living Centres, Canadian Association for Community Living, Canadian Down Syndrome Society, Developmental Disabilities Resource Centre of Calgary, Inclusion Press, Laidlaw Foundation, L'Arche Canada Foundation and the Philia Dialogue on Caring Citizenship.

The initiative is guided by the principle that one of the most significant dimensions of well-being is a sense of belonging – a feeling that human worth is recognized and valued. The effort hopes to raise $50 million for a "No One Alone" Fund in support of a campaign to end isolation and loneliness among persons with disabilities.

The campaign will foster the development of relationships and the creation of inclusive communities. The Belonging Initiative will also build a learning network to share expertise and disseminate knowledge. It will seek to influence public policy in order to draw attention and resources to the problem of social isolation.

ii. Links to literacy

The Toronto Public Library uses its public space creatively to foster engagement and promote literacy.[42] It has 98 branches, two bookmobiles, dozens of specialized book and materials collections, 22 special services, two reference and research libraries, and the second-largest collection of materials on the continent (only the Boston Public Library is larger). Its estimated 11 million books, periodicals, CDs, maps, pictures and videos include items in more than 100 languages.

In addition to serving the needs of Toronto residents, the provincial government conferred special library status, which helps fund its Virtual Reference Library. Several subject gateways have been designed that provide access to digital collections on-line. These include newsgathering services, historic and artistic collections, and child-friendly services developed in collaboration with community partners.

The library pays special attention to the needs of seniors, persons with disabilities, new Canadians, people without Internet access in their homes, areas currently without a library, and children and youth. Friends of the Library is a volunteer organization that supports library programs and services through fundraising, promotion and the provision of personal and professional services. Volunteers help run the adult and child literacy programs, after-school homework clubs for elementary-aged children, and homework and reading clubs for students in Grades 7 to 12.

New technologies are opening up worlds of information to individuals who previously had been excluded from participation. The library makes available technical aids and adapted materials. Its services include a centre for persons with disabilities, sign language interpretation, disability resource collection and special study rooms. Home library deliveries benefit residents who are housebound because of illness or disability.

The library has extended the concept of accessibility beyond the provision of materials and building access. It welcomes the public to a wide array of cultural events, including lectures by artists and writers, open dialogue with an author-in-residence and presentations of art, music and dance – free of charge.

The immigrant settlement organization, CultureLink, works with the library to offer English conversation programs at selected branches. The Settlement and Education Partnerships in Toronto allows settlement workers from various agencies to use the library to help newcomers with information and interpretation. Workers also introduce library services to adults and children. Legal aid lawyers provide free advice and guidance at specific branches. In co-sponsorship with the Toronto Public and Catholic Boards of

Education, many branches offer classes in English conversation, grammar and writing at a beginner, intermediate or advanced level.

The City of Chicago is another example of the power of libraries, dubbed by the mayor as "community anchors." In little more than a decade, the city built 32 neighbourhood branch libraries and renovated nine others. No longer simply a repository of books and information, the new library is an active participant that sparks community engagement in various activities and events.

The neighbourhood branches function effectively as community centres with book discussions, readings, classes, homework help and displays of local art. All branches reach out to local schools and tailor their collections and programs to the character of the neighbourhood. The branch libraries also narrow the digital divide by providing access to the Internet.

A particular effort is noteworthy for its creativity: One book is chosen each year and the entire city is encouraged to read it, just like a book club. When the program was initiated in 2001, the book *To Kill a Mockingbird* was chosen. While the program is intended to encourage reading, it is also consistent with the library's role in fostering social connection and improvement.

The City of Hamilton recently embarked upon a One Book, One City project. Its purpose is both to raise awareness about poverty and to promote literacy through a focus on the arts. Students in schools throughout the city are reading *Looking for X*.[43] A public festival was organized to highlight its key themes through various forms of cultural expression including art, dance, drama and music.

Engagement and opportunity

A comprehensive community initiative in the Saint-Michel neighbourhhood of Montréal has developed an ambitious plan to reduce poverty and social exclusion and to revitalize the area. Saint-Michel is one of the Trail Builders in the Vibrant Communities initiative.[44]

Its work builds on a strong local base. The neighbourhood had created *Vivre Saint-Michel en santé* in 1991 as part of the healthy communities movement. The organization became the focal point for linking residents and bringing together groups to promote numerous local projects.

The community's identity in the past had been built largely around its role as a dumping ground for garbage as a result of the closure of huge local quarries. A core feature of the current revitalization effort is to foster a positive identity with citizens actively engaged in the process of neighbourhood change. The renewed vision of the neighbourhood is based on a broad articulation that emerged from a long participatory process.

> Saint-Michel is a pleasant neighbourhood within which to live, supportive of family life and multicultural exchanges, an active and unified community, which takes charge of its affairs and also contributes to the vigour of Montréal.

About 800 people – at least 500 of whom were local residents – helped formulate a plan of action through various consultations including polls, focus groups and large community meetings. The plan is founded on four major pillars selected by residents: low individual and family incomes; poor quality of housing; lack of local cultural, sports and recreational, and commercial facilities; and the fear of living in an unsafe and insecure environment.

With respect to the income objective, the strategic plan focuses on training linked to employment opportunities, attracting and retaining businesses, and reducing household expenses. Accommodation targets include renovating designated areas of the neighbourhood, creating mixed housing and supporting access to homeownership – especially cooperative arrangements.

Access to culture, recreation and sports facilities lies at the heart of the neighbourhood plan to engage residents. These activities have become the basis for broader economic and social renewal. Perhaps more than any other Trail Builders that comprise the Vibrant Communities initiative, Saint Michel is developing a dynamic weave of recreation, sports and cultural practices to stimulate citizen engagement. It has opened a new community centre and is working with the City of Montréal to ensure the availability of active cultural and recreational programs. A physical centre with no programming, in the view of community leaders, actually can create problems rather than produce solutions.

The neighbourhood is home to the international headquarters of *Cirque du Soleil*, which is a leading partner in the School of Circus and TOHU, a community centre that employs job training to promote circus arts, the environment and social inclusion. The company trains young people in circus performance to help keep them off the streets and find employment in *Cirque du Soleil* and other theatrical shows. These forms of engagement have become an important base for building opportunity, the fourth core resilience cluster.

Around policy

Play Works is a movement of interested parties committed to helping youth by encouraging and promoting greater investment in youth play and access to all forms of recreation.[45] Partners include Parks and Recreation Ontario, the Ontario Physical and Health Education Association, 4-H Ontario, Arts Network for Children and Youth, Sportalliance, the Laidlaw Foundation, Boys and Girls Clubs of Ontario, YMCA Ontario and young people.

The initiative has carried out extensive research that documents the benefits of youth participation in play, barriers to this participation and the components of a "positive youth development framework." It is encouraging local governments to adopt within their recreational programs the principles embedded in that framework, which include the engagement of young people in decisions that affect them and in programs intended for them.

Through annual awards, Play Works recognizes communities functioning in this youth-friendly manner and has developed a compendium of good practice to support Youth-Friendly communities. It provides financial support to youth-led initiatives that enhance opportunities for recreation in communities. It also documents and shares the results of these 'do it yourself' efforts.

While provinces throughout the country generally provide some funding for recreation, its planning and delivery are a municipal responsibility. Play Works focuses its policy efforts primarily upon local governments. The initiative calls upon municipalities to eliminate user fees that can act as a barrier to participation. It encourages recreation departments to work more closely with children's programs and the Ontario Ministry of Children and Youth Services, in particular, to replace compartmentalized funding with joined-up investment. Play Works also supports the use of community spaces as friendly play areas and the practice of school as hub, considered in *Advancing Adaptation*.

Reviewing:

Monitoring progress

The BC Capital Region's Quality of Life CHALLENGE discussed in *Supporting Sustenance* is one of the most advanced initiatives in the country in terms of ongoing monitoring and review. In addition to its work on housing and income earlier described, the CHALLENGE is concerned with various forms of engagement. It regularly tracks selected indicators of participation including charitable giving, voting, attendance at festivals, recycling practices, use of a recreation centre and leisure time physical activity.[46]

Recent results have found that use of the Greater Victoria Public Library, for example, has risen steadily over the past few years. Between 2001 and 2004, there was an increase in registered borrowers, visits to the library, number of items borrowed and total population served. The rise was interpreted as positive, given the central role of libraries with respect to both engagement and literacy.

Voter turnout at local elections varies widely across the region, ranging in 2002 from a low of 25 percent to a high of 61 percent. There appears to have been no discernible trend over time. Neither was there a noticeable change in the attendance at festivals and community events. In 2004, the City of Victoria funded 26 diverse festivals with an estimated attendance of 1.3 million people, less than 50 percent of whom were residents of the region.

There is growing evidence that community events and celebrations – such as festivals, parades and block parties – are important to communities not just because they are fun. These celebrations promote appreciation of other cultures and build social capital. They keep neighbours in touch with each other and reinforce the networks and associations that make neighbourhoods strong. The CHALLENGE concluded that, in light of this evidence, it will be important to encourage participation in these events to strengthen the community's collective story and sense of place.

The CHALLENGE reported an improvement in measures related to leisure time physical activity. It also noted the positive impact of the Leisure Involvement for Everyone

(LIFE) program, which seeks to reduce barriers to participation in recreation and ensure equitable access for all residents, regardless of ability to pay. This program was cited as a positive way to ensure broad participation in physical recreation.

In respect of its commitment as a Trail Builder in Vibrant Communities, the CHALLENGE tracks as a measure of engagement the numbers of participants in various initiatives. Since its inception in 2002, 2,255 people have been engaged in its work. Some 201 community groups, 153 private sector organizations, 47 public sector organizations and 879 individuals from all sectors have committed time, effort or resources to improve the quality of life in BC's Capital Region.

These numbers are monitored on a regular basis to track participation from all sectors and citizens. In fact, the CHALLENGE has created an action task force composed of people living in poverty to ensure their authentic participation in the initiative.

All this to say...

Active engagement contributes dramatically to the well-being of individuals and the quality of life in communities. Comprehensive communities facilitate access to social opportunities – because of their intrinsic benefits as well as the fact that they provide a positive means to reach other goals.

Engagement means social opportunity. Equally important to well-being is economic opportunity – the final core dimension of resilience. Unlike engagement, however, work in the opportunity cluster moves away from the emotional dimensions of resilience and involves instrumental methodologies – concerned with skills, jobs and assets. It is that opportunity to which we now turn.

Endnotes

[1]   Bowen, P. (2004). *Investing in Canada: Fostering an Agenda for Citizen and Community Participation*, Ottawa, March. *www.sportmatters.ca*

[2]   See, for example, Donnelly, P. and J. Coakley. (2002). *The Role of Recreation in Promoting Social Inclusion*. Perspectives on Social Inclusion Series. Toronto: Laidlaw Foundation.

[3]   Yashinsky, D. (2005). *Suddenly They Heard Footsteps: Story-Telling for the Twenty-First Century*. Toronto: Vintage Canada, p. 5.

[4]   Yashinsky, D. *Ibid*, p. 5.

[5]   See *www.projectresilience.com*

[6]   Desetta, A. and S. Wolin. (nd). "Youth Communications: A Model Program for Fostering Resilience Through the Art of Writing." See *www.projectresilience.com*

[7]   Hall, M., D. Lasby, G. Gumulka and C. Tryon. (2006). *Caring Canadians, Involved Canadians: Highlights from the 2004 Survey of Giving, Volunteering and Participating*. Ottawa: Minister of Industry.

[8]   United Nations Conference on Environment and Development. (1993). *Earth Summit '92*. Rio de Janeiro. London: The Regency Press.

[9]   Commission on Sustainable Development. (1992). *Agenda 21: Rio Declaration on Environment and Development*. New York: Division for Sustainable Development, United Nations Department of Economic and Social Affairs.

[10] Young, J. (2006). "The building that fought back." *The Globe and Mail,* January 7, F9.

[11] Technical Advisory Committee on Tax Measures for Persons with Disabilities. (2004). *Disability Tax Fairness*. Report to the Minister of Finance and the Minister of National Revenue. Ottawa: Finance Canada, December.

[12] Bill 118: An Act respecting the development, implementation and enforcement of standards relating to accessibility with respect to goods, services, facilities, employment, accommodation, buildings and all other things specified in the Act for persons with disabilities.

[13] Torjman, S. (2000). *Proposal for a National Personal Supports Fund*. Ottawa: Caledon Institute of Social Policy, October.

[14] These findings are discussed in Hadley, T. (2006). "Community engagement more important to happiness and productivity than material wealth." Vancouver: Wosk Centre for Dialogue, March.

[15] See a description of this study at *www.ciar.org*

[16] Wallis, C. (2005.) "The Science of Happiness: What Makes the Human Heart Sing?" *Time Magazine*, January 17.

[17] Canadian Parks and Recreation Association (CPRA). (1997). *The Benefits Catalogue*. Ottawa: CPRA and Health Canada.

[18] Results from the National Longitudinal Survey on Children and Youth are posted at *www.statcan.ca*

[19] Browne, G., C. Byrne, J. Roberts, A. Gafni and S. Whittaker. (2001). "When the Bough Breaks: Provider-Initiated Comprehensive Care Is More Effective and Less Expensive for Sole-Support Parents on Social Assistance." *Social Science and Medicine.* 53(12).

[20] McKay, S., I. Reid, M. Tremblay and R. Pelletier. (1996). "The Impact of Recreation on Youth in Transition to Adulthood: A Focus on Youth at Risk." In B. Galaway and J. Hudson eds. *Youth in Transition: Perspectives on Research and Policy.* Toronto: Thompson Educational Publishing Inc.; Reid, I., M. Tremblay, R. Pelletier and S. McKay. (1994). "Impact and Benefits of Physical Activity and Recreation on Canadian Youth-at-Risk." Joint Initiative of the Inter-Provincial Sport and Recreation Council, Fitness Directorate of Health Canada and Canadian Parks and Recreation Association, December.

[21] Wright, R., L. John, D. Offord and W, Rowe. (2004). *Highlights. National Arts and Youth Demonstration Project.* Montreal: School of Social Work, McGill University.

[22] Burton, J., R. Horwitz and H. Abeles. (1999). "Learning in and through the Arts: Curriculum Implications." In E. Fiske ed. *Champions of Change: The Impact of the Arts on Learning.* Washington, DC: The Arts Education Partnership and the President's Committee on the Arts and the Humanities. Online report, pp. 49-60. *www.aep-arts.org/files/publications/ChampsReport.pdf*

[23] Catterall, J., R. Chapleau and J. Iwanaga. (1999). "Involvement in the Arts and Human Development: General Involvement and Intensive Involvement in Music and Theater Arts." In E. Fiske ed. *Champions of Change: The Impact of the Arts on Learning.* Washington, DC: The Arts Education Partnership and the President's Committee on the Arts and the Humanities. Online report, pp. 15-32. *www.aep-arts.org/files/publications/ChampsReport.pdf*

[24] National Governors Association Center for Best Practices. (NGA Center). (2001). "The Role of Arts in Economic Development." *Issue Brief, Economic and Technology Policy Studies.* Washington DC, June.

[25] Ubelacker, S. (2006). "Art therapy eases pain, fatigue of cancer, study finds." *The Globe and Mail*, January 3, A11.

26 Stern, M. and S. Seifert. (1998). *"Community Revitalization and the Arts in Philadelphia."* Working Paper #8. Social Impact of the Arts Project. Philadelphia: University of Pennsylvania School of Social Work.

27 Azmier, J. (2002). *Culture and Economic Competitiveness: An Emerging Role for the Arts in Canada.* Calgary: Canada West Foundation, March, p. 6.

28 Kotkin, J. (2000). *The New Geography: How the Digital Revolution is Reshaping the American Landscape.* New York: Random House, p. 41.

29 Kotkin, J. *Ibid,* p. 159.

30 Azmier, J. (2002). *Culture and Economic Competitiveness: An Emerging Role for the Arts in Canada.* Calgary: Canada West Foundation, March, p. 10.

31 A description of the Community Inclusion Initiative can be found at *www.cacl.ca.* See also BC Association for Community Living. (2004). "12 Inclusive Activities: A Guide for Youth Group Leaders." Vancouver.

32 See *www.diasporadialogues.com*

33 Torjman, S. (2005). *The Group of Six.* Ottawa: Caledon Institute of Social Policy, April.

34 This initiative is profiled at *www.cpra.ca*

35 The Arts Network is described at *www.artsnetwork.ca*

36 See *www.creativecity.ca*

37 For more information on the Learning Through The Arts initiative, see *www.ltta.ca*

38 Torjman, S. (2000). *Proposal for a National Personal Supports Fund.* Ottawa: Caledon Institute of Social Policy, October.

39 Provincial Equipment and Assistive Devices Committee (PEADC). (2006). *A Participation Model for a Personal Supports Program for People with Disabilities in British Columbia.* Vancouver, June.

40 For more information, see *www.sketch.ca*

41 See The Belonging Initiative at *www.philia.ca*

42 Makhoul, A. (2004). *Celebrating Access at the Toronto Public Library.* Ottawa: Caledon Institute of Social Policy, March.

43 Ellis, D. (1999). *Looking for X.* Toronto: House of Anansi Press.

44 See Saint-Michel Community Plan at *www.vibrantcommunities.ca*

45 Play Works Partnership. (2005). *The Cost of Excluding Ontario's Youth from Play. Call to Action.* Toronto.

46 See *www.qolchallenge.com*

Chapter 7

Optimizing Opportunity

In summary

The goal of the communities agenda is to build resilience in communities in order to ensure their strength and vibrancy. Resilience is the result of actions taken in four independent but related clusters – or areas of shared space.

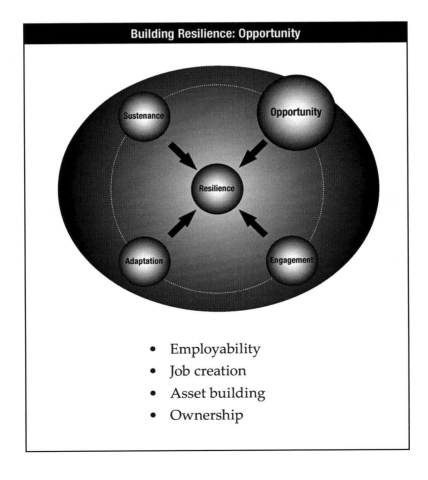

Building Resilience: Opportunity

- Employability
- Job creation
- Asset building
- Ownership

This chapter focuses primarily upon opportunity from an economic perspective. It considers employability enhancement, job creation and the building of financial assets. As in the case of the other clusters, work on various forms of opportunity is an essential component of the well-being equation. But taken alone, it is not sufficient. Ideally, actions in the opportunity cluster link to the three other domains that comprise resilience.

The context

Resilience refers to the capacity to survive, adapt to change, engage in the community and thrive in response to opportunity. The preceding chapter on *Ensuring Engagement* talked primarily about social opportunity. This chapter focuses upon economic opportunity, the fourth core dimension of resilience.

Work in the shared space begins with a clear knowledge base. It then involves a set of actions that seek to create collaborative relationships within the cluster, between clusters and around policy. Finally, work in the shared space involves monitoring progress against identified outcomes.

Knowing:

Creating the evidence base

As in the other clusters that comprise resilience, opportunity is the result of investments in individuals, opportunities and the links between them. Certain measures focus upon individual workers by ensuring that they have appropriate skills to bring to the labour market. Other interventions are concerned with job creation, through support for initiatives such as self-employment and small business development.[1] Still other actions within the cluster help households build financial assets.

On the individual side of the equation, labour market integration strategies include pre-employment preparation, skills training, reducing personal barriers, job retention and career advancement. The one consistent theme that emerges from the wide and diverse literature on employability is that there is no consistent theme.

There is no magic bullet solution to labour market integration – just as there is no single answer to unemployment or poverty. Each strategy is a node on a continuum of possible interventions. Each approach has its strengths and weaknesses and, ideally, is used in combination depending upon the demands of the labour market and the capacities of the prospective worker.

On the job side of the equation, recent years of labour market restructuring and rapid technological change have had a profound impact upon work. Labour market restructuring has taken many forms, including the outsourcing of manufacturing and other production to cheaper labour out of the country. While many jobs have gone offshore, freer trade has opened up additional markets – though the news had not been good for all sectors (read softwood lumber).

This formula for opportunity is not new. It is a function of both adequate demand for skills and sufficient capacity to meet that need. The problem is that this traditional model relies upon the invisible hand of supply and demand to sort out the matching function. But the market does not function perfectly and, as a result, there are too many people unable to take advantage of available opportunities. They are left on or outside the margins.

In some cases, the pool of available skills in a community does not keep pace with its changing economic base. Part of the problem arises from the fact that most communities lack ongoing upgrading and training to ensure that its skill set keeps pace with changing demands.

Many jobless workers did not have access to retraining supported through Employment Insurance because they did not have sufficient hours to qualify for the employment benefits associated with this support. Only four in ten un-employed workers are eligible for this program on a national basis. At other times, those with requisite skills cannot get a job because of barriers, such as non-recognition of creden-tials acquired offshore or lack of access to affordable quality child care.[2]

A related barrier is the difficulty accessing work-relat-ed training. A national survey found that larger companies provide training more frequently than medium- and small-er firms. But with more than 75 percent of new jobs being created by small enterprises, fewer employees will have op-portunities for workplace training in future.[3]

Another problem stems from the fact that communities typically lack information about the skills that might be re-quired down the road. Employment data generally provide an historic rather than a predictive perspective, looking at the shape of the labour market over the past few years. But retrospective figures tell little about how this market might evolve. It is difficult to prepare for the future when all the available information is rooted in the past.[4]

An equally tough challenge arises from trying to apply national information to the local level. There are technical problems involved in disaggregating national data to prov-inces and territories, let alone to regions and local areas. But it is precisely this type of disaggregation that is required if local economies are to act as engines of growth.

Other cases call for a better matching of skills and jobs. Both economic shifts and changing technology have creat-ed a need for continual training and upgrading. Higher ex-pectations in the labour market have compounded the prob-lem. The requirements of the knowledge economy make it increasingly difficult for individuals with limited literacy to find decent work, let alone a job that pays more than sub-poverty wages.[5]

Even entry-level requirements in most training programs and apprenticeships are tougher than ever. The knowledge society has also raised the bar in terms of educational requisites. Basic readiness now involves higher levels of formal schooling and mastery of numeracy, computer and communications skills.

Far too many workers are excluded from the labour market because they cannot meet these tougher skill requirements. One in four high school graduates lack adequate literacy skills, effectively blocking them from postsecondary learning.[6] The poorly educated tend to be excluded from or marginalized in the labour market and pay the price throughout their lives. Access to postsecondary education is more difficult for lower socioeconomic groups and people with special needs.

Moreover, attention in the opportunity cluster is shifting increasingly to severe labour shortages in certain professions, such as the skilled trades, construction, heavy equipment operators and health care workers. Some parts of the country, notably Alberta and BC, are experiencing labour shortages in virtually all sectors, skilled and unskilled alike.[7] The problem is only expected to get worse in the face of an aging population.

In other regions, notably parts of Atlantic Canada, the challenge stems not only from skill requirements but also the lack of suitable year-round employment. There is a wealth of experience in the creation of jobs for those considered hard to employ through the social economy, a term used in Québec to refer to the entrepreneurial, not-for-profit sector. Its work is based on democratic values and seeks to enhance the social, economic and environmental conditions of communities, often with a focus on their disadvantaged members.[8]

In the rest of Canada, the social economy is most closely associated with community economic development – a unique form of practice that seeks to bridge economic and social well-being.[9] Community economic development comprises a wide range of activities. It can involve co-operatives or community-based businesses that serve the needs of their members' owners. It is difficult, however, to set up microenterprise in the absence of capital investment – an asset well beyond the reach of most low-income Canadians.

In response to this identified problem, there is an emerging body of literature and practice on building financial assets, in particular, as a means of fostering economic self-sufficiency. Specific measures include individual development accounts, community loans for microenterprise, learning bonds and ownership of homes, property and businesses. Building personal and community assets is considered a powerful key to the door of opportunity. Interest in this area – at least in North America – was prompted by the book *Assets and the Poor*, which made the case for focusing on assets as an important lever to reduce poverty.[10]

The rationale for building financial assets is based on several arguments. There is growing evidence that assets make a real difference to well-being, given the positive correlation between assets and increases to income over the long term. Assets are associated with reduced financial strain and enhanced economic security. They also have an impact upon neighbourhood stability through improved property maintenance and associated values. Ownership confers a sense of choice and security; it helps create a personal safety net that can be used in the event of emergency or as leverage for raising funds for other assets, such as work tools and equipment, business or residence.

The research results have been borne out in practice throughout the world. The impact of the microcredit movement is a case in point. The Nobel Peace Prize for 2006 was awarded to Muhammad Yunus and the Grameen Bank that he established in recognition of their efforts to tackle poverty.[11] Their loans of very small amounts have benefited millions, not only in Bangladesh but throughout the world. The work is based on the philosophy that lasting global peace cannot be achieved unless large population groups find ways to break out of poverty. Microcredit is one such means – particularly in societies where women, in particular, struggle against repressive social and economic conditions.

Despite the crucial role of assets, there is vast inequality in the distribution of wealth and assets – both within developed nations and between North and South. The disparities derive from the fundamental structure of market economies and their control by multinational corporations.[12] But there are additional barriers that individuals face in trying to play the assets game on an uneven field. The disparity in distribution is exacerbated, for example, by problems of access to financial information and to credit through traditional banking institutions.

Major savings and assets incentives, such as measures to facilitate home ownership and tax assistance for retirement savings, disproportionately benefit middle- and high-income earners.[13] Low- and modest-income workers are unable to afford the basics of life, let alone put aside extra for savings. Neither do these individuals rank high on banks' list of preferred clients. Welfare recipients must divest themselves of most of their assets in order to be eligible for financial assistance.

Banks and credit unions can help low- and middle-income customers by offering alternatives to high-fee payday loans. These are short-term loans of small amounts with interest rates typically so high that they result in annualized percentage rates of between 391 and 572 percent. A study supported by the US-based Annie E. Casey Foundation explored various ways to replace these costly payday loans.[14]

Comprehensive local governance mechanisms play a significant role in all dimensions of the opportunity cluster. They must ensure that the pieces comprising individual capacity and community infrastructure are in place and are functioning well. They must then foster links among these component parts. For example, skills training must line up with market needs. Information must drive the training. The left hand in the form of skills training must know what the right hand is doing with respect to job prospects. As in the other clusters, comprehensive community initiatives need to work in the shared space between and among the component parts.

Governments can create an enabling environment for work in the opportunity cluster. Local governments can support favourable conditions for poverty reduction and economic growth, more generally. The economic health of any given region can be bolstered, for example, through internal market opportunities. Governments can promote awareness about locally produced goods and available services as well as the benefits of supporting community business. Local sourcing of supplies and labour for government activities keeps more money in the community.

Municipal governments can foster economic development by protecting tracts of land for designated purposes, such as community business. They can also support the growth of these enterprises, as they did in Halifax.[15] The Human Resources Development Association (HRDA) was created in 1978 with $275,000 from the Halifax social assistance budget. Through its subsidiary, HRDA Enterprises Ltd., the Association created small businesses that placed more than 1,400 welfare recipients in newly-created jobs in environmental care services, painting, property management, bakery, consultation and training, and sewing contracting.

The City of Hamilton designated an enterprise zone in support of economic renewal. Taxes from increased assessment resulting from the redevelopment or improvement of properties within the limits of the Downtown Business Improvement Area are returned to the developer in the form of a grant. The City also adopted an Environmental Remediation and Site Enhancement Community Improvement Plan to make available grants for financial relief to property owners who undertake and complete brownfield redevelopment projects. (Brownfield is land previously used for industrial or commercial purposes, and may be contaminated by low concentrations of hazardous waste or pollution. It has the potential to be reused if properly cleaned up.)

In short, communities must be able to foster links among the wide-ranging and disparate parts of the system. They provide a focal point so that any individual can go to a place that helps them through the required steps on the continuum. Most communities have no coordinating mechanism that can assist people – particularly workers considered vulnerable – to move along the continuum and ensure that they are supported in this journey. Comprehensive local initiatives can play this integrative role.

Doing:
Creating links within the cluster
Leadership
While financial resources are important, the time, energy and leadership of the business sector sometimes represent an even greater contribution. In Saint John, for example, a network of more than 100 businesses came together in 1997 to form the Business Community Anti-Poverty Initiative (BCAPI).[16] While spearheaded by the private sector, the collaborative includes a wide range of nonprofit organizations working together to assist low-income residents.

Based on an analysis of poverty trends, current initiatives and feedback from people living in poverty, BCAPI decided initially to target the circumstances of teenagers and young single parents. Saint John County has an annual birth rate of 33 births per 1,000 teenagers – twice the rate of New Brunswick as a whole. The project focused on preventing teen pregnancy and, for young teens already pregnant, to ensuring a healthy birth. For young single parents, the community initiative sought to help them complete their high school education, move off social assistance and find employment.

BCAPI is also working on quality affordable housing, described in *Supporting Sustenance,* and employment readiness programs. It has encouraged the provincial government to adjust policies that create barriers for social assistance recipients trying to move into the labour market. The collaborative is urging local businesses to examine how they can create economic opportunities for disadvantaged residents, and has helped secure 40 new positions of employment for people living in poverty.

In Trois Rivières, by contrast, a nonprofit economic development group spearheaded the comprehensive local initiative. The *Corporation de développement économique communautaire de Trois-Rivières* (ECOF) involved at least 75 organizations in creating a five-year (2007-2012) strategic plan entitled *Tout commence par un rêve (Everything Starts with a Dream)* for the Trois Rivières region.[17] The plan proposes a platform of key interventions, including social economy enterprises to support entrepreneurship and create jobs.

Information

As noted, one of the difficulties of the opportunity cluster is rooted in the weaknesses related to labour market information. Numbers of vacancies typically are counted but there is usually no precise indication of the skills required for these jobs, especially in emerging sectors. Some communities are developing unique ways to improve their knowledge about labour market needs and associated responses.

In Vancouver, for example, a web-based Fast Track to Employment Social Purchasing Portal was established to create sustained employment for hard-to-employ individuals, such as many residents in the Downtown East Side. The Portal links job seekers with community-based training, educational expertise and employers.[18]

In addition to acting as an electronic bridge for joining supply and demand, the Portal provides purchasers of goods and services an opportunity to practise socially responsible procurement. In purchasing goods and services, companies can choose suppliers – such as food services/catering, printing, packaging, couriers, promotional materials, building maintenance, recycling and landscaping – based on values of quality, service and price. Cook Studio Catering, for example, is a Downtown East Side company that also acts as a training program for youth at risk and welfare recipients moving to work.

Coordination

Some communities face employment barriers related not to skills and jobs but to public transit. As a result of local transit problems, many households spend inordinate amounts of their limited budgets on work-related transportation, leaving less for food or utility payments.

Municipal governments can play a significant role in easing access to transit. They can reduce fares for persons trying to move off welfare into work or participating in training after a spell of unemployment. Bus passes can be distributed through selected social agencies, as in the City of Victoria. Lower fares can also be introduced during off-peak hours, making public transit more affordable for all community members.

In many cases, the problem goes beyond affordability. The issue can be summed up in a nutshell: You can't get there (easily) from here. In theory, it is possible to respond to this problem by encouraging prospective workers or students simply to move closer to their work or school. But here they may come smack up against the lack of affordable housing – discussed in *Supporting Sustenance*.

Where possible, local transit systems should be regionalized or at least coordinated to ensure easy access. Niagara Region did just that through the guidance of Opportunities Niagara, a comprehensive community initiative concerned with employment and poverty. It convened transit authorities, private transportation companies, community agencies, local government and job seekers to devise an intervention that linked both opportunity and sustenance.[19]

Niagara Region is composed of 12 municipalities, covers 1,841 square kilometers and has a population of 430,000. The drive from the Township of West Lincoln on the region's western edge to the casinos, restaurants and hotels in Niagara Falls takes 20 to 25 minutes by car. Because there is limited inter-municipal public transportation, it was hard for residents to get to work or school if they had to travel outside their home municipality.

Recent layoffs and plant closures in the Niagara Region had left many residents unemployed. Despite the growing pool of local labour and a stated commitment to hire residents, employers imported 2,000 entry-level workers from outside the country in 2004 because local job seekers were unable to obtain affordable, convenient transit. Opportunities Niagara recognized the need to close the region's transportation gap in order to ease access to education, training and work.

Due to its higher-than-average unemployment rate and close proximity to Niagara Falls, Port Colborne was selected as the target community for a transportation pilot.

In collaboration with PORT CARES, an employment support agency, the Region's Community Services Department and Opportunities Niagara, job seekers were offered both résumé and interview clinics on applying for the position of room attendant for the Niagara 21st Group, a Niagara Falls hotel consortium. An agreement was reached for the employer and employees to share the costs of a "Job Bus" from Port Colborne to Niagara Falls. The Job Bus commenced operations in June 2005, providing round trip transportation to the employment.

Nearly one-third of the participants were receiving some form of public pension or social assistance. Within six months, the project saved the region $250,000 from its social assistance budget. There are now five Job Bus runs – an indicator of the project's success.

Access to capital

Far too many new Canadians have difficulties finding employment as a result of barriers related to accreditation, training and upgrading. The irony is that there are serious skill shortages in a wide range of fields. To address this problem, representatives from the Calgary Foundation brought together the Alberta Network of Immigrant women and other community groups to establish the Immigrant Access Fund.[20] The program provides microloans for new Canadians for a period of study, examination and license fees, tuition, books and supplies – basically whatever assistance they require to work in their respective fields.

The Fund is administered by the Mennonite Central Committee Employment Development and receives operating support from the United Way and Alberta Lottery Fund, with contributions from Suncor, PetroCanada and immigrant-owned businesses. As the loans are repaid, they are deposited in an endowment fund – with a $2 million loan capital pool as the goal.

In another example of access to financial assistance, the Manitoba Government has joined with the 38 community foundations throughout the province to offer greater educational assistance for rural and northern students pursuing postsecondary education. Students who must leave their home community to attend college or university often face significant additional costs beyond the expense of tuition and books incurred by urban residents.

The $500,000 Manitoba Scholarship and Bursary Building Incentive Program, administered by The Winnipeg Foundation, provides up to $100,000 each year over five years to match funds raised by community foundations for scholarships and bursaries. The incentive funds have been successful in leveraging gifts from local donors resulting in permanent educational endowments. The goal of raising $1 million appears within reach. The program has championed community-building efforts through creative and 'fun fundraising.' Students have already benefited from the creation of more than 30 new scholarships.

Customized training

Another example of joined-up work within the opportunity cluster involves a unique form of skills development, known as 'customized training.'[21] It arises in response to fast-paced advances in knowledge and technology, which mean that it is not just nice – but indeed essential – to have access to continual upgrading of knowledge and skills upgrading. Actual and looming skill shortages are driving this need for training.

Few communities make provision for ongoing upgrading – particularly for workers employed in small firms. Current practice is out of sync with economic needs. There is a disjuncture between changing educational and skill requirements, and opportunities for the renewal of human capital. The training offerings currently in place have not yet been designed – at least on a broad scale – to match the learning pace that the economy demands.

Customized training has been found to be an effective response to this rapidly changing environment. But in order to be effective, it is a response that, by definition, requires local collaboration.

There is no single approach to customized training but rather a range of models. While the specifics vary, the general story goes like this: A designated organization assumes responsibility for identifying job opportunities in various sectors of the local economy and in specific workplaces. These include current vacancies and impending job openings.

Typically, the identification of employment opportunities involves more than a cursory review of ads in newspapers. It entails a systematic, methodical and in-depth exploration of the local labour market. In some programs, this process is referred to as 'job development.' Job developers meet with local employers and often find positions that were not advertised. Sometimes they uncover work opportunities that employers themselves had not explicitly classified as a discrete job but nonetheless recognize as work that must be done.

The task of job developers is not simply to identify vacancies. They must determine the skill requirements associated with the vacancies and local employment opportunities, more generally. The designated organization also assesses the skills, knowledge and abilities of the individuals currently unemployed or underemployed. Participants in customized training programs tend overwhelmingly to be social assistance recipients, although the approach need not be limited to this population.

The designated organization helps match trained participants with appropriate job opportunities. Local companies that have been engaged in the process generally use the designated organization as their hiring window because prospective employees have been pre-screened for their suitability to the work. They have been trained explicitly to fill the *precise* job requirements identified by local employers. While there is no guarantee that trainees will be hired by the firm, it is clearly in the interest of business to employ workers with job-ready skills.

Partners for Jobs is an example of customized training rooted in a collaborative local model. The Chairman of the Regional Municipality of Ottawa-Carleton (who subsequently became the Mayor of Ottawa) created the initiative in 1998 to tackle unemployment and underemployment in the region. A multisectoral working group was convened that included representatives from all orders of government, anti-poverty groups, labour, social organizations, training bodies, the Caledon Institute of Social Policy and key employment sectors in the region – technology, life sciences, and tourism and hospitality.

Its work focused upon market-relevant training programs for the unemployed and underemployed; supports for self-employment and the creation of community business; policies to promote transition to work and job retention; and the collection of timely and relevant local labour market information. More specifically, the training targeted major clusters in the Ottawa economy including high tech, biotechnology, photonics (the application of laser technology) and tourism. Training for the first three clusters focused upon manufacturing positions.

The program was successful in its results – nearly 1,300 unemployed workers were trained and found good work in less than two years. Part of its success was due to the fact that the training was market-relevant. Partners for Jobs also helped participants with associated problems related to child care and lack of funds for transition to work or business start-up.

The initiative subsequently was rolled over into a region-wide employment partnership called TalentWorks and turned over for implementation to the Ottawa Centre for Research and Innovation. What began as a small project for training the hard-to-employ evolved into a broad effort to redress skill shortages in key economic clusters including high tech, biotech and photonics.

Customized training is an effective methodology not just for tackling unemployment. It is also useful for meeting shortages in selected sectors such as skilled trades, and in certain regions of the country such as Alberta and BC. The Shapotowak Programme in Fort McMurray is an example of a joined-up effort that seeks to redress these shortages while helping develop the skills of Aboriginal workers.[22]

The company 2000 Plus identified the need to get more of its young Aboriginal employees involved in skilled trades. 2000 Plus is a contractor to Syncrude and is owned by the Miksew Cree First Nation of Fort Chipewyan, Alberta. It provides Syncrude with casual labour, grounds-keeping services and labour support for maintenance shutdowns. Shapotowak is a pilot program set up as a partnership among 2000 Plus, Keyano College, Syncrude Canada Ltd, Alberta Apprenticeship and Industry Training, the Athabasca Tribal Council and the Mikisew Cree First Nation.

The initiative is designed to meet the needs of young Aboriginal workers who require skills upgrading but cannot afford to quit working full time to attend school. Tuition and other academic expenses are covered by 2000 Plus and the Athabasca Tribal Council, funded primarily by the federal government.

Most of the customized training programs are organized in the evening and are delivered at Keyano College.

Syncrude allows up to 60 hours of release time per student to participate in workshops that may occur during a scheduled job shift. The company also contracted with a psychologist to work with students on personal or family problems that could affect their success. The pilot started with 12 students and is expected to expand to an estimated 90 full-time employees.

Despite its apparent strengths, customized training should not be considered a magic bullet to the problem of skills upgrading or unemployment. No one solution to employability challenges is intended to stand on its own. Customized training is linked intrinsically to literacy proficiency discussed in *Advancing Adaptation* and to other labour market interventions, such as the removal of barriers to employment.

Between clusters
Opportunity and sustenance

The Toronto City Summit Alliance is a coalition of civic leaders created in 2003 to tackle social and economic challenges facing the Toronto Region, such as expanding research-driven industry, the poor economic integration of immigrants and decaying infrastructure. Since its inception, the Alliance has initiated and developed nine major projects.[23]

The Toront03 Alliance, for example, was created to bolster tourism after the drop related to SARS. It partnered with the three orders of government, Tourism Toronto and a range of corporate partners to promote the city and to launch a long-term brand strategy. Another project, the Toronto Region Research Alliance, brings together public and private institutions involved in research and its commercialization. It seeks to build the research and development capacity of the Golden Horseshoe region, to enhance the commercialization of research, and to attract and expand knowledge-based industry.

While several of its efforts focus upon opportunity, the Alliance is also working actively on the links to sustenance. The Affordable Housing Coalition united the private and community sectors to advocate greater access to quality affordable housing. The Alliance initiated the Strong Neighbourhoods Task Force, which articulated a vision for strong neighbourhoods in Toronto, defined the important role of community infrastructure and established benchmarks to assess neighbourhood health. The Neighbourhood Vitality Index was described in *Supporting Sustenance*.

Its Task Force on Modernizing Income Security for Working-Age Adults convened a broad-ranging coalition to identify flaws in Canada's income security system. The Task Force's report *Time for a Fair Deal* described the barriers to work embedded in social assistance, the coverage and disincentive problems related to Employment Insurance and insufficient income from paid employment.[24] Among its suite of recommendations, the Task Force proposed a Working Income Tax Benefit to be paid through the federal income tax system to low- and modest-income workers. The federal government did proceed to introduce this measure in its 2007 federal Budget. It is one of a series of measures that help make work pay, discussed in *Supporting Sustenance*.

Opportunity and adaptation

The chapter on *Advancing Adaptation* made clear that working parents require a range of supports to enhance their parenting capacity, ease conflicts between work and home, and deal with problems that income alone cannot solve. Child care, early childhood development and supplementary health care are core components of positive supports for families with children.

Even the Organisation for Economic Co-operation and Development has documented the fact that accessible and affordable child care is a smart investment in a competitive economy.[25] Without it, parents cannot participate fully in the labour force. Good child care eases access to education, training and employment for parents. It is vital to promoting women's equality by enabling them to train for, find and maintain paid work. Most important, high-quality child care contributes to healthy child development.

The Learning Enrichment Foundation, based in Toronto, is an example of an organization which recognizes that most prospective participants would not be able to partake of its programs – whether language, skills training or job search – unless they had access to affordable, high-quality child care. In response to this need, the Foundation set up its own network of child care centres, currently operating 18 licensed centres throughout the city as well as 15 before- and after-school programs.[26]

This work is an example of how an organization functioning primarily in the opportunity cluster can forge strong links with another core component of resilience – the adaptation cluster. Another illustration was discussed in *Supporting Sustenance* in which the Quint Development Corporation, concerned primarily with co-operative housing, built into the accommodation plans a training and skills component. It thereby joined the sustenance and opportunity clusters.

Opportunity and engagement

In recent years, immigration has become a major contributor to Canada's population and labour force growth. Between 1991 and 2001, 71 percent of net labour force growth was attributable to newcomers. By 2011, it is estimated that this figure will rise to near 100 percent.[27]

Despite high overall levels of education and skill, many new Canadians face barriers to work because their knowledge and experience acquired offshore are not recognized in this country. Workplace discrimination also presents obstacles to the efforts of immigrants to secure employment and climb the job ladder. In this case, the solution lies not in acquiring new skills but in recognizing or upgrading the credentials they already have.

In 2003, the Maytree Foundation partnered with the Toronto City Summit Alliance in creating the Toronto Region Immigrant Employment Council to promote the appropriate inclusion of immigrants in the labour market.[28] The Council is a multistakeholder collaboration composed of members representing employers, occupational regulatory bodies, postsecondary educational institutions, assessment service providers, community organizations and the federal, provincial and local governments. Its goal is to remove barriers that skilled newcomers face when they try to work in their respective fields of practice.

The program creates partnerships with employers to help skilled immigrants find employment, internships or appropriate mentors. As of April 2006, an estimated 1,000 mentoring matches were made, resulting in an employment rate of nearly 70 percent for those who completed the four-month program. TD Bank Financial Group played a significant role in providing both financial support and mentors.

A related program called Career Bridge encourages employers to offer Canadian work experience to immigrants. It acts as a bridge between industry and immigrants by creating paid internships ranging from between four and ten months. With support from Proctor and Gamble, an estimated 340 internships were developed involving more than 130 employers. The top five Career Bridge hosts included Hudson's Bay Company, GE Canada, TD Bank Financial Group, Filogix Incorporated and Manulife Financial. The program not only generated employment for immigrants but also ensured the diversity of workplaces.

The Mentoring Partnership creates connections that enable immigrants to make links to employment. More than

35 corporate partners participate in this component of the work. It is intended to help newcomers engage actively in the economy and society, more generally. The program itself represents a collaborative approach. The Mentoring Partnership is funded by a consortium of government, private and voluntary partners including Service Canada, TD Bank Financial Group, Ontario Trillium Foundation, Maytree Foundation, Region of Peel and United Way of Peel Region.

Finally, *the hireimmigrants.ca* component of the work is an interactive website that provides resources to support a learning community of employers and human resource professionals. It presents weekly tips on how to integrate skilled immigrants into the workplace and hosts a discussion forum that answers questions about assessment, recruitment and employment of newcomers. An associated Intergovernmental Relations Committee has been organized with representatives from all orders of government.

A similar partnership in Ottawa was spearheaded by the Canadian Labour Business Council, Local Agencies Serving Immigrants/WorldSkills and United Way/*Centraide* Ottawa. Other partners have been engaged in this community-wide effort to remove barriers to participation and help employers understand the labour market needs of immigrants.[29]

It is of interest that the Government of Ontario introduced in December 2006 a new law that will make it easier for foreign-trained professionals to become licensed in their respective areas of expertise. Ontario is the first province to require professions to speed up the certification and licensing of internationally trained specialists. The *Fair Access to Regulated Professions* Act obliges the 34 regulated professions to assess as quickly as possible educational credentials and professional experience gained in other countries.

In another example of opportunity linked to engagement, Community Futures South Fraser secured funding from the federal Cooperative Development Initiative program to set up an artists' cooperative, which markets the artwork of federal inmates. The InsideArt Cooperative was launched in 2004. Its work is sold through an e-commerce website, at various art shows and through sales representatives. The initiative encourages engagement through artistic expression while providing a vehicle for economic opportunity. The Cooperative also enables members to purchase supplies at reasonable cost for the production of fine craft and artwork.

Around policy

The earlier discussion on the evidence base pointed to the importance of assets as a core component of opportunity. One way to create assets is through a measure, known as individual development accounts, in which private household savings are matched on the basis of a set ratio – say three-to-one. In this case, one dollar in household savings generates three dollars in matched contributions. A savings of one dollar results in a total of four.

The concepts of asset-based policy and individual development accounts (IDAs) were first introduced in Canada by Social and Enterprise Development Innovations (SEDI). The first pilot of IDAs was launched as part of a comprehensive community initiative called Opportunities 2000 based in Waterloo Region. The accounts gave low-income households an opportunity to save and accumulate assets over a set period of time. The Co-operators Insurance Group of Guelph contributed the matching funds on a 3:1 basis. These were directed toward a specific goal – education, job training or small business start-up – that increased income or employability.[30]

Other pilots were launched separately in Calgary and Winnipeg by local nonprofit development organizations that had taken part in SEDI's initial consultation process. In 2000, these small local efforts were complemented by the introduction of a federal *learn*$ave initiative in 10 pilot sites to test the value of an IDA instrument to support adult learning for low- and modest-income Canadians. The project was designed and implemented by SEDI, evaluated by the Social Research and Demonstration Corporation and is funded by Human Resources and Social Development Canada. Community partners are involved in each of the pilot sites as was RBC Royal Bank, *Caisse Desjardins* (in Montreal) and Assiniboine Credit Union (in Winnipeg).

The Learn$ave project enabled low-income individuals, including many social assistance recipients, to save up to $1,500 for a range of activities related to adult learning. Deposits are matched on a 3:1 basis, resulting in a maximum $6,000 in financial assets available to accountholders. While participants have unrestricted access to their own deposits, matching contributions are paid out only to eligible providers of goods and services, such as training providers or schools. Participants are investing these accumulated resources in postsecondary education, skills development, microenterprise capitalization and learning aids, such as computer equipment or disability supports.[31]

As a result of this work, the 2004 federal Budget introduced a new Canada Learning Bond to help low- and modest-income families save for their child's education after high school. Human Resources and Social Development Canada deposits an amount in respect of the Canada Learning Bond directly into the Registered Education Savings Plan of a child whose parent is eligible for the National Child Benefit Supplement – which means families with net annual income below $37,000 in 2007.

Qualifying households also receive additional annual payments of $100 for up to 15 years, as long as they qualify for the National Child Benefit Supplement – for a total maximum $2,000. In addition, the federal government accelerated for low-income families its contribution to Canada Education Savings Grants. If families contribute $5 per week to their Registered Education Savings Plan, then the federal Grant and Learning Bond potentially could result in estimated combined savings for postsecondary education of up to $12,000 per child.

While asset-based approaches have generated positive response, they are not without controversy. Some argue that governments should invest more in redistributive policy and bolster household income to ensure adequate housing and good nutrition instead of individual savings for the future. In a presentation on October 28, 2004, to the Standing Committee on Human Resources, Skills Development, Social Development and the Status of Persons with Disabilities, seven organizations including the Canadian Federation of Students, Canadian Association of University Teachers and National Anti-Poverty Organization called the government-sponsored savings plan "fundamentally flawed."[32]

The groups opposed the plan on several grounds including the fact that it did not come close to meeting the rapidly rising costs of tuition in most colleges and universities. They claimed that it imposed a middle-class philosophy of personal investment onto people with a different reality and challenges. The groups could not support an approach that diverts government investment away from public education – moving instead toward private savings. They argued that the biggest winners would be RESP providers – not households in need of assistance for education.

So far, the take-up of this measure has been low. "Although no official statistics are available on the participation rate for the Canada Learning Bond program, informal inquiries of a number of financial institutions that offer Educational Savings Plans suggest that the participation percentage among those who would qualify for the Canada Learning Bond is currently in the single digit and perhaps the low single digits."[33] There are many possible reasons for the scant take-up of this measure.

Even in the absence of debate over the efficacy of asset-based approaches, there is another policy concern. The federal initiative potentially can be sabotaged for many households if they happen to be welfare recipients. The payments come smack up against welfare rules known as liquid asset exemption guidelines. Households with cash or cash-convertible assets are expected by the social assistance rules to use these assets for personal support. The level of allowable assets typically is so low that the guidelines could be more appropriately named the 'must-be-in-dire-poverty-to-qualify' rules.[34]

In order to ensure that households do not lose the benefit of the savings accruing from Learning Bonds or individual development accounts, communities have had to raise the issue with provincial and municipal (in Ontario) social service departments. In some cases, the jurisdiction has agreed to ignore the savings in respect of the fact that these derive from a pilot project. In other cases, provincial governments have taken steps to explicitly disregard certain assets for the purposes of determining welfare eligibility. Nova Scotia, for example, announced its intent to disregard the Canada Learning Bond as an asset.

This specific example reflects a more general issue. Policy needs to line up between jurisdictions in order to ensure that advances in one domain are not reduced or negated by other policies that have the opposite effect. Unfortunately, the burden is often upon communities to make certain that all parties are on the same page.

Reviewing:

Monitoring progress

The work on monitoring progress undertaken by BC Capital Region's Quality of Life CHALLENGE was described in the chapters on *Supporting Sustenance* and *Ensuring Engagement*.

Its review process applies equally well to the opportunity cluster.

As part of the ongoing assessment in which this comprehensive community initiative is involved, it tracks several measures related to employability and employment.[35] Industry diversity, for example, is examined to determine whether the local economy is healthy and robust.

The most recent review found that occupations in the service sector in BC Capital region have been changing. At the same time, the proportion of workers in sales and service occupations with traditionally lower wages grew from 17 percent to 31 percent in that same period. The proportion of employees in business, finance and administrative jobs, which generally pay higher wages, declined from 20 percent in 1998 to 17.5 percent in 2003.

There was a substantial impact upon jobs in the public sector due to cuts to government in the Capital Region. The construction industry is experiencing skill shortages; an estimated 1,700 job openings between 1998 and 2008 are expected as a result of the local construction boom. High tech is one of the fastest growing industries in the area with more than 800 firms now in that sector. In response to this information, the Quality of Life CHALLENGE concluded that the region needs an economic development strategy in order to reduce the heavy reliance on tourism and to diversify the economy.

In terms of labour force participation, the local unemployment rate has declined since measures taken in 1999, 2001 and 2004. Not surprisingly, this drop was considered a good sign.

There was no discernible trend, however, in the percentage of waged poor – those who are employed but whose earnings still fall below poverty levels. The percentage of these workers had dropped only marginally to 11 percent by 2000 from 11.8 percent in 1995. In assessing this data, the CHALLENGE proposed that several actions be taken. These included paying sustainable incomes and reducing the costs of housing, transportation and other essential goods.

The Quality of Life CHALLENGE also holds annual reflection sessions in which its key partners are invited to provide their perspectives on the effectiveness of the effort. This qualitative assessment combines with the quantitative picture to redraw the pathway of its future efforts.

All this to say...

Work in the shared space – not only in the opportunity cluster but in the sustenance, adaptation and engagement clusters as well – goes only so far. At the end of the day, comprehensive community initiatives can succeed only to the extent that they function in a context that works with and not against them. *Creating an Enabling Environment* for the communities agenda is a vital piece of the complexity puzzle.

Endnotes

[1] Torjman, S. and K. Battle. (1999). *Good Work: Getting It and Keeping It.* Ottawa: Caledon Institute of Social Policy, February.

[2] Torjman., S. (2000). *Survival-of-the-Fittest Employment Policy.* Ottawa: Caledon Institute of Social Policy, April.

[3] Statistics Canada (nd). *Workplace and Employee Survey.* See *www.statcan.ca/english/survey/business/wes.htm*

[4] Torjman, S. (2002). *The Bases Are Loaded.* Ottawa: Caledon Institute of Social Policy, September.

[5] Human Resources Development Canada. (2002). *Knowledge Matters: Skills and Learning for Canadians.* Ottawa: Her Majesty the Queen in Right of Canada.

[6] Human Resources Development Canada. (2002). *Ibid.*

[7] See, for example, Harding, K. and S. Chase. (2007). "Deal to ease Alberta's serious labour shortage." *The Globe and Mail*, March 5, A4.

[8] The work of *Le Chantier* and its 'vales added campaign' are described at *www.chantier.qc.ca*

[9] See the work of CCEDNet at *www.ccednet-rcdec.ca*

[10] Sherraden, M. (1991). *Assets and the Poor: A New American Welfare Policy.* Armonk, NY: FE Sharpe, Inc. See also M. Sherraden. (2001). "Asset-building policy and programs for the poor." In T. Shapiro and E. Wolff eds. *Assets for the Poor: The benefits of spreading asset ownership.* New York: Russell Sage Foundation, Chapter 9.

[11] Westley, F., B. Zimmerman and M. Quinn Patton. (2006). *Getting to Maybe: How the World is Changed.* Toronto: Random House Canada, pp. 58-60.

[12] Korten, D. (2001). *When Corporations Rule the World.* 2nd ed. New York: Kumarian Press.

[13] Boshara, R. (nd). "The Rationale for Assets, Asset-Building Policies and IDAs for the Poor." In R. Boshara ed. *Building Assets: A Report on the Asset-Development and IDA Field.* Washington, DC: Corporation for Enterprise Development, December.

[14] Bair, S. (2005). *Low-Cost Payday Loans: Opportunities and Obstacles.* Baltimore: Annie E. Casey Foundation.

[15] Lewis, M. (1999). "Community Economic Development." In K. Battle and S. Torjman eds. *Employment Policy Options.* Ottawa: Caledon Institute of Social Policy, pp. 181-214.

[16] For information on the Business Community Anti-Poverty Initiative, see *www.bcapi.ca*

[17] *Corporation de développment économique de Trois Rivières.* (2006). *Tout commence par un rêve. Démarche des premiers quartiers. Planification stratégique 2007-2012.* Trois Rivières.

[18] Lepage, D. (2004). *Social Purchasing – Buying Locally, Helping Locally.* Ottawa: Caledon Institute of Social Policy, September.

[19] Makhoul, A. and E. Leviten-Reid. (2006). *Opportunities Niagara: Untying the Knots, Connecting the Dots.* Ottawa: Caledon Institute of Social Policy, May.

[20] Community Foundations of Canada. (2006). *Working Together for Lasting Change.* Annual Report 2005, Ottawa.

[21] Torjman, S. (1999). *Reintegrating the Unemployed through Customized Training.* Ottawa: Caledon Institute of Social Policy, June.

[22] Brisbois, R. and R. Saunders. (2006). "Skills Upgrading Initiatives in Canada: Evidence from Alberta and the Northwest Territories." In Organisation for Economic Co-operation and Development. *Skills Upgrading: New Policy Perspectives.* Paris, pp. 290-292.

[23] For a description of the work of the Toronto City Summit Alliance, see *www.torontoalliance.ca*

[24] St. Christopher House and the Toronto City Summit Alliance. (2006). *Time for a Fair Deal.* Report of the Task Force on Modernizing Income Security for Working-Age Adults. Toronto.

[25] Organisation for Economic Co-operation and Development (OECD). (2006). *Starting Strong II: Early Childhood Education and Care.* Country Profiles. Paris.

[26] For a description of the work of the Learning Enrichment Foundation, see *www.lef.ca*

[27] Lochhead, C. (2003). *Perspectives on Immigration: Findings from the Canadian Labour and Business Centre's Survey of Canadian Business, Labour and Public Sector Leaders.* Final Report. Ottawa: Canadian Business and Labour Centre, March; Wall Street Journal Online. (2005). "Canada's open door to immigrants is crucial, May 23; Mahoney, J. (2007). "All immigration by 2030." *The Globe and Mail,* March 14, A1; A10.

[28] Toronto Region Immigrant Employment Council. (TRIEC). (nd). The *2005 TRIEC Annual Review,* Toronto.

[29] See *www.ottawa-worldskills.org*

[30] Rail, D. (2001). *Opportunity Development Accounts.* Ottawa: Caledon Institute of Social Policy, March.

[31] See the description of *Learn$ave* under Asset Building at *www.sedi.org*. See also Kingwell, P., M. Dowie, B. Holler, C. Vincent, D. Gyarmati and H. Cao. (2005). *Design and Implementation of a Program to Help the Poor Save: The Learn$ave Project*. Ottawa: Social Research and Demonstration Corporation, August.

[32] Canadian Federation of Students. (2004). "The Canada Education Savings Act (Bill C-5). Testimony to the Standing Committee on Human Resources, Skills Development, Social Development and the Status of Persons with Disabilities." Ottawa, October 28.

[33] Minister of Finance's Expert Panel on Financial Security for Children with Severe Disabilities. (2006). *A New Beginning*. Ottawa: Finance Canada, December.

[34] Torjman, S. (1998). *The Don't-Make-Sense Welfare Rules*. Ottawa: Caledon Institute of Social Policy, November.

[35] See *www.qolchallenge.com*

Chapter 8
Creating an Enabling Environment

In summary

The previous chapters set out the substance of the communities agenda in terms of its focus upon resilience. Each of the four major clusters that comprise resilience can be understood as an area of shared space. The process of the communities agenda involves working in the shared space within each cluster, between clusters and in relation to policy.

Work within each cluster involves creating an evidence base, forming collaborative relationships where appropriate and monitoring progress with continual course correction as required. Knowing, doing and reviewing are the three core elements of work within each resilience cluster.

But communities can do only so much on their own. They need to be supported in their work by governments and other organizations, including the voluntary sector and the private sector, through their roles as exemplars, investors and enablers. The enabling role involves support for community work undertaken to promote resilience. But it also means that government policies and practices themselves must line up to enhance rather than inhibit comprehensive community efforts.

The context

The wide-ranging interventions that comprise the communities agenda in no way minimize the need for a strong core of public goods and services. *Community interventions both supplement and complement – but can never replace – public measures concerned with the well-being of individuals, households and neighbourhoods.*

Governments must act like governments if the communities agenda is to succeed. They must carry out more effectively their traditional roles as *exemplars* and *investors*. They must live up to their obligations to citizens and as citizens – in their capacity as signatories to international agreements and covenants.

But the communities agenda also needs another form of support. Work in the shared space requires an appropriate context. Governments, other funders and the private sector can act as *enablers* of the communities agenda by supporting its major functions – how it organizes for complexity and the knowing, doing and reviewing that comprise this work.

This enabling role is consistent with the practice of cluster-based economic development. As explained in the chapter on *Working in the Shared Space*, clusters do not function independently from one another. Neither do they operate in a vacuum. They must be bolstered and sustained by a supportive infrastructure. Within the model of cluster-based economic development, this base is referred to as quality foundations. These include an appropriate regulatory framework, physical amenities such as roads and sewers, access to financial capital and a pool of skilled workers.

Similarly, the core resilience clusters that comprise the substance of the communities agenda also need an environment that supports their activity. This enabling role is a new element required by the evolving work in the shared space.

Governments are not the only players responsible for creating an enabling environment. Funders such as family foundations, community foundations and United Ways must line up their own policies and practices in support of the communities agenda.

Employers can promote resilience through interventions in the four core clusters. Concrete actions include payment of a living wage, flexible and humane employment conditions, workplace accommodation of special needs and customized training. The growing awareness of corporate social responsibility means that firms are looking increasingly at the impact of their practices upon employees and the world outside their own doors.

There are many efforts under way to increase employer awareness of the unique contribution they can make to social and economic well-being. Credit unions such as VanCity, *Caisse de dépôt Desjardins* and Coast Capital Savings have played leading roles in demonstrating corporate social responsibility through their support for local economic development and various social investments. The national Imagine Canada program is the nation's leading corporate citizenship initiative, which encourages members of the private sector to demonstrate social responsibility through their practices, procurement and contributions.[1]

Many corporate social responsibility efforts, such as the Global Reporting Initiative and the Dow Jones Sustainability Index, involve the monitoring and reporting of company performance. Human resource policies deal with issues such as wages and benefits, worker health and safety, training and skills development, and diversity of the company workforce. Indicators of good governance, such as transparency and shareholder engagement, focus mainly upon company relations with shareholders.[2]

Another category of measures in these international initiatives is concerned with the application of negative screens, by which companies gauge their ethical performance – such as child labour or exploitive images in advertising. The use of negative screens is intended to curb these inappropriate practices.

This chapter focuses largely upon the role of governments and the federal government, in particular, in creating an enabling environment for work in the shared space. But the elements of the enabling environment apply equally well to employers, and to private and community foundations. They all act – or should act – as exemplars, investors and enablers in support of the communities agenda.

Traditional roles
Exemplar

As *exemplar,* governments set the moral, legal and fiscal context within their respective jurisdictions. Leadership by government involves translating into action the conventions and obligations which they have signed and the legislation they have written.

At the federal level, both international commitments and national legislation establish regulatory and policy frameworks, which set the parameters for household and business transactions in economic, social and environmental domains. We literally eat, drink and breathe public policy. It affects the food we eat – its harvest, importation, distribution, sale and price. It controls the quality of the water supply and sets limits on air emissions.

Provincial governments play an important role in the communities agenda. Many of the substantive areas with which this agenda is concerned – decent affordable housing, social assistance, early childhood development, literacy, and training and employment – fall primarily within provincial domain.

While provinces may provide funding for recreation, municipalities typically are responsible for the design and implementation of recreational programs and amenities. In Ontario, local governments have broad social responsibility, including social assistance and child care, social housing and supports at home. This wider responsibility resulted from the exchange of authority known as 'disentanglement' – though some billed it as an exercise in disengagement.[3]

The role of local government with respect to economic and social well-being is particularly significant in light of comprehensive community initiatives which are developing a new forum for addressing local issues. As described in *Organizing for Complexity*, these emerging structures are filling a significant void in decision-making processes that have not been designed to respond effectively to complexity. As community governance structures become increasingly common, there is a growing need to clarify the roles of local government relative to the local governance body.

Most community governance structures have tried to link with municipal governments in some way – and for good reason. These governments are profoundly important to the success of comprehensive initiatives. In fact, there are examples in which the two bodies are collaborating exceptionally well together.

The President of the Hamilton Community Foundation and the Director of the Department of Community Services, City of Hamilton, for example, co-chair the Poverty Roundtable. The City of Edmonton participates on the voluntary local governance structure of Vibrant Communities Edmonton. In Niagara Region, a member of the governance body is also an elected city councillor, who tries to ensure the links between the two bodies.

As leaders, local councils can raise awareness about social needs and the importance of social investment. They can encourage responsibility for social well-being. They can foster social capital by acting as a bridge among neighbourhoods, community organizations and social institutions, and by convening citizens and representatives from diverse sectors in local dialogue. Municipal governments can create opportunities for developing a shared vision for the community.

Exemplary employment practices

Governments act as exemplars by practising desirable behaviour. They can start in their own backyard through model employment practices. Governments also establish bottom-line pay standards for employers in the country though minimum wage legislation.

The federal government's minimum wage covers, under the Canada Labour Code, private sector industries that are interprovincial or international in scope such as air, marine, rail and road transportation; telecommunications; banks; and some federal crown corporations. The federal government also applies in practice the federal minimum wage to its own employees.

The federal minimum wage is equal to the provincial/territorial rate for federally protected workers in each jurisdiction. Provincial and territorial governments establish and enforce minimum wages for both private sector and public sector workers in their respective jurisdictions. Current rates range from a low of $7.00 an hour in Newfoundland, New Brunswick and Alberta to a 'high' of $8.50 an hour in Nunavut.

It is clear that minimum wages are just that – bare minima required for subsistence. The after-tax income of a minimum wage worker, both from wages and refundable tax credits, falls short of the poverty line for the largest city in every province.

A recent study identified the minimum housing wage that would be required for accommodation in major urban centres.[4] For an average bachelor apartment in Toronto or Vancouver, for example, workers would have to earn more than $13 an hour compared to the current minimum hourly wage of $7.45 and $8.00 in those cities, respectively. In these same centres, an hourly wage of more than $20 would be required for a single-earner family while wages in eight other cities would have to exceed $17 an hour more than double the minimum wage in all provinces.

At the end of March 2006, the Royal Bank of Canada (RBC) reported in its *Housing Affordability Index* that the affordability of homes was the worst seen in a decade – though by the end of December 2006, there had been modest improvement in some centres. An RBC economist attributed much of the drop in affordability to slower growth in household income, making it far more difficult to offset increases in mortgage rates, house process and utility costs.[5]

The low rate relative to poverty standards has given rise throughout North America to a living wage movement. 'Living wage' refers to the fact that statutory minimum wages are not high enough to allow workers with children to adequately support their families. The chapter on *Supporting Sustenance* noted that comprehensive community initiatives in Edmonton, Calgary, Niagara and Waterloo have embarked upon living wage campaigns to convince public and private sector employers to improve their wages and associated employment practices.

The Vibrant Communities effort in Calgary, for example, is collaborating with several employers to create, implement and sustain living wages in these sectors. This Living Wage Business Engagement initiative is supported with funding from a community grant through The Calgary Foundation. The City of Calgary actually passed a Sustainable Environmental and Ethical Procurement Policy in January 2007. The intent is to require provision for a living wage for suppliers and sub-contractors to the City.

Though relatively new to Canada, this movement is strong in the US. Hundreds of businesses have voluntarily adopted living wage covenants. At least 62 living wage ordinances have been passed by cities, counties and school districts in 24 states. The ordinances require employers that receive contracts or financial support from local governments to pay their workers a living wage. While the required wage level varies by jurisdiction, the rate is typically well above the minimum wage.[6]

Beyond living wages, employers can help meet sustenance needs by providing associated benefits, such as pensions and extended health care coverage. Pro-rated benefits ideally are made available to employees working less than full time. The provision of health- and disability-related benefits is crucial, especially for those with disabilities who are trying to make the transition from welfare to work.

Welfare generally covers these additional costs while paid work usually does not. The special assistance budget within welfare provides for these needs in the form of wheelchairs, hearing aids, prosthetic equipment, medications and personal services required for independent living or work. Because special assistance is intended only for this program's recipients, this policy virtually ties many individuals to welfare because they have no other source of support for the required aids and equipment. Many low-wage employees find that they are worse off working if they must cover health- and disability-related costs as well as employment expenses, such as clothing and transportation, from their meagre pay cheques.[7]

Ideally, supplementary health benefits should extend to a broader segment of Canadians and not just to those on social assistance. The goal should be to make these benefits available to all low-income households not currently covered by employer-supplied or individually purchased private insurance, notably most of the working poor and those with modest earnings.[8]

Exemplary employers also introduce model employment practices, such as flexible working arrangements, job sharing and unpaid leaves of absence for family reasons, which help balance the demands of work and family. Parents may need to take time occasionally for children's medical appointments and attendance at school events. Progressive employers enable contributions to the community, such as allowing a set number of paid hours per month for voluntary service.

Several of the comprehensive community initiatives that comprise the Vibrant Communities project encourage through written materials, workshops and public recognition the widespread adoption of positive employment practices. The local effort in Waterloo Region, for example, developed in association with the private sector a booklet entitled "Human Resources Options for Action." It includes 50 human resources ideas, employer and employee benefits, and case studies.

BC Capital Region's Quality of Life CHALLENGE has built on the Waterloo work. It has produced practical materials and actively recognizes private sector employers that have made significant contributions to well-being. It has presented 36 Quality of Life Awards and has acknowledged 18 employers that made changes to their human resource practices, affecting 108 employees. These companies have increased their wages, extended the hours of paid employment and introduced benefits and profit-sharing.

Exemplary employers also seek diversity in their workforce. In fact, diversity has been identified in the literature on resilience as a critical factor in the success of complex adaptive systems.

Local government in York Region, for instance, developed in association with community partners an Inclusivity Plan to ensure the accessibility of all its programs and services.[9] It also sought to act as role model to business and community organizations. The plan focused upon several areas including a welcome and resource centre, English language development programs, learning opportunities for children, leadership and volunteer prospects for immigrants, and an awareness campaign.

The Government of Manitoba has introduced a diversity plan as part of its human resources work. It has integrated Diversity and Employment Equity policies and practices in its activities related to staffing, retention and human resource development. The "Diversity Within" program, which operates within the Department of Family Services and Housing, includes workshops on valuing diversity and the duty to accommodate.

The Maytree Foundation recently published a resource guide entitled *Diversity Matters*. It is part of the abcGTA project, which seeks to ensure a pool of qualified visible minority candidates are available for acting as governors and trustees on the boards of public agencies and voluntary organizations. The document serves as an action plan for improving diversity in public appointments by setting out models of exemplary practice and guidelines for establishing targets and measuring progress. It discusses relevant training for these positions and the recruitment and selection of qualified diverse candidates.

Progressive employers also make an effort to accommodate the special needs of actual or prospective workers who typically are marginalized from the labour market, such as persons with disabilities, new Canadians and racialized youth. With respect to young people, employers can offer mentoring, establish internships and accept students for co-op placements. As described in *Optimizing Opportunity*, the demands of the knowledge economy have created pressures for employers to encourage continual staff training and upgrading.

Another important contribution: Employers can explore alternatives to layoffs. They can consider a shorter workweek or job sharing for those who prefer this arrangement because of caregiving responsibilities. A reduction in the use of overtime can help create new jobs.

A different option takes the form of a community-based early warning system that can organize preventive rescue missions before problems actually occur. In the late 1980s, for example, a community development corporation called RÉSO (*Regroupement pour la relance économique et social du sud-ouest de Montréal*) established an early warning system to counteract the dramatic decline of business in an economically vulnerable part of Montreal. Trade union members were encouraged to contact RÉSO about companies that appeared to be experiencing difficulties, such as an owner retiring with no apparent successor in place, financial troubles or worker layoffs. In these cases, RÉSO staff offered technical assistance in product development, marketing and other aspects of business operation.

Finally, employers can be exemplars when it comes to responsible procurement. They can make a conscious decision to 'buy green' from producers and suppliers with a strong environmental record. They can also purchase from private companies that pay decent wages or from local social economy enterprises, thereby supporting work in the sustenance and opportunity clusters, respectively.

Investor

Clearly governments do more than set frameworks and lead by example. They also make *strategic investments* – in both citizens and communities.

At the individual level, governments invest in income security and in educational and training opportunities that enable citizens to participate in the knowledge economy. Governments can make a substantial dent in poverty by bolstering benefits delivered through income security programs, such as the federal Canada Child Tax Benefit and provincial and territorial child benefits for families with children, and the Guaranteed Income Supplement for seniors. Community investments include decent affordable housing, early childhood development centres, schools, recreational facilities and cultural programs.

Governments can make individual and community investments in all four resilience clusters. They play an especially important role in sustenance by ensuring income security and access to decent affordable housing. The latter involves direct support for building new affordable units and indirect assistance in the form of rent supplements, reduced taxes for land and supplies used for social housing, and bylaws that allow secondary suites.

In adaptation, governments can provide funding for early childhood development, literacy programs and settlement services for newcomers. In respect of engagement, governments can fund recreational spaces and programs, and accommodation efforts. They can protect public space, support voluntary organizations and create opportunities for engaging citizens in local decision-making. Funds for training, job creation and financial asset-building are all significant investments around opportunity.

Governments and funders more generally can also improve the way in which they support voluntary organizations. There has been some important work recently undertaken in this area. In 2005, the federal government launched the Task Force on Community Investments. The Task Force consisted of representatives from 20 federal departments and was guided by an external advisory group. Its mandate was to examine federal policies and practices relating to the use of transfer payments and to make recommendations to achieve more consistent and coherent funding practices across the government and seamless, horizontal approaches to community investments.

In its report entitled *Achieving Coherence in Government of Canada Funding Practice in Communities*, the Task Force pointed to the significant variation in the design of transfer programs.[10] There are an estimated 700 grant and contribution programs – each with its own unique terms and community conditions. While every program reflects its respective departmental priorities, the system lacks the overall coherence required to support comprehensive approaches.

The Task Force made numerous recommendations, including the development of umbrella terms and conditions for the funding of programs with similar objectives. Terms and conditions should encourage experimentation; collaboration across programs, departments and jurisdictions; and flexibility for community-based responses and innovation.

As part of the Federal Accountability Action Plan, the Treasury Board appointed an Independent Blue Ribbon Panel on Grants and Contributions. Its mandate included the identification of barriers of access for applicants of government grant and contribution programs. They were asked to consider eliminating legislative barriers and constraints to the effective and efficient delivery of these programs.

The report of the Panel, released in February 2007, pointed to the need for fundamental change in the way in which the federal government understands, designs, manages and accounts for grants and contributions. It made 32 recommendations to cut red tape and strengthen accountability.[11]

The Panel proposed improvements to horizontal coordination in program administration based on a "single view of the client" perspective. It also recommended that the Treasury Board Secretariat work with departments to simplify the grant and application process to make it more transparent and easily accessible. Current accountability documents were seen as too complex, time-consuming and expensive.

The private sector also has an important investment role through the contribution of financial and in-kind resources. In British Columbia, for example, Coast Capital

Savings supports persons with disabilities in their efforts to establish microenterprises.

Coast Capital entered into an arrangement with Western Economic Diversification Canada to deliver the Advice and Business Loans for Entrepreneurs with Disabilities program. It administered loans of up to $75,000 to entrepreneurs with disabilities. The government contributions helped pay for managers' salaries, marketing activities, costs associated with operating an advisory committee and loan loss reserve. Coast Capital Savings also provided business advice and mentorship.[12]

Finally, by virtue of their legislative authority, governments play a significant regulatory role in respect of the communities agenda. They can both enable and discourage certain forms of investment, behaviour and purchase. As part of the (former) federal Social Economy Initiative, the Department of Industry was exploring how its policies intended for small business, such as various loan programs, could also apply to nonprofit business enterprises.

But the communities agenda has created a new role for governments and, in fact, for other funders. Beyond the traditional functions of exemplar and investor, there is a novel set of activities required to create the context for and sustain the activities within this agenda. The emerging role requires funders to act as enablers of complex community processes.

Emerging role
Enabler

Work in the shared space involves knowing, doing and reviewing – building the evidence base, developing collaborative relationships and reviewing progress on an ongoing basis in respect of identified goals. Each of these areas is discussed below.

i. Knowing

Governments have substantial expertise in the area of evidence and the broader foundational knowledge base. They continually collect, store and analyze information, which is crucial not only for understanding current context. This activity is also helpful for tracking trends and determining whether progress has been made over time – all part of the vital accountability agenda.

Understanding the Early Years described in *Advancing Adaptation* is a significant model of strategic support. Human Resources and Social Development Canada funds consultants to assist communities in the collection, analysis, interpretation and application of data and information on various dimensions of child development. The Department also provides support to the Community Social Data Strategy run by the Canadian Council on Social Development. This initiative makes available relevant local data related to employment and poverty.

As noted, Agriculture and Agri-Food Canada's Rural Secretariat recently launched a national statistical website. It enables communities across the country to access economic and demographic information, which can be used as the basis for planning and revitalization work.

Another significant need discussed in *Optimizing Opportunity* relates to the fact that national labour market surveys cannot be readily disaggregated to the local level. But the federal government, which collects and analyzes this data, can provide expertise in helping cities and regions determine their labour market trends and emerging skill needs. Alternatively, it can support selected organizations to gather and interpret this information.

Working in the Shared Space described how the Government of Newfoundland and Labrador has created a mechanism to supply relevant data at no charge to local communities. Community Accounts make available a range of data organized by locality and region.

Based on this example, governments and other funders could consider the development of local multi-organization information systems, which the entire community can use and manage.[13] Protocols would be established for the protection of confidentiality, where appropriate. There could be provision for technical assistance around information technology and data collection. Ideally, the proposed information system would be linked to the tracking of system-wide outcomes – an essential component of work in the shared space.

In addition to data, governments and other funders can support research and the strategic collection of information related to the core resilience clusters. The research could focus on substantive questions regarding decent affordable housing, income security, skills training and community economic development. It could identify barriers in housing or welfare policies that make it difficult to build affordable accommodation or help the unemployed move from social assistance into the labour market.

Research can also examine new approaches to community work that involve linkages between and among clusters. As described, the nonprofit Quint Development Corporation in Saskatoon set up a housing co-operative, which created a component for skills development around home maintenance and upgrading. The housing serves both the traditional role of ensuring a decent home and nontraditional function as a base for future employment.

Governments can enable the process of knowledge development by linking community practitioners with policy institutes and university researchers. This type of work would connect comprehensive local efforts to a steady stream of knowledge and ideas for innovation. Grant criteria could require the active engagement of community advisors to define the focus of the research and its methodology.

In fact, there has been important progress in this area. The Community-University Research Alliances program, introduced by the Social Sciences and Humanities Research Council in 2002, is designed to facilitate such collaboration. It is based on the assumption that most challenges created by globalization and changing technologies are best addressed by local and regional groups that understand the needs of particular communities. Under the program, post-secondary institutions and community organizations build new knowledge and capabilities around issues of common interest.

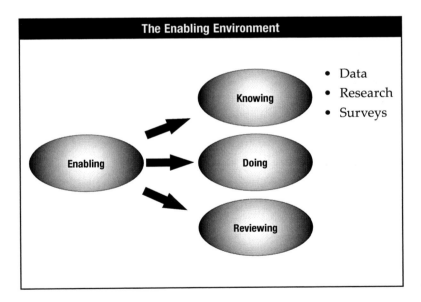

Additional areas of knowledge development in support of comprehensive community initiatives involve exemplary practice both within and outside Canada. Governments and other funders can create opportunities for documenting and sharing innovative local practice.

The chapter on *Supporting Sustenance* described the housing work under way in Saint John as an example of how governments can provide technical assistance around the evidence base and associated interventions. Six representatives from the Saint John business and voluntary sectors were invited to make a 10-minute presentation each to the national information-gathering tour undertaken by the (then) federal Housing Minister. The Saint John team asked the Minister to assign one employee from the Canada Mortgage and Housing Corporation to help them develop a strategic plan for affordable housing. This technical assistance has been invaluable to the formulation of their evidence base and related set of actions.

ii. Doing

By definition, all communities engaged in comprehensive efforts are trying to tackle complex issues. They begin their work by organizing for complexity. The main task in this process involves the creation of a diverse and multisectoral structure that assumes responsibility for the governance of the comprehensive initiative.

The chapter on *Organizing for Complexity* described how these governance bodies play a foundational role in the communities agenda. They provide a focal point for local expression and act as its champion. They set out a guiding vision for the community effort and associated strategic plan. They determine the resilience clusters and areas of shared space upon which to focus. They identify and bring together key players from diverse sectors to make these decisions.

Local governance processes also harness resources, including financing and technical expertise. They link the comprehensive initiative with relevant organizations, projects and resources in the wider community. They provide opportunities for learning and monitor results on an ongoing basis.

Governments and other funders can enable the do-ing component of work in the shared space. They can support the local convening role and other collaborative efforts within each cluster.

As noted, community governance bodies do not simply emerge on their own. These processes and their respective conveners require assistance to sustain their efforts over time. They need opportunities to develop skills and expertise, especially in light of the myriad relationship challenges embedded in these complex local efforts. 'Leading between' requires an ability to foster links among citizens, groups and decision-makers in order to work effectively.

Another area worthy of support involves assistance in the formulation of theories of change. This is a time-consuming, resource-intensive task that requires several iterations, good facilitation and access to information. Stakeholders need to be guided through the process of thinking strategically about change, drawing connections among identified problems and proposed interventions, identifying the possible effects of their actions and understanding potential interactions among the components of their initiatives.[14]

But funds are not generally available for these purposes. Public dollars typically flow to projects rather than to community processes, such as local governance mechanisms, which support problem-solving capacity. A collaborative structure to grapple with complex problems usually does not achieve swift measurable results. It is concerned with identifying and convening key players. It generally does not meet funder criteria – which tend to be short-term, often over the course of a fiscal year. These requirements are also results-based with expectations for near-immediate, clearly identified and quantifiable outcomes.

Many funders are not interested in supporting more complex, less certain forms of community process. Most prefer to invest in the start-up phase of promising ventures.

Most look for a prescriptive methodology that proceeds without diversion from point A to point B. They want to know precisely the results that the process intends to achieve and over what period. Unfortunately, the expectations of most funders run counter to the time and flexible support that communities require in order to build resilience.

Neither is it easy for funders to work with 'emergence' or processes that unfold over time. They prefer a clear pathway in which the actions are clearly spelled out and in which fluctuations and deviations from the stated plan are minimized. The J.W. McConnell Family Foundation provides insightful advice to funders in this regard – especially in respect of lessons from the growing body of literature on complexity theory.

> One is not working entirely in the dark, however. Complexity theory provides some insights into what to expect and how to work on change in complex organizations. Understanding complexity can serve to reassure boards and participants that the lack of a precise blueprint is not an omission or a fault; rather, that the dynamics they are seeing and experiencing is normal. … Funders can, however, request a well-articulated vision, a case for support, and a good sense of strategy, while being ready for significant variability as the social change initiative is spread and implemented. Above all, funders should accept that complex is not synonymous with unmanageable, and that there are recognized guidelines that can help maintain a consistent direction at all stages, from choosing an initiative to assessing its potential.[15]

Substantial time and energy are spent trying to secure funding to achieve sustained benefits for communities. Promising initiatives are often unable to realize their potential because they never move beyond the pilot phase. Lack of stable funding makes it difficult to maintain staff on a sustained basis. High rates of staff turnover undermine efforts to learn, acquire knowledge and pursue innovative action.

But local processes do not simply require dollars. They need a certain kind of money. Significant changes, by their very nature, take place over an extended period of time. They evolve continually – a good thing from the perspective of community process but difficult from the vantage of funders, who generally prefer predictable and early returns on their investment. Patient capital is essential for long-term changes in collaborative relationships and the policy work that comprise the communities agenda.

> While assessing progress is ideally carried out continuously, most if not all of the major outcomes of neighbourhood interventions are very slow to develop. Practitioners often cite 3-5 year time frames. Staff administering the Vancouver Urban Development Agreement cite time frames in excess of 20 years. Few practitioners and even fewer funders are willing to wait that long to determine if they are on the right track. The problem is compounded by the fact that progress is not only slow, it is not consistent. For example, improving employment systems may require skills development. However, over the period in which future workers are in training, the employment rates will not increase. Gains in the key indicator will not begin until later in the process, even if the process is entirely successful. In many areas of community development, progressions are geometric, not mathematical, with most of the change happening in the last stages of the process.[16]

But governments and other funders can do more than simply provide financial support for a local convening process and other collaborative work. They can participate as active partners. They can share information as to research and projects under way in other regions of the country or throughout the world that can guide the local effort. They can be part of the doing. In fact, they can start in their own backyards.

If funders want to achieve positive impact, they must demonstrate their commitment to coordinated strategies and systemic solutions by incorporating joined-up methods into their respective activities.[17] They can structure their own giving by funding communities and systems. They can support collaborative initiatives within neighbourhoods rather than the individual components of a comprehensive effort. They can pool resources in support of an enabling infrastructure – such as the one around community access to information. Funders alone and together can support technical assistance, policy knowledge and learning-based evaluation.

> Before we can really take a serious step towards reversing it [the fragmented funding approach] or changing the community on a permanent basis, we've got to look at our own behaviour [as a funding organization] in that regard. We've got to reduce the number of institutions with outside resources, to reduce the categorization of our support and encourage a collaborative effort at the community level that rallies around an agenda, a framework for accountability, and an elected authentic leadership base that is empowered to partner with other institutions.[18]

There is still more to changing funder behaviour than through financing practices alone. Just like comprehensive initiatives in community work, collaborative relationships in government in particular create value by bringing new resources, insights and expertise to the table. These relationships can increase efficiency and effectiveness through shared investment and reduced conflict. Government departments and agencies need to collaborate – horizontally across mandates rather than vertically within their sole jurisdiction – in order to work effectively on complex files, such as homelessness, urban Aboriginal issues and climate change.

Horizontality involves managers from different departments working together to tackle a common concern beyond the areas for which they are primarily responsible. The need for horizontal approaches arises from the fact that many objectives which governments seek to achieve are complex and relate to the mandates of two or more departments, jurisdictions or voluntary organizations. Treasury Board Secretariat points out in *The Development of Results-based Management and Accountability Frameworks for Horizontal Initiatives* that the ability to build alliances, form partnerships and manage horizontal initiatives is considered an essential ingredient for delivering high-quality, cost-effective public services.[19] Too bad that it is so hard to do.

> The absence of common performance indicators, and the means to report against them, as well as the lack of ability to aggregate funding and programming data across issues and departments, undermines transparency and accountability. At the same time, frequent staff turnover amongst federal employees at all levels challenges the capacity of the public service to build and maintain relationships across time as well as policy issues. Treasury Board Secretariat has suggested that the lack of capacity for horizontal integration impedes the government's ability to provide seamless, responsive service to people in communities.[20]

Collaborative work is being driven partly by the pressure to enhance performance and achieve measurable improvements in service delivery. The 2005 Budget was just one more node in a string of federal documents that highlighted the need to strengthen and modernize public sector management. The most recent was a January 2007 report commissioned by the Task Force on Community Investments entitled *Horizontal Tools and Relationships: An International Survey of Government Practices Related to Communities*. Horizontality is seen as a way to ensure that the federal government acts as a vibrant, cohesive and coherent national institution.

Even the Auditor General has pointed to the need for the federal government to step up its efforts around horizontal management.[21] The lack of appropriate coordination causes inertia and is detrimental to the effective functioning of individual departments within government. Central agencies were instructed to provide stronger and more explicit guidance for improving horizontal practice. This guidance ideally would apply to common application procedures, funding instruments, data collection, reporting practices and evaluation frameworks.

The report of the Task Force on Community Investments, earlier described, proposed various ways to improve horizontality within government. It cites Action for Neighbourhood Change as an example of horizontal management within government. Action for Neighbourhood Change was a pan-Canadian initiative that involved four national organizations, five local United Ways and five federal partners in an effort to improve the quality of life in selected neighbourhoods across the country.

The national partners were United Way of Canada-*Centraide Canada*, Tamarack – An Institute for Community Engagement, National Film Board of Canada and Caledon Institute of Social Policy. The local partners were United Ways in Halifax, Thunder Bay, Toronto, Regina and Surrey. The federal partners were the National Secretariat on Homelessness, Office of Learning Technologies and National Literacy Secretariat (all of Human Resources and Social Development Canada); Canada's Drug Strategy (Health Canada); and the National Crime Prevention Strategy (Public Safety and Emergency Preparedness Canada).[22]

The government partners pooled their efforts in support of a common goal – strengthening neighbourhoods. They crafted two contribution agreements from five separate funding streams. The project employed a coordinated reporting procedure in respect of its financing. A single monthly report was prepared for all five funders. Through a special policy dialogue created for this project, the government partners joined together several of their procedures.

There are still other opportunities for consolidation that would advance the communities agenda. If governments truly want to support collaborative community efforts, they could work to combine their extensive submission procedures that currently involve different, and sometimes conflicting, information and multiple letters of support. Ideally, the application process in respect of the same or similar initiatives should be coordinated to promote program coherence, and to reduce the administrative burden on both communities and funders.

Horizontality is not a magic bullet for governments seeking solutions to complex issues, but rather an emerging alternative style of partnership involving multiple relationships and lines of accountability. Horizontal practice is best applied to complex issues requiring collaboration among multiple partners sustained over long periods of time. Horizontality requires agreement among partners on policy outcomes, collaborative programs and structural leadership mandates and budgets that cross departmental lines. Horizontality involves strong, connected networks into communities, which are often a key asset of voluntary organizations.

Governments at all levels have begun to explore ways to more effectively support multifaceted community initiatives. Experiments in horizontal management, such as the Sustainable Communities Initiative based in Nova Scotia, sought to change the culture and operating practices of government to enable various departments and orders of government to pool their interventions and resources in support of local development strategies. The Sustainable Communities Initiative brought together federal, provincial, municipal and First Nations governments to help selected communities in Nova Scotia work together on the environmental, economic, social and cultural dimensions of sustainability.

Other governments have taken similar steps. The Manitoba Community and Economic Development Initiative employs an integrated social and economic lens for shaping government policies and programs. An interdepartmental committee of Cabinet oversees the effort and provides a forum for decision-makers to align the efforts of their respective departments.

Evaluation of community efforts represents another potential area for consolidation. Because all government departments and funders, for that matter, require an assessment of the projects they support, communities must collect information from diverse sources. Considerable yet scarce resources end up being invested in project accountability. While essential, this activity diverts local efforts from their primary focus. Fortunately, the work of the five neighbourhoods involved in Action for Neighbourhood Change was assessed through a common evaluation framework.

A positive recent example was the formulation of a joint evaluation framework for the (former) Social Economy Initiative in which several departments collaborated in respect of a common goal – to support and grow the practice of community economic development.[23] Federal partners included Human Resources and Social Development Canada, Industry Canada, Western Economic Diversification, the Federal Economic Development Initiative in Northern Ontario, the Atlantic Canada Opportunities Agency, Canada Economic Development (Québec), and the Social Sciences and Humanities Research Council.

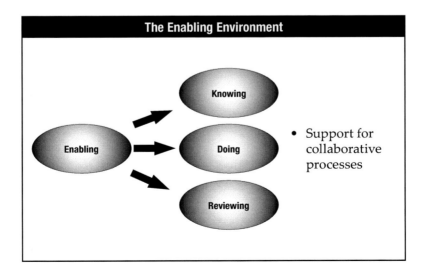

- Support for collaborative processes

The joint evaluation framework developed for this purpose created a logic model for conceptualizing the work of the social economy, including its broad societal objectives, underlying guiding principles, and major investments and supports required to sustain local activity. The framework set out the range of possible results at the household, organizational, community and sector levels.

If the benefits of joined-up work are so obvious, then why is it not the accepted practice? Why is it more the exception than the rule? While there is no definitive answer, it appears that there are basic human factors at play that have little to do with logic and more to do with the psychology of risk and reward.

In terms of risk, anyone working in government knows that they must protect their higher-up in the ladder from surprise, embarrassment or negative press. The rule is nothing less than a commandment when it comes to safeguarding the reputation of the Minister. The system is inherently risk averse, which means that it tends to stifle the untried as though it is automatically untrue. There is safety in predictability.

The Task Force on Community Investments devoted considerable attention to the issue of risk. It explored how to balance concerns about risk with the government interest in achieving clear outcomes and results. Its report considered the question of accountability and the need to clarify information expectations while reducing the reporting burden on community organizations.[24]

In fact, the structures of government tend to be driven by public accounts – and accountability. Ministers are assigned responsibility for a certain amount of expenditure for which they must answer to Parliament. The so-called clear lines of reporting become muddied when a joint initiative involves the pooling of funds from several different sources. The question of accountability also arises in horizontal initiatives because of the many cooks contributing to the collective broth.

While more complex, the accountability challenge need not be insurmountable. The most reasonable solution is to designate a given Minister as lead in a common effort with primary responsibility for reporting on funding. The other departments clearly must monitor their expenditures but recognize that the outcomes may be somewhat more broad or different from those they typically see.

The very reason for working in this way is to create a whole that is greater than its constituent parts. Someone with the designated authority needs to state that joined-up efforts are the expected method of operation when collaborative work is likely to lead to better results. Government workers must get the green light from their superiors, who need to hear from higher ranks that this is, indeed, the expectation.[25]

Even Deputy Ministers who are in charge of their respective departmental ships need direction from their bosses. They must get the signal from Privy Council Office to work in this way. They must hear the message from Treasury Board, the Auditor General and the political level.

If politicians do not understand the need for joined-up efforts, then it is unlikely they will communicate this message to public servants. Moreover, if government caucus members are vying for the attention of the Prime Minister in hopes of a Cabinet position, the last thing they may want is to share credit with their colleagues. They will seek to shine the spotlight upon themselves – in which case they will not likely want to pursue collaborative work.

Politicians and government officials need to learn the same lessons as communities when it comes to leading between. Collaborative work involves a sharing of responsibility, risk and reward. If any progress is to be made in government around horizontal efforts, there needs to be clear direction on this expectation from the highest possible source. That is the lesson from the UK experience in joined-up solutions to joined-up problems, which is probably the most sophisticated example in the world of government involvement in joint ventures.

Joined-up government is an explicit political strategy that seeks to coordinate the development and implementation of policies across departments in order to address complex social problems, such as social exclusion and poverty, in a comprehensive way.[26] But it moves beyond government to include a range of private sector and voluntary organizations. The approach is based on the principle that joined-up solutions are created by involving as many interested parties as possible in relevant policy design and implementation.

One of the first joined-up initiatives was introduced in 1997 when (former) Prime Minister Tony Blair established a Social Exclusion Unit to improve local action to enhance social cohesion. The Unit was housed within the (then) Office of the Deputy Prime Minister and worked on projects agreed to by the (former) Deputy Prime Minister in consultation with the Prime Minister.

The Unit's central place in government encouraged cooperation among departments because its mandate derived directly from the Prime Minister. This authority helped cut through red tape and encouraged cooperation among staff from different departments and between public and private concerns. In May 2006, the Social Exclusion Unit moved to the newly-created Department for Communities and Local Government.

Similarly, the Neighbourhood Renewal Unit was designated as responsible for overseeing the UK government's comprehensive neighbourhood renewal strategy. Created in 2001, the Neighbourhood Renewal Unit had also been housed in the Office of the Deputy Prime Minister and now resides in the Department for Communities and Local Government. Its purpose was to harness the hundreds of billions of pounds currently being spent by diverse departments. The Unit worked with Neighbourhood Renewal Teams throughout the country to monitor and support local strategic partnerships in the 88 most deprived districts.[27]

The national production of neighbourhood statistics helped track progress in communities and identify areas considered vulnerable or at risk of decline. The Unit created a knowledge management system to share evidence of effective practice and to ensure that community workers had adequate training and skills. It also monitored the progress of the National Strategy on Neighbourhood Renewal, which set clear targets around five identified problems – poor job prospects, high levels of crime, educational underachievement, poor health, and problems with housing and the physical environment. The targets and associated actions were determined and carried out by individual departments but monitored and coordinated by the overarching Neighbourhood Renewal Unit.

In the area of employment, for example, the Department for Education and Employment and the Department of Social Security set three-year targets to raise employment rates in the 30 districts with the poorest employment records. The intent was to narrow the gap between these areas and overall rates for the country, and similarly to narrow the gap for disadvantaged groups. Several key policies were identified to achieve these targets, including £40 million for 32 Action Teams for Jobs and a large investment in child care and transportation. The plan also sought to 'make work pay' through changes to the income security and tax systems. A new small Business Service was created and £96 million Phoenix Fund was set up to encourage small enterprise in deprived areas. Additional funding was allocated for regional development agencies.

The Home Office set a target to reduce burglary by 25 percent and to ensure that no district has a burglary rate more than three times the national average. Policies to support this goal and other crime reduction objectives included a £1.6 billion increase over three years in spending on police, an £18.5 million Neighbourhood Wardens Fund, a three-year crime Reduction Program with more than £200 million committed to more than 1,000 projects and a new National Drug Treatment Agency for which funding would rise by an average 10 percent a year over three years. New Crime and Disorder Reduction Partnerships were established throughout the country to unite police, local authorities and community members in tackling crime. Each partnership produced a Crime and Disorder Strategy with associated local goals.

Educational targets spelled out the expected national standards of literacy and numeracy for students and educational performance. The policies included the extension of Sure Start to cover one-third of infants, setting up a Children's Fund to work with vulnerable young people ages 5 to 13, creating a Connexions service to keep 13- to 19-year-olds in learning and an Adults Basic Skills Strategy to help 750,000 improve basic skills.

The Department of Health committed itself to narrowing the health gap between socioeconomic groups, and between the most deprived areas and the rest of the country. Major policy changes over three years included long-term investment through the National Health Service with a 6.1 percent increase in funding each year; making reduced health inequalities a key criterion for allocating health resources; incentives to recruit and retain primary care staff in deprived areas; 200 personal medical service pilots, mainly in deprived areas, to improve primary care; and free national interpretation and translation services in all premises of the National Health Service.

The Department of the Environment, Transport and the Regions set out to reduce by 33 percent the number of households living in sub-standard social housing, with the greatest improvement to be made in the most deprived local areas. Significant actions included an extra £1.6 billion pounds in housing over three years, an additional £80 million extra each year for housing management, the transfer of local authority homes to registered social landlords and the creation of measures to tackle low demand and abandonment.

In addition to monitoring the implementation of designated plans and targets, the Neighbourhood Renewal Unit played an important coordination role. It encouraged active engagement through a £96 million initiative to develop local participation infrastructure. A neighbourhood management process helped agencies improve and link their services. Communities were further supported in their efforts through a skills and knowledge program that offered practical assistance to those directly involved in neighbourhood renewal.

As noted, this joined-up approach is one of the most elaborate examples of collaboration to be found anywhere in government. But the degree of central government involvement naturally raises questions about the extent to which the neighbourhood renewal process was community driven. On the positive side, it is an example of extensive government collaboration – coupled with significant support for comprehensive community work.

While the UK may be the most comprehensive example of joined-up work, the notion and practice of partnership are alive and well throughout Europe. The European Commission makes available special funds for partnership development and supports a variety of mechanisms to encourage the exchange of good practice between countries. The Structural and Cohesion Funds are the main instruments for supporting social and economic restructuring across the European Union, accounting for more than one-third of its budget. The funds are used to redress regional disparities through infrastructure and telecommunications, human resources, and research and development. Multisectoral and cross-sectoral collaboration are the primary methodologies employed to achieve identified goals.

The Organisation for Economic Cooperation and Development is similarly active in its support of collaborative work. In 2003, the OECD Council established, in co-operation with the Italian government and the Province of Trento, an OECD Centre for Local Development, known as the LEED Centre. Its mission is to build the capacity for local development in OECD countries, with a special focus on central and eastern European nations. It actively supports the creation of local collaborative efforts, or area-based partnerships, to carry out the development mission.

All institutions and organizations involved in the management of area-based partnerships may become members of LEED's Forum on Partnerships and Local Governance. The mandate of the Forum is to facilitate the transfer of expertise and exchange of experience on partnerships within and between OECD member and non-member countries.

At a meeting of the Forum held in Vienna in March 2007, participants agreed to a support a Vienna Action Statement on Partnerships that had been developed by representatives from several European nations, New Zealand and Canada. The purpose of the Action Statement is to improve dialogue and cooperation between policy-makers and stakeholders at the local, regional and national levels in the areas of economic development, social cohesion, environmental sustainability and the quality of life. The intent of the Action Statement is to underscore the important role of partnerships involving communities and government in the policy process.

In short, there are significant developments throughout the world that are actively recognizing and supporting the value of collaborative work. They are effectively creating an enabling environment through direct funding of community process and through indirect support of learning opportunities.

Here at home, there are some interesting provincial and local examples of joined-up work. A study of horizontal policy-making among provincial governments concludes that Newfoundland and Labrador may have the most ambitious process in the country.[28] Its roots can be traced to 1988 when the Community Services Council Newfoundland and Labrador took the initiative to promote the need for strategic and joined-up planning in respect of economic and social well-being. The Council organized meetings with government officials and made numerous presentations to Cabinet in an effort to encourage joint planning for future development in the province.

The 1993 Throne Speech announced the Government's intent to develop a Strategic Social Plan. The Premier initiated the process by establishing a high-level Strategic Planning Group composed of Deputy Ministers. The fact that the Premier's chief of staff chaired the group lent considerable weight to the process. It also included one nongovernmental representative from the Community Services Council.

More recently in 2005, the Government of Newfoundland and Labrador announced in its Speech from the Throne a commitment to transform itself over a ten-year period from the province with the highest rate of poverty to the jurisdiction with the lowest rate. A background paper entitled *Reducing Poverty in Newfoundland: Working Towards a Solution* subsequently helped inform the wide-ranging public consultations and workshops held throughout the province.

In June 2006, the Government released *Reducing Poverty: An Action Plan for Newfoundland and Labrador*. The Plan acknowledged that it is virtually impossible to tackle this complex problem in the absence of a long-term, comprehensive and integrated approach, which involves horizontal management at the highest level of government and close collaboration with other sectors.

As part of its commitment, the Government established a Ministerial Committee with seven participating ministers responsible for the following portfolios: human resources, labour and employment; Aboriginal affairs; education and the status of women; finance; health and community services; innovation, trade and rural development; and justice. The Action Plan points to the need to ensure, through streamlined eligibility and application procedures, the accessibility of programs and services to households living in poverty. The Government also stated its intent to engage low-income residents in helping to develop new policy directions.

At the local level, one of the most comprehensive examples of joined-up work is the Integrated Service Strategy developed by the Community Services Department of the City of Edmonton. It is based on a clear vision.

> Edmonton is a collection of urban villages, each with its own unique assets and strengths. Urban villages as vibrant places where people live in affordable housing, care about their neighbours, walk the streets in safety and live their lives with dignity, regardless of their circumstances. They are brimming with opportunities for the arts, culture, leisure, recreational pursuits for citizens of all ages.[29]

The Strategy is organized around six major themes – citizens first, community building, focused efforts, urban wellness, ribbons of green and blue (its environmental focus), and community places. Perhaps most important is the identification of roles that the government must play in effecting this strategic vision. These involve sharing knowledge, brokering services, shared funding, coaching capacity and stewardship.

Sharing knowledge means that ensuring information is accurate, readily available and publicly accessible. *Brokering services* involves putting together the right people at the right time in order to mobilize and enhance community efforts. To effect *shared funding*, the City of Edmonton creates partnerships to maximize its financial resources and is exploring new grant relationships with communities to enable access to arts, culture, recreation and sport. As part of *coaching capacity*, the City shares its experience and expertise to foster community leadership. Its *stewardship* role involves the preservation and protection of urban parks, open spaces, natural areas and built assets.

Finally, joining up is important not just from the perspective of more effective service delivery. It also reduces the likelihood of unanticipated negative consequences in which one order of government withdraws or shrinks its benefits in the face of improvements made by another. This concern was discussed in *Optimizing Opportunity* in which provincial social assistance rules could penalize recipients who accumulate savings, for example, under the new federal Canada Learning Bond.

iii. Reviewing

While governments at all levels recognize the value of learning, they usually express this interest by investing in traditional educational institutions. These investments are necessary but not sufficient. Governments – and other funders for that matter – should support learning within and between communities. The value of this investment derives from the fact that communities can learn from each other and thereby raise the bar of practice.

Moreover, comprehensive community initiatives are demanding and complex. Participants are continually challenged to innovate in response to a changing environment. Learning sessions help ensure that they do not lose perspective and feel abandoned. Funders can support reflective practice among social innovators.[30] A strong community of practice allows members to assist each other in struggling with tough problems, sharing new approaches and applying effective methods.

But learning does not simply emerge spontaneously in communities. The process must be carefully developed and strategically pursued. Comprehensive local efforts require support in respect of these goals, and both governments and other funders are uniquely poised to enable this learning role. The Vibrant Communities initiative has demonstrated the value of a national system of supports, including peer learning coupled intensive with local coaching.

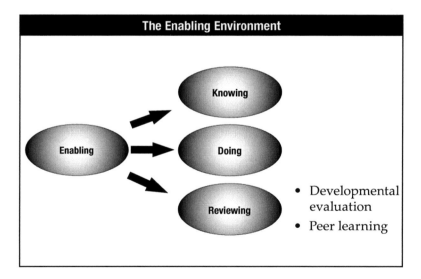

Communities that seek to tackle complex economic, social and environmental problems often require technical assistance to address these difficult areas. Technical assistance refers to the critical guidance that enables communities to carry out their identified goals effectively and efficiently. It may apply either to the development of generic skills or specific skills.

Generic skills refer to the areas of knowledge and expertise that all communities require regardless of focus. These skills pertain to the processes embedded in local decision-making – involving partners from diverse sectors, engaging marginalized groups, formulating theories of change, developing strategic plans, raising funds, creating learning networks, devising evaluation plans and monitoring systems for assessing progress.[31] Technical assistance in specific areas focuses upon substantive issues, such as creating affordable housing, setting up licensed child care, financing a community loan fund and organizing a home care co-operative.

The importance of strategic learning cannot be underestimated – particularly in a knowledge economy in which both information and technology change continually. Success in the knowledge economy is the result of effective knowledge management. As in organizing for complexity, the strategic management of knowledge is not something that simply happens on its own. Opportunities need to be created for reflecting upon these actions. These reflection sessions help build knowledge about community change.

> It is possible to envision a more *commonly determined, collective knowledge development enterprise* [italics in original] than currently exists in all the stand-alone comprehensive community initiatives and stand-alone evaluations. This endeavor would begin with taking stock of the existing knowledge base in the field, followed by efforts to organize systematic learning around core questions, challenges, and unknowns.[32]

It is also helpful to facilitate exchange either in groups or even in pairs whereby two communities join together for the purpose of peer learning. In one example, the comprehensive local initiative in Edmonton invited a colleague from a similar effort in Niagara Region to share their respective experiences. There was a presentation by a Canada Revenue Agency official who spoke of how important it had been to work with the local effort to identify hard-to-reach citizens. (Edmonton's Make Tax Time Pay campaign was described in *Supporting Sustenance*.) At the end of the presentation, the Niagara visitor committed himself publicly to a similar campaign in his region.

It is important to note that shared learning on community practice is beginning to take place increasingly within government. Vibrant Communities convenes a Government Learning Circle in which officials from all orders of government who are involved in the project have an opportunity to discuss areas of shared interest. More recently, a community of practice called the Federal Family – Collaborative Community Initiatives was formed in which officials from 25 departments and agencies meet regularly to expand their knowledge and skills on various aspects of the communities agenda.

In fact, the Task Force on Community Investments made special reference to learning. It recommended that funding programs be enhanced by encouraging learning about effective approaches and practices. It noted that: "A number of federal departments are moving in this direction, creating feedback loops from program evaluation to policy and from policy to program implementation, enabling knowledge development to inform practice."[33] The Task Force called for appropriate training about the nonprofit sector and on the core elements of program design and implementation. This new knowledge effectively comprises the foundation for future work – whether undertaken by funders or by communities.

All this to say...

So it goes – a virtuous circle of knowing, doing and reviewing. The end does not end. It simply becomes the starting point for improved local practice. When all is said and done, the communities agenda is basically about hope and renewal – of self, of place and of interventions to improve the quality of life.

Endnotes

1 See program description at *www.imaginecanada.ca*

2 Torjman, S. and D. Minns. (2005). *Sustainable Development Framework for Science and Technology: Social and Cultural Dimensions*. Ottawa: Caledon Institute of Social Policy, February.

3 Torjman, S. (1997). *Disentanglement – or Disengagement?* Ottawa: Caledon Institute of Social Policy, January.

4 Canadian Housing and Renewal Association. (2007). *Minimum Housing Wage 2006: Housing Continues to Move out of Reach for Minimum Wage Workers*. Ottawa: Canadian Housing and Renewal Association, January. *www.chra-achru.ca*

5 Perkins, T. (2006). "Affordability of homes worst in decade: RBC." *The Globe and Mail*, March 30: B6.

6 Employment Policy Foundation. (2003). "The Living Wage Movement: Gaining Momentum." *www.epf.org/LWsite/factsheets/ overview.asp*; Department for International Development. (1999). *Sustainable Livelihoods Guidance Sheet: Introduction. www.livelihoods.org/ info/info_ guidancesheets.html#1*

7 Battle, K. and S. Torjman. (1993). *Breaking Down the Welfare Wall*. Ottawa: Caledon Institute of Social Policy, July.

8 Battle, K., M. Mendelson and S. Torjman. (2006). *Towards A New Architecture for Canada's Adult Benefits*. Ottawa: Caledon Institute of Social Policy, June.

9 Human Services Planning Coalition. (2005). *The Road to Inclusivity: An Action Plan for York Region*. Report of the Inclusivity Summit. York Region, January.

10 Task Force on Community Investments. (2006). *Achieving Coherence in Government of Canada Funding Practice in Communities*. Ottawa: Human Resources and Social Development Canada, October, pp. 14-15.

11 Treasury Board of Canada Secretariat. (2007). *From Red Tape to Clear Results*. Report of the Independent Blue Ribbon Panel on Grants and Contributions. Ottawa, February.

12 Makhoul, A. (2002). *The ABLED Initiative: Encouraging Entrepreneurship for Persons with Disabilities*. Ottawa: Caledon Institute of Social Policy, July.

13 Connor, J. and S. Kadel-Taas. (2003). *Community Visions, Community Solutions: Grantmaking for Comprehensive Impact*. St. Paul: Amherst H. Wilder Foundation, pp. 38-41.

[14] Auspos, P. and A. Kubisch. (2004). *Building Knowledge about Community Change: Moving Beyond Evaluations.* Aspen Institute Roundtable on Community Change, November, p. 15.

[15] Pearson, K. (2006). *Accelerating Our Impact: Philanthropy, Innovation and Social Change.* Montreal: The J.W. McConnell Family Foundation, November, p. 12.

[16] Meager, S. (2006). *A Neighbourhood Vitality Index: An Approach to Measuring Neighbourhood Well-Being.* Toronto: United Way of Greater Toronto, p. 9.

[17] Connor, J. and S. Kadel-Taas. (2003). *Community Visions, Community Solutions: Grantmaking for Comprehensive Impact.* St. Paul: Amherst H. Wilder Foundation, p. 42.

[18] Yates, G. (2004). "Rebuilding Communities." *Ideas That Matter.* 3(2): 16.

[19] Treasury Board of Canada Secretariat. (2002). *The Development of Results-based Management and Accountability Frameworks for Horizontal Initiatives.* Ottawa. *www.tbs-sct.gc.ca*

[20] Elson, P., M. Struthers and J. Carlson. (2007). *Horizontal Tools and Relationships: An International Survey of Government Practices related to Communities.* Ottawa: Task Force on Community Investments, Government of Canada, pp. 6-7.

[21] See both the 2005 and the 2006 Report of the Auditor General of Canada to Parliament. Ottawa: Government of Canada.

[22] See *www.anccommunity.ca*

[23] Leviten-Reid, E. and S. Torjman. (2006). *Evaluation Framework for Federal Investment in the Social Economy: A Discussion Paper.* Ottawa: Caledon Institute of Social Policy, January.

[24] Task Force on Community Investments. (2006). *Achieving Coherence in Government of Canada Funding Practice in Communities.* October, 2006, p. 42.

[25] Torjman, S. (2006). *There's Madness to this Method.* Ottawa: Caledon Institute of Social Policy, January.

[26] V. Bogdanor ed. (2005). *Joined-Up Government.* Oxford: Oxford University Press.

[27] Social Exclusion Unit. (2001). *A New Commitment to Neighbourhood Renewal: A National Strategy Action Plan.* London: Cabinet Office, UK Government, January. *www.neighbourhood.gov.uk*

[28] Peach, I. (2004). *Managing Complexity: The Lessons of Horizontal Policy-Making in the Provinces.* Regina: Saskatchewan Institute of Public Policy, University of Regina, Spring/Summer.

[29] City of Edmonton. (2000). Towards 2010. *A New Perspective: An Integrated Service Strategy*. Edmonton: Community Services, City of Edmonton, p. 9.

[30] Westley, F., B. Zimmerman and M. Quinn Patten. (2006). *Getting to Maybe: How the World is Changed*. Toronto: Random House Canada, p. 181.

[31] Torjman, S. (2003). *Think Piece: Policy Conversation on Community Learning*. Ottawa: Caledon Institute of Social Policy, July.

[32] Auspos, P. and A. Kubisch. (2004). *Building Knowledge about Community Change: Moving Beyond Evaluations*: Aspen Institute Roundtable on Community Change, November, p. 7.

[33] Task Force on Community Investments. (2006). *Achieving Coherence in Government of Canada Funding Practice in Communities*. Ottawa: Human Resources and Social Development Canada, October, p. 14-15.

Chapter 9
Facing the Future

The communities agenda is alive and well throughout the country, and throughout the world, though it is not typically recognized as such.

The communities agenda is about resilience. It is essentially a message of strength – and of hope. Communities are involved in actions related to sustenance, adaptation, engagement and opportunity in their efforts to promote well-being.

Communities are also seeking ways to respond to tough challenges more strategically than in the past. The wide-ranging local activity speaks clearly to the move away from single organizational efforts to more comprehensive interventions that involve multiple groups and sectors.

The many examples presented in this book illustrate how organizations in the same cluster are joining together to reach a desired objective and moving beyond the bounds of their cluster to attain related goals. Moreover, local efforts increasingly are incorporating a policy dimension in order to achieve larger systemic impact.

The fact that substantial work is under way is a good thing. Community interventions have become more sophisticated and intentional in their approaches. But the rich and growing body of case evidence does not mean that these efforts come without their own challenges.

With respect to *knowing*, the scope and complexity of information which communities require in order to carry out their work effectively can be overwhelming. Questions always arise as to how much evidence is needed to understand a problem or make the case for a particular intervention. When is enough enough?

The challenge of creating a persuasive and informed evidence base will only become more complex as communities embark increasingly upon policy change. The balancing act is to find good information that is good enough. Without a solid case, they will be sent back by policy-makers to the proverbial drawing board. At the same time, communities can spend so much time at that drawing board that they lose the momentum for action – the very strength of local initiatives.

There is a need for a more strategic and organized approach to the collection and interpretation of data and research on the various dimensions of resilience. The chapter on *Creating an Enabling Environment* discussed a community-wide information base as one possible approach to facilitating comprehensive local work.

The *doing* component of the work in the shared space comes with its unique challenges. The chapter on *Organizing for Complexity* cited the emerging art of 'leading between' or collaborative leadership as a difficult skill.

Many organizations have a difficult time working collaboratively because they have been stripped of adequate resources. They lack sufficient funds to carry out their own mandate, let alone spend time with colleagues on broader areas of joint intervention. While it is true that the sum is usually greater than the parts, the individual components still need to be strong and healthy.

Of course, it is not the responsibility of funders alone to change the broader landscape. The fact that all organizations function in a competitive culture with an economy rooted in competitive practice does not make easy the culture shift required to support collaborative work.

It is also a culture shift that values the role of citizen voices and that makes a place for them at decision-making tables. The emerging communities agenda is concerned with a new way to distribute resources. But it also deals fundamentally with a new way to share power – through access to information, distributed resources and links with policy-makers. However, the inherent power shift also raises questions about the respective roles of local government and local governance – far more profound than the mere four-letter difference would imply.

Finally, the *reviewing* dimension of work in the shared space comes with its own challenges. Again, the question arises as to how much information is enough to make the case? How much data must be gathered to determine how well a particular effort is doing?

The chapter on *Working in the Shared Space* described the complexities of attribution when myriad factors play a role in achieving the desired results. This difficulty is all the more challenging in a culture of accountability, which expects identified resources and actions to result in clear outcomes.

A world that sees cause and effect as discrete points on a straight line has a hard time with winding roads and changing pathways. A world that views relationships only as black and white typically is uncomfortable with the varying shades of gray that characterize comprehensive community initiatives.

Perhaps the best guidance in facing the future derives from the concept of resilience itself – the capacity to thrive in a changing world. The new approaches to community interventions, through work in the shared space within and between clusters and around policy, require an environment that enables this emerging form of complex work.

But it also needs a culture that embraces continual change rather than absolute certainty. It is a culture in which ongoing adaptation rather than definitive endpoints is the desired goal. It is a culture in which hope for a better future is deeply valued – especially for those who have lived for too long on its margins. In the true spirit of resilience, it is a culture of hope for a better future.

About the Author

Sherri Torjman is Vice-President of the Caledon Institute of Social Policy. She has written in the areas of welfare reform, customized training, disability income and supports, the social dimension of sustainable development and community-based poverty reduction. She has also written many Caledon reports including *Reclaiming our Humanity; Strategies for a Caring Society; Proposal for National Personal Supports Fund; Survival-of-the-Fittest Employment Policy; The Social Dimension of Sustainable Development; The Key to Kyoto: Social Dimensions of Climate Change; The Social Role of Local Government; The Canada Pension Plan Disability Benefit; Reintegrating the Unemployed through Customized Training;* and *How Finance Re-formed Social Policy.*

Sherri wrote the vision paper In Unison: *A Canadian Approach to Disability Issues* for the Federal/Provincial/Territorial Ministers Responsible for Social Services. She has authored four books on disability policy: *Income Insecurity, Poor Places, Nothing Personal and Direct Dollars.* Sherri wrote the welfare series of reports for the National Council of Welfare, including *Welfare in Canada: The Tangled Safety Net; Welfare Reform; and Welfare Incomes 1989, 1990, 1991, 1992, 1993 and 1994.*

Sherri was co-Chair of the Technical Advisory Committee on Tax Measures for Persons with Disabilities that reported to the Minister of Finance and the Minister of National Revenue in December 2004. She has worked for the House of Commons Committee on the Disabled and the Handicapped, the House of Commons Special Committee on Child Care and the Royal Commission on New Reproductive Technologies.

Sherri taught a course in social policy at McGill University and is a former Board Member of the Ontario Trillium Foundation.